College Reading Series

"Thinking It Through!"

Revised Printing

John A. Garcia, Ed. R.S., ABD
Harvard Reading Specialist & Reading Instructor

Loretta W. Rodgers, MS
Reading Coordinator & Reading Instructor

Kendall Hunt
publishing company

www.kendallhunt.com
Send all inquiries to:
4050 Westmark Drive
Dubuque, IA 52004-1840

Contents

SECTION FOUR—CONTENT-AREA

SECTION FIVE—TEACHING GUIDES

DEDICATION

To—

Wesley—for being by my side, as my husband, and sharing your love of 'rummaging' through used books at book stores to find the special treasures that we discovered together!

Jonathan & David—for allowing me to be a part of your 'curiosity' from the moment that each of you were born. While you allowed me to experience many miracles, you were my greatest miracles—my dear and loving sons!

My Parents, George and Rosa Woodruff and my Brothers, Carl, Gerald, and Larry—for always believing in me.

Prof. Loretta W. Rodgers, M.S.

To—

Mom—for taking the time to read a story to me every night when I was a child!
Esmeralda—for the support and encouragement that you have always given me!
Dean Ricardo Rodriguez—for supporting us and letting us 'run' with our project!
Dr. George Keating—for changing my life by 'sending' me to Harvard University!
Dr. Jeanne Chall—for mentoring, guiding, and 'teaching' me while I was at Harvard!
G. Denise Griffin—for encouraging me to become an author, before you left this world!

Prof. John A. Garcia, Ed.R.S., ABD

For—

Zach 'Todd' Fitzgerald, In His Memory—here was an exceptional student who had much to live for and many dreams to accomplish. You died too young and will never be able to achieve the goals (dreams) you once envisioned. We will always remember you as the vibrant young man who made our class and our lives better. The energy you brought to our class plus your enthusiasm for learning were passed on to everyone in class. You made an impact on each and every one of us in class, and you will be missed each day. Thank you for calling me a couple of days before you passed away, to share how much you enjoyed the class and how much you learned over the semester. We're very saddened by the news of your passing—you will never be forgotten. Rest In Peace!!

Prof. John A. Garcia, Ed.R.S. ABD

Our Sincere Gratitude To—

Our students—former and current—for giving us the opportunity to pass on some of the knowledge you sought by going to college. You allowed us to provide you the many 'adventures' that you never expected to encounter. We strongly believe that each of you can, and will, achieve well-above your expected potential. The ultimate success, that you seek, is just around the next corner. Do not lose faith; you must keep trying! In the many years that we have spent teaching, our greatest reward has been your success! We will always be here for you and because of you! Believe it or not, you have probably taught us more than we have taught you—we must take each day to learn something new and to use that knowledge to better ourselves. Learning must be constant and continuous as we progress through life—through our daily learning, we can teach others later on in life! So, don't ever let anyone tell you that you are being unrealistic and cannot achieve what you have set out to—you will never know whether or not you can truly accomplish something unless you try, regardless of the obstacles. You do not want to wake up one day and say to yourself, "what if." And always remember one thing: do not 'rest easy' until you have achieved each of your goals and fulfilled all of your dreams!!

Prof. John A. Garcia, Ed.R.S., ABD
Harvard Reading Specialist & Instructor
&
Prof. Loretta W. Rodgers, MS
Reading Coordinator & Instructor

From the Students at Eastfield College (DCCCD):

1—This textbook helped me in more ways than I could have imagined. It not only helped me to develop college-level vocabulary and comprehension, but it helped me actually enjoy reading, something I never did before. Also, the Reading Systems in our text, that Professor Garcia developed (especially his 'HQA5R'), were very instrumental in building my confidence about my reading and in fine-tuning my analysis of college-level material and in developing better note taking and study skills. I now feel that I can be successful in any content-area course that I take for my degree.

Alimatu Turay

2—What I really loved about this textbook is that it offered high-interest reading selections, multi-cultural readings, and personal experiences that sometimes 'hit home' with me. Learning the 'HQA5R' system, which is in our text, made my reading worthwhile because it is guaranteed to help us succeed in other courses. The selections about personal experiences made me realize that we all face obstacles, but there is light at the end of the tunnel—that light is success!

Mayra Vega

3—The selections in this textbook were not only very interesting, but they were quite helpful in building my reading skills to college-level comprehension—they made me want to read and analyze more. And in turn. I tested out of reading without a struggle. I found many of the short excerpts, taken from novels, to be very motivating and inspiring—they were a great choice by the authors. In addition, the activities that went along with each selection actually "packed a punch" in getting me to college level so quickly. Finally, the Reading Systems & Learning Strategies were extremely valuable. They have helped to increase my success in other classes. This book is a must-have for any reading course in colleges!

Charles 'Mark' Ragsdale

4—The reading selections in this text are very informative. I was also able to relate to many of the personal experiences that could be found in the readings. I have found that, besides elevating my comprehension level and learning how to retain material that I read, I can now feel confident that I can be successful in college. The text and the teaching methods used were highly effective—I am now very confident and self-assured of my future successes.

Paula 'Renee' Bryant

5—My reading level was quite low, but by the end of the semester, I was able to test very high in comprehension. I feel that I accomplished this because of our text and the teaching methods in our class—the reading selections got me motivated, and my professor challenged us each day with new activities from the text. It was never boring—some of the selections got me to think more of my life and what I want in the future. This textbook actually motivated me to do well. This textbook 'beats out' all other programs that I have been through. It is the best tool for college reading courses!

Bianca Hinojos

6—Because of this textbook, I now find that I want to read more. The interesting selections offered what my professor calls "experiential learning." I discovered that, many times, others share personal experiences that are similar to ones I have been through. This text was one of the major factors in having me do very well in the course and raising my comprehension to college level in one semester. I don't think I would have done as well without this text because I really didn't like to read before taking this course. All reading courses should use this text as a valuable guide to success!

Taiwo 'Raymond' Akinsuroju

7—I discovered that our textbook provided a foundation for my overall success in my reading course. What I liked most about the textbook were the many activities, i.e., writing, critical thinking, and vocabulary, which were what made me do so well in the course. I have never been 'turned on' to reading—I always found it boring, but this text has changed my view of reading. Reading is now something I look forward to because I actually can comprehend what I am reading and can participate in discussions with confidence. I give this book an 'A' for helping to make me an avid reader.

Yessenia Eguia

8—This text really helped me achieve the goal of testing out of reading! While I was in a lower level reading course and thought I would need a couple of semesters of reading to get to college-level comprehension, I actually was able to achieve my goal of testing out in one semester. I am now ready to achieve my next goal of graduating from college, a goal that I was once just a dream. I now know that the problems that I've always had in reading were due to my lack of essential reading skills, but that is not the case anymore. I am happy to say that I am now at college level and give all the credit to my professor and his textbook. Both instilled a love of reading in me that I never had before! And now, I'm on my way!

Jakari Jones

Section One

High Interest

In Praise of the 'F' Word

by
Mary Sherry

Image © Yuganov Konstantin, 2012. Used under license from Shutterstock, Inc.

Tens of thousands of 18-year-olds will graduate this year and be handed meaningless diplomas. These diplomas won't look any different from those awarded their luckier classmates. Their validity will be questioned only when their employers discover that these graduates are semi-literate.

Eventually a fortunate few will find their way into educational-repair shops—adult-literacy programs, such as the one where I teach basic grammar and writing. There, high school graduates and high school dropouts pursuing graduate-equivalency certificates will learn the skills they should have learned in school. They will also discover they have been cheated by our educational system.

As I teach, I learn a lot about our schools. Early in each session I ask my students to write about an unpleasant experience they had in school. No writers' block here! "I wish someone would have had made me stop doing drugs and made me study." "I liked to party and no one seemed to care." "I was a good kid and didn't cause any trouble, so they just passed me along even though I didn't read well and couldn't write." And so on.

I am your basic do-gooder, and prior to teaching this class I blamed the poor academic skills our kids have today on drugs, divorce and other impediments to concentration necessary for doing well in school. But, as I rediscover each time I walk into the classroom, before a teacher can expect students to concentrate, he has to get their attention, no matter what distractions may be at hand. There are many ways to do this, and they have much to do with teaching style. However, if style alone won't do it, there is another way to show who holds the winning hand in the classroom. That is to reveal the trump card of failure.

I will never forget a teacher who played that card to get the attention of one of my children. Our youngest, a world-class charmer, did little to develop his intellectual talents but always got by. Until Mrs. Stifter.

Our son was a high school senior when he had her for English. "He sits in the back of the room talking to his friends," she told me. "Why don't you move him to the front row?" I urged, believing the embarrassment would get him to settle down. Mrs. Stifter looked at me steely-eyed over her glasses. "I don't move seniors," she said. "I flunk them." I was flustered. Our son's academic life flashed before my eyes. No teacher had ever threatened him with that before. I regained my composure and managed to say that I thought she was right. By the time I got home I was feeling pretty good about this. It was a radical approach for these times, but, well, why not? "She's going to flunk you," I told my son. I did not discuss it any further. Suddenly English became a priority in his life. He finished out the semester with an A.

I know one example doesn't make a case, but at night I see a parade of students who are angry and resentful for having been passed along until they could no longer even pretend to keep up. Of average intelligence or better, they eventually quit school, concluding they were too dumb to finish. "I should have been held back," is a comment I hear frequently. Even sadder are those students who are high school graduates who say to me after a few weeks of class, "I don't know how I ever got a high school diploma."

Passing students who have not mastered the work cheats them and the employers who expect graduates to have basic skills. We excuse this dishonest behavior by saying kids can't learn if they come from terrible environments. No one seems to stop to think that—no matter what environments they come from—most kids don't put school first on their list unless they perceive something is at stake. They'd rather be sailing.

Many students I see at night could give expert testimony on unemployment, chemical dependency, abusive relationships. In spite of these difficulties, they have decided to make education a priority. They are motivated by the desire for a better job or the need to hang on to the one they've got. They have a healthy fear of failure.

People of all ages can rise above their problems, but they need to have a reason to do so. Young people generally don't have the maturity to value education in the same way my adult students value it. But fear of failure, whether economic or academic, can motivate both.

Flunking as a regular policy has just as much merit today as it did two generations ago. We must review the threat of flunking and see it as it really is—a positive teaching tool. It is an expression of confidence by both teachers and parents that the students have the ability to learn the material presented to them. However, making it work again would take a dedicated, caring conspiracy between teachers and parents. It would mean facing the tough reality that passing kids who haven't learned the material—while it might save them grief for the short term—dooms them to longterm illiteracy. It would mean that teachers would have to follow through on their threats, and parents would have to stand behind them, knowing their children's best interests are indeed at stake. This means no more doing Scott's assignments for him because he might fail. No more passing Jodi because she's such a nice kid.

This is a policy that worked in the past and can work today. A wise teacher, with the support of his parents, gave our son the opportunity to succeed—or fail. It's time we return this choice to all students.

I. Reading Comprehension Activities

My Title: _____

Main Idea Statement: This story is about _____

_____

_____

Supporting Details / Specific Info / Facts & Details (5W's + H) :

1. _____

2. _____

3. _____

4. _____

5. _____

6. _____

7. _____

8. _____

9. _____

10. _____

Inferences (Educated Guesses/Possibilities/R-B-T-L):

1. _____

2. _____

3. _____

4. _____

5. _____

6. _____

7. _____

8. _____

II. Using Vocabulary In Context

1. Write a complete sentence using 'unknown' word in context: _____

_____

   A. New Word/Unknown Word: _____

   B. Dictionary Definition: _____

_____

   C. Synonyms: i. _____

               ii. _____

2. Write a complete sentence using 'unknown' word in context: _____

_____

   A. New Word/Unknown Word: _____

   B. Dictionary Definition: _____

_____

   C. Synonyms: i. _____

               ii. _____

3. Write a complete sentence using 'unknown' word in context: _____

_____

   A. New Word/Unknown Word: _____

   B. Dictionary Definition: _____

_____

   C. Synonyms: i. _____

               ii. _____

4. Write a complete sentence using 'unknown' word in context: _____

_____

   A. New Word/Unknown Word: _____

   B. Dictionary Definition: _____

_____

   C. Synonyms: i. _____

               ii. _____

III. Critical Reading & Thinking, Part One

A. The author's purpose in writing this was to _____

_____

_____

B. I know this because of the following traits included in this reading: _____

_____

C. Of the following tone words, discuss with a partner or in your group which words more appropriately describe the tone of the selection. Support your choices—reasons why you made the choice that you did.

accurate	factual	impartial	truthful	matter-of-fact
calm	angry	direct	dramatic	serious
informal	formal	optimistic	pessimistic	biased
neutral	objective	subjective	emotional	unbiased

D. A graphic organizer is the most effective way to show the visual connection between ideas. The best graphic organizer to use for this selection would be:

_____

_____

Why? _____

_____

E. Complete a graphic organizer, a map, or an outline of main points of selection.

IV. Critical Reading & Thinking, Part Two

Directions: Your instructor will guide you based on which of the sections below students will be working on (individually or in groups). Students are to use the back of this page (Notes Page) to list their information and ideas based on evaluation, analysis, or discussion of the chosen Issues, Readings, or Topics below. This is a teacher-guided activity.

Argument is the ability to exchange ideas, opinions, and conclusions between two or more students based on readings or writings that cover contemporary issues or author's ideas.

Issue #1: _____

Issue #2: _____

Issue #3: _____

Issue #4: _____

Inferences are educated guesses or educated possibilities based on what is already known (past information or background information). These are not assumptions, opinions, or personal points of view.

Reading #1: _____

Reading #2: _____

Reading #3: _____

Reading #4: _____

Points of View are ideas that students come to conclude (draw conclusions) based on their own personal experience or information gained from past knowledge or experiences. These ideas can be personal opinions if they have an educational foundation and are not just personal feelings or beliefs.

Topic #1: _____

Topic #2: _____

Topic #3: _____

Topic #4: _____

V. Summary Page –or– Precis Page

Summary / Precis (Circle One): This story is about _____

_____

_____

_____

_____

_____

_____

_____

_____

_____

_____

_____

_____

_____

_____

_____

_____

_____

_____

_____

_____

_____

_____

_____

_____

<u>Source Information (Citation):</u>

Title of Selection: _____

Author: _____

Publisher: _____

Copyright Date: _____

Notes: _____

Five Parenting Styles

by
Mary Ann Lamanna and Agnes Riedman

Image © Flashon Studio, 2012. Used under license from Shutterstock, Inc.

Considering the lack of consensus about how to raise children today, it may seem difficult to single out styles of parenting. From one point of view there are as many parenting styles as there are parents. . . . Yet certain elements in relating to children can be broadly classified. One helpful grouping is provided in E. E. LeMasters' listing of five parenting styles: the martyr, the pal, the police officer, the teacher-counselor, and the athletic coach. . . . We will discuss each of these.

The Parent as Martyr. Martyring parents believe "I would do anything for my child." . . . Some common examples of martyring are parents who habitually wait on their children or pick up after them; parents who nag children rather than letting them remember things for themselves; parents who buy virtually anything the child asks for; and parents who always do what the children want to do.

This parenting style presents some problems. First, the goals the martyring parent sets are impossible to carry out, and so the parent must always feel guilty. Also, . . . martyring tends to be reciprocated by manipulating. In addition, it is useful to ask if persons who consistently deny their own needs can enjoy the role of parenting and if closeness between parent and child is possible under these conditions.

The Parent as Pal. Some modern parents, mainly those of older children and adolescents, feel that they should be pals to their children. They adopt a **laissez-faire** policy, *letting their children set their own goals, rules, and limits,* with little or no guidance from parents. . . . According to LeMasters, "pal" parents apparently believe that they can avoid the conflict caused by the generation gap in this way.

Pal parenting is unrealistic. For one thing, parents in our society *are* responsible for guiding their children's development. Children deserve to benefit from the greater knowledge and experience of their parents, and at all ages they need some rules and limits, although these change as children grow older. Much research points to the conclusion that laissez-faire parenting is related to juvenile delinquency, heavy drug use, and runaway behavior in children. . . .

LeMasters points out that there are also relationship risks in the pal-parent model. If things don't go well, parents may want to retreat to a more formal, authoritarian style of parenting. But once they've established a buddy relationship, it is difficult to regain authority. . . .

The Parent as Police Officer. The police officer (or drill sergeant) model is just the opposite of the pal. These parents make sure the child obeys all the rules at all times, and they punish their children for even minor offenses. Being a police officer doesn't work very well today, however, and **autocratic discipline**, *which places the entire power of determining rules and limits in the parents' hands*—like laissez-faire parenting—has been associated with juvenile delinquency, drug use, and runaway teen-agers. . . .

There are several reasons for this. First, Americans have tended to resist anything that smacks of tyranny ever since the days of the Boston Tea Party. Hence, children are socialized to demand a share of independence at an early age.

A second reason why policing children doesn't work well today is that rapid social change gives the old and the young different values and points of view and even different knowledge. In our complex culture, youth learn attitudes from specialized professionals, such as teachers and school counselors, who often "widen the intellectual gap between parent and child." . . . For example, many young people today may advocate Judy Blume's novel for teens, *Forever* (1975), which is explicit about and accepting of premarital sex. Many parents, however, disapprove of the book.

A third reason why the police officer role doesn't work is that children, who find support from their adolescent peers, will eventually confront and challenge their parents. LeMasters points out that the adolescent peer group is "a formidable opponent" to any cop who insists on strict allegiance to autocratic authority. . . .

A fourth reason is that autocratic policing just isn't very effective in molding children's values. One study of 451 college freshmen and sophomores at a large western university found that adolescents were far more likely to be influenced by their parents' referent or expert power . . . than by coercive or legitimate power. The key was respect and a close relationship; habitual punishment or the "policing" of adolescents were far less effective modes of socialization. . . .

The Parent as Teacher-Counselor. The parent as teacher-counselor acts in accord with the **developmental model of child rearing**, *in which the child is viewed as an extremely plastic organism with virtually unlimited potential for growth and development.* The limits to this rich potential are seen as encompassed in the limits of the parent to tap and encourage it. . . . This model conceptualizes the parent(s) as almost omnipotent in guiding children's development. . . . If they do the right things at the right time, their children will more than likely be happy, intelligent, and successful.

Particularly during the 1960s and 1970s, authorities have stressed the ability of parents to influence their children's intellectual growth. Psychologist J. McVicker Hunt, for example, stated that he believes "you could raise a middle-class child's I.Q. by twenty points with what we know about child-rearing." . . .

The teacher-counselor approach has many fine features, and children do benefit from environmental stimulation. Yet this parenting style also poses problems. First, it puts the needs of the child above the parents' needs. It may be unrealistic for most parents to always be there, ready to stimulate the child's intellect or to act as a sounding board. Also, parents who respond as if each of their child's discoveries is wonderful may give the child the mistaken impression that he or she is the center of everyone's universe. . . .

A second difficulty is that this approach expects parents to be experts—an expectation that can easily produce guilt. Parents can never learn all that psychologists, sociologists, and specialized educators know. Yet If anything goes wrong, teacher-counselor parents are likely to feel they have only themselves to blame. . . .

Finally, contemporary research suggests more and more that this view greatly exaggerates the power of the parent and the passivity of children. Children also have inherited intellectual capacities and needs. Recent observers point instead to an interactive perspective, *which regards the influence between parent and child as mutual and reciprocal*, not just a "one-way street." . . .

The "athletic coach" model proceeds from this perspective.

The Parent as Athletic Coach. Athletic-coach parenting incorporates aspects of the developmental point of view. The coach (parent) is expected to have sufficient ability and knowledge of the game (life) and to be prepared and confident to lead players (children) to do their best and, it is hoped, to succeed.

This parenting style recognizes that parents, like coaches, have their own personalities and needs. They establish team rules, or *house rules* (and this can be done somewhat democratically with help from the players), and teach these rules to their children. They enforce the appropriate penalties when rules are broken, but policing is not their primary concern. Children, like team members, must be willing to accept discipline and, at least sometimes, to subordinate their own interests to the needs of the family team.

Coaching parents encourage their children to practice and to work hard to develop their own talents. But they realize that they can not play the game for their players. LeMasters says:

> The coach's position here is quite analogous to that of parents; once the game has begun it is up to the players to win or lose it. . . . [He] faces the same prospect as parents of sitting on the sidelines and watching players make mistakes that may prove disastrous.

LeMasters also points out that coaches can put uncooperative players off the team or even quit, but no such option is available to parents.

I. Reading Comprehension Activities

My Title: _____

Main Idea Statement: This story is about _____

_____

_____

Supporting Details / Specific Info / Facts & Details (5W's + H) :

1. _____

2. _____

3. _____

4. _____

5. _____

6. _____

7. _____

8. _____

9. _____

10. _____

Inferences (Educated Guesses/Possibilities/R-B-T-L):

1. _____

2. _____

3. _____

4. _____

5. _____

6. _____

7. _____

8. _____

II. Using Vocabulary In Context

1. Write a complete sentence using 'unknown' word in context: _____

_____

_____

    A. New Word/Unknown Word: _____

    B. Dictionary Definition: _____

_____

    C. Synonyms: i. _____

                ii. _____

2. Write a complete sentence using 'unknown' word in context: _____

_____

    A. New Word/Unknown Word: _____

    B. Dictionary Definition: _____

_____

    C. Synonyms: i. _____

                ii. _____

3. Write a complete sentence using 'unknown' word in context: _____

_____

    A. New Word/Unknown Word: _____

    B. Dictionary Definition: _____

_____

    C. Synonyms: i. _____

                ii. _____

4. Write a complete sentence using 'unknown' word in context: _____

_____

    A. New Word/Unknown Word: _____

    B. Dictionary Definition: _____

_____

    C. Synonyms: i. _____

                ii. _____

III. Critical Reading & Thinking, Part One

A. The author's purpose in writing this was to _____

_____

_____

B. I know this because of the following traits included in this reading: _____

_____

C. Of the following tone words, discuss with a partner or in your group which words more appropriately describe the tone of the selection. Support your choices—reasons why you made the choice that you did.

accurate	factual	impartial	truthful	matter-of-fact
calm	angry	direct	dramatic	serious
informal	formal	optimistic	pessimistic	biased
neutral	objective	subjective	emotional	unbiased

D. A graphic organizer is the most effective way to show the visual connection between ideas. The best graphic organizer to use for this selection would be:

_____

_____

Why? _____

_____

E. Complete a graphic organizer, a map, or an outline of main points of selection.

IV. Critical Reading & Thinking, Part Two

Directions: Your instructor will guide you based on which of the sections below students will be working on (individually or in groups). Students are to use the back of this page (Notes Page) to list their information and ideas based on evaluation, analysis, or discussion of the chosen Issues, Readings, or Topics below. This is a teacher-guided activity.

<u>Argument</u> is the ability to exchange ideas, opinions, and conclusions between two or more students based on readings or writings that cover contemporary issues or author's ideas.

Issue #1: _____

Issue #2: _____

Issue #3: _____

Issue #4: _____

<u>Inferences</u> are educated guesses or educated possibilities based on what is already known (past information or background information). These are not assumptions, opinions, or personal points of view.

Reading #1: _____

Reading #2: _____

Reading #3: _____

Reading #4: _____

<u>Points of View</u> are ideas that students come to conclude (draw conclusions) based on their own personal experience or information gained from past knowledge or experiences. These ideas can be personal opinions if they have an educational foundation and are not just personal feelings or beliefs.

Topic #1: _____

Topic #2: _____

Topic #3: _____

Topic #4: _____

V. Summary Page –or– Precis Page

Summary / Precis (Circle One): This story is about _____

_____

_____

_____

_____

_____

_____

_____

_____

_____

_____

_____

_____

_____

_____

_____

_____

_____

_____

_____

_____

_____

_____

_____

_____

_____

Source Information (Citation):

Title of Selection: _____

Author: _____

Publisher: _____

Copyright Date: _____

Notes:

Section One—High Interest

A Beloved Professor's Last Lessons

by
Mitch Albom

Image © bioraven, 2012. Used under license from Shutterstock, Inc.

The old man who lay dying before me was a friend and a respected professional. But mostly he was a teacher. I still thought of him that way. A teacher. *My* teacher. And I was his student.

Never mind that in 16 years since my college graduation, I had lost track of him, building a work-stuffed life as a journalist. And although Morrie Schwartz, my former sociology professor, had thinning gray hair now and sunken eyes, he still offered me the same delightful smile that <u>engaged</u> me as a freshman at Brandeis University. The moment we were reunited, I was back in class again, my ego much smaller, my sense of wonder renewed.

Good teachers do that.

If I could wish anything for students today, it would be that they might find their own Morrie, and see how much learning goes on when you put down the books. With the trend today toward larger classes on some campuses, and less personal <u>interaction</u> with professors, many students are missing something special.

For me, such an impersonal situation would have meant missing one of my life's most important relationships, forged with a man who taught me how to live when he was healthy and now, even more, was teaching me how to live through his dying.

"Which do you prefer, Mitch or Mitchell?" Morrie asked me that first day at Brandeis.

I was taken aback. No teacher had ever asked this before.

"My friends call me Mitch," I replied.

"Well then, Mitch it is. And Mitch?"

"Yes?"

"I hope one day you will think of me as your friend."

Two decades earlier, that was our first conversation.

We had now reunited to share our last.

Morrie was dying of Lou Gehrig's disease, amyotropic lateral sclerosis, a terrible illness that melts your nerves like a candle's flame and leaves your body a pile of wax. Morrie had but a few months left.

I had learned about his fate while watching "Nightline." I had lost track of Morrie in pursuit of my career in newspapers, television and radio. I was successful, financially if not spiritually. I lived in suburban Detroit with my wife, in a large house on a hill. It was there, one night, that I was startled to see my old professor talking earnestly with Ted Koppel. I felt ashamed at losing touch, yet was immediately drawn to his soothing conversation and engaging intelligence. Once teachers touch you, I believe they always will.

Watching the program that night, I learned that the silver lining to Morrie's illness—the only one—was that his mind would remain intact. As long as he had that, he could do what he loved most: teach.

And that is what he did with me. He taught me one last class, on the meaning of life.

Shortly after I saw Morrie on "Nightline," we reunited, rediscovered our affection for each other and began to meet at his home every Tuesday, the same day we used to meet for most of his classes in college.

In those years, it was an office at Brandeis; now it was the study in his house in West Newton, Mass., where he lived with his wife and a small visiting army of health care workers who tended to him around the clock. Back in college, I would scurry up the campus hill to Morrie's classes, always late, always out of breath. Now I flew in from Detroit each week to sit by my old teacher's side.

But there was still the same magic, the teacher-student chemistry, a relationship I have never really duplicated since.

Each Tuesday, Morrie would rest in a reclining chair, where he could watch his beloved hibiscus plant on the windowsill. He was unable to move his legs or torso. He needed me to wipe his brow and place his glasses on the bridge of his nose. He was weak and frail, 78 years old.

We talked about life, a different topic every week. I asked about things that perplexed many Americans. Marriage. Career. Aging. Death. Morrie saw these things through the eyes of a man who knew his fate. His wisdom was a precious fountain, offering answers to that eternal question: how would I change my life if I knew I had only a few months left?

So I asked about wealth. "I can tell you right now, as I'm sitting here dying," Morrie said, "when you need it most, neither money nor power will give you the feeling you're looking for."

I asked about aging. Morrie answered: "Aging is not just decay. It's growth. If you've found meaning in your life, you won't want to go back."

Often, I asked about his new specialty, death. "It ends a life," he said, "but not a relationship."

Throughout the process, we laughed. We held hands. I took notes and taped our conversations for the book we would do together, "Tuesdays With Morrie," something Morrie called our last thesis. As the weeks went on, my old professor spoke more and more about compassion, being fully human. He whispered warnings for the young and healthy. "Love each other or perish," he said, echoing Auden[1].

I wrote it all down, just as I had years ago.

Finally, one Tuesday, I arrived at the house in West Newton, but Morrie was no longer in his study. He was tucked in bed, his body shriveled to the size of a boy's. He was crying. I began to cry, too.

Our last class was brief, only a few words, and a funeral followed instead of graduation.

At the memorial service, hundreds of former students paid their respects. I found a common theme: few of us remembered textbooks and papers; all of us remembered Morrie. The way he spoke with us in his office. The way he listened to our student angst. The walks we took. The coffees we drank. The jokes we made.

Maybe they don't do this on college campuses anymore. Maybe you get something from large lecture halls and graduate assistants. Maybe it is a more efficient use of time, of resources. I don't know.

All I know is that I was never quite as good as I was when I was by my favorite professor's side, once in the prime of his life, once in his final days.

---

[1]W. H. Auden was a well-known British poet of the 1930s.

Selection 3: A Beloved Professor's Last Lessons

I. Reading Comprehension Activities

My Title: _____

Main Idea Statement: This story is about _____

_____

_____

Supporting Details / Specific Info / Facts & Details (5W's + H) :

1. _____

2. _____

3. _____

4. _____

5. _____

6. _____

7. _____

8. _____

9. _____

10. _____

Inferences (Educated Guesses/Possibilities/R-B-T-L):

1. _____

2. _____

3. _____

4. _____

5. _____

6. _____

7. _____

8. _____

II. Using Vocabulary In Context

1. Write a complete sentence using 'unknown' word in context: _____

_____

    A. New Word/Unknown Word: _____

    B. Dictionary Definition: _____

    _____

    C. Synonyms: i. _____

                ii. _____

2. Write a complete sentence using 'unknown' word in context: _____

_____

    A. New Word/Unknown Word: _____

    B. Dictionary Definition: _____

    _____

    C. Synonyms: i. _____

                ii. _____

3. Write a complete sentence using 'unknown' word in context: _____

_____

    A. New Word/Unknown Word: _____

    B. Dictionary Definition: _____

    _____

    C. Synonyms: i. _____

                ii. _____

4. Write a complete sentence using 'unknown' word in context: _____

_____

    A. New Word/Unknown Word: _____

    B. Dictionary Definition: _____

    _____

    C. Synonyms: i. _____

                ii. _____

III. Critical Reading & Thinking, Part One

A. The author's purpose in writing this was to _____

_____

_____

B. I know this because of the following traits included in this reading: _____

_____

C. Of the following tone words, discuss with a partner or in your group which words more appropriately describe the tone of the selection. Support your choices—reasons why you made the choice that you did.

accurate	factual	impartial	truthful	matter-of-fact
calm	angry	direct	dramatic	serious
informal	formal	optimistic	pessimistic	biased
neutral	objective	subjective	emotional	unbiased

D. A graphic organizer is the most effective way to show the visual connection between ideas. The best graphic organizer to use for this selection would be:

_____

_____

Why? _____

_____

E. Complete a graphic organizer, a map, or an outline of main points of selection.

IV. Critical Reading & Thinking, Part Two

Directions: Your instructor will guide you based on which of the sections below students will be working on (individually or in groups). Students are to use the back of this page (Notes Page) to list their information and ideas based on evaluation, analysis, or discussion of the chosen Issues, Readings, or Topics below. This is a teacher-guided activity.

Argument is the ability to exchange ideas, opinions, and conclusions between two or more students based on readings or writings that cover contemporary issues or author's ideas.

Issue #1: _____

Issue #2: _____

Issue #3: _____

Issue #4: _____

Inferences are educated guesses or educated possibilities based on what is already known (past information or background information). These are not assumptions, opinions, or personal points of view.

Reading #1: _____

Reading #2: _____

Reading #3: _____

Reading #4: _____

Points of View are ideas that students come to conclude (draw conclusions) based on their own personal experience or information gained from past knowledge or experiences. These ideas can be personal opinions if they have an educational foundation and are not just personal feelings or beliefs.

Topic #1: _____

Topic #2: _____

Topic #3: _____

Topic #4: _____

V. Summary Page –or– Precis Page

Summary / Precis (Circle One): This story is about _____

_____

_____

_____

_____

_____

_____

_____

_____

_____

_____

_____

_____

_____

_____

_____

_____

_____

_____

_____

_____

_____

_____

_____

<u>Source Information (Citation):</u>

Title of Selection: _____

Author: _____

Publisher: _____

Copyright Date: _____

Notes:

The Yellow Ribbon

by
Pete Hamill

Image © Richard F Cox, 2012. Used under
license from Shutterstock, Inc.

They were going to Fort Lauderdale, the girl remembered later. There were six of them, three boys and three girls, and they picked up the bus at the old terminal on 34th Street, carrying sandwiches and wine in paper bags, dreaming of golden beaches and the tides of the sea as the gray cold spring of New York vanished behind them. Vingo was on board from the beginning.

As the bus passed through Jersey and into Philly, they began to notice that Vingo never moved. He sat in front of the young people, his dusty face masking his age, dressed in a plain brown ill-fitting suit. His fingers were stained from cigarettes and he chewed the inside of his lip a lot, frozen into some personal cocoon° of silence.

Somewhere outside of Washington, deep into the night, the bus pulled into a Howard Johnson's, and everybody got off except Vingo. He sat rooted in his seat, and the young people began to wonder about him, trying to imagine his life: Perhaps he was a sea captain, maybe he had run away from his wife, he could be an old soldier going home. When they went back to the bus, the girl sat beside him and introduced herself.

"We're going to Florida," the girl said brightly. "You going that far?"

"I don't know," Vingo said.

"I've never been there," she said. "I hear it's beautiful."

"It is," he said quietly, as if remembering something he had tried to forget.

"You live there?"

"I did some time there in the Navy. Jacksonville."

"Want some wine?" she said. He smiled and took the bottle of Chianti and took a swig. He thanked her and retreated again into his silence. After a while, she went back to the others, as Vingo nodded in sleep.

In the morning they awoke outside another Howard Johnson's, and this time Vingo went in. The girl insisted that he join them. He seemed very shy and ordered black coffee and smoked nervously, as the young people chattered about sleeping on the beaches. When they went back on the bus, the girl sat with Vingo again, and after a while, slowly and painfully and with great hesitation, he began to tell his story. He had been in jail in New York for the last four years, and now he was going home.

"Four years!" the girl said. "What did you do?"

"It doesn't matter," he said with quiet bluntness°. "I did it and I went to jail. If you can't do the time, don't do the crime. That's what they say and they're right."

"Are you married?"

"I don't know."

"You don't know?" she said.

"Well, when I was in the can I wrote to my wife," he said. "I told her, I said, Martha, I understand if you can't stay married to me. I told her that, I said I was gonna be away a long time, and that if she couldn't stand it, if the kids kept askin' questions, if it hurt her too much, well, she could just forget me. Get a new guy—she's a wonderful woman, really something—and forget about me. I told her she didn't have to write me or nothing. And she didn't. Not for three and a half years."

"And you're going home now, not knowing?"

"Yeah," he said shyly. "Well, last week. when I was sure the parole was coming through I wrote her. I told her that if she had a new guy, I understood. But if she didn't, if she would take me back, she should let me know. We used to live in this town, Brunswick, just before Jacksonville, and there's a great big oak tree just as you come into town, a very famous tree, huge. I told her if she would take me back, she should put a yellow handkerchief on the tree, and I would get off and come home. If she didn't want me, forget it, no handkerchief, and I'd keep going on through."

"Wow," the girl said. "Wow."

She told the others, and soon all of them were in it, caught up in the approach of Brunswick, looking at the pictures Vingo showed them of his wife and three children, the woman handsome in a plain way, the children still unformed in a cracked, much-handled snapshot. Now they were twenty miles from Brunswick and the young people took over window seats on the right side, waiting for the approach of the great oak tree. Vingo stopped looking, tightening his face into the ex-con's mask, as if fortifying himself against still another disappointment. Then it was ten miles, and then five and the bus acquired a dark hushed mood, full of silence, of absence, of lost years, of the woman's plain face, of the sudden letter on the breakfast table, of the wonder of children, of the iron bars of solitude.

Then suddenly all of the young people were up out of their seats, screaming and shouting and crying, doing small dances, shaking clenched fists in triumph and exaltation°. All except Vingo.

Vingo sat there stunned, looking at the oak tree. It was covered with yellow handkerchiefs, twenty of them, thirty of them, maybe hundreds, a tree that stood like a banner of welcome blowing and billowing in the wind, turned into a gorgeous yellow blur by the passing bus. As the young people shouted, the old con slowly rose from his seat, holding himself tightly, and made his way to the front of the bus to go home.

I. Reading Comprehension Activities

My Title: _____

Main Idea Statement: This story is about _____

_____

_____

Supporting Details / Specific Info / Facts & Details (5W's + H) :

1. _____

2. _____

3. _____

4. _____

5. _____

6. _____

7. _____

8. _____

9. _____

10. _____

Inferences (Educated Guesses/Possibilities/R-B-T-L):

1. _____

2. _____

3. _____

4. _____

5. _____

6. _____

7. _____

8. _____

II. Using Vocabulary In Context

1. Write a complete sentence using 'unknown' word in context: _____

_____

_____

    A. New Word/Unknown Word: _____

    B. Dictionary Definition: _____

    _____

    C. Synonyms: i. _____

                   ii. _____

2. Write a complete sentence using 'unknown' word in context: _____

_____

    A. New Word/Unknown Word: _____

    B. Dictionary Definition: _____

    _____

    C. Synonyms: i. _____

                   ii. _____

3. Write a complete sentence using 'unknown' word in context: _____

_____

    A. New Word/Unknown Word: _____

    B. Dictionary Definition: _____

    _____

    C. Synonyms: i. _____

                   ii. _____

4. Write a complete sentence using 'unknown' word in context: _____

_____

    A. New Word/Unknown Word: _____

    B. Dictionary Definition: _____

    _____

    C. Synonyms: i. _____

                   ii. _____

III. Critical Reading & Thinking, Part One

A. The author's purpose in writing this was to _____

_____

_____

B. I know this because of the following traits included in this reading: _____

_____

C. Of the following tone words, discuss with a partner or in your group which words more appropriately describe the tone of the selection. Support your choices—reasons why you made the choice that you did.

accurate	factual	impartial	truthful	matter-of-fact
calm	angry	direct	dramatic	serious
informal	formal	optimistic	pessimistic	biased
neutral	objective	subjective	emotional	unbiased

D. A graphic organizer is the most effective way to show the visual connection between ideas. The best graphic organizer to use for this selection would be:

_____

_____

Why? _____

_____

E. Complete a graphic organizer, a map, or an outline of main points of selection.

IV. Critical Reading & Thinking, Part Two

Directions: Your instructor will guide you based on which of the sections below students will be working on (individually or in groups). Students are to use the back of this page (Notes Page) to list their information and ideas based on evaluation, analysis, or discussion of the chosen Issues, Readings, or Topics below. This is a teacher-guided activity.

Argument is the ability to exchange ideas, opinions, and conclusions between two or more students based on readings or writings that cover contemporary issues or author's ideas.

Issue #1: _____

Issue #2: _____

Issue #3: _____

Issue #4: _____

Inferences are educated guesses or educated possibilities based on what is already known (past information or background information). These are not assumptions, opinions, or personal points of view.

Reading #1: _____

Reading #2: _____

Reading #3: _____

Reading #4: _____

Points of View are ideas that students come to conclude (draw conclusions) based on their own personal experience or information gained from past knowledge or experiences. These ideas can be personal opinions if they have an educational foundation and are not just personal feelings or beliefs.

Topic #1: _____

Topic #2: _____

Topic #3: _____

Topic #4: _____

V. Summary Page –or– Precis Page

Summary / Precis (Circle One): This story is about _____

_____

_____

_____

_____

_____

_____

_____

_____

_____

_____

_____

_____

_____

_____

_____

_____

_____

_____

_____

_____

_____

_____

_____

_____

_____

Source Information (Citation):

Title of Selection: _____

Author: _____

Publisher: _____

Copyright Date: _____

Notes:

The Unseen Homeless Women

by
Bettijane Levine

Image © John T Takai, 2012. Used under license from Shutterstock, Inc.

Don't worry about Joanna—she'll be warm tonight. She will park in her old neighborhood, on a street with no security patrol and tall hedges in front of the houses, so no one will notice her car.

She will open the window a crack, lock the doors, curl up in warm clothes beneath blankets.

Tomorrow she will visit the Beverly Center, one of Los Angeles' upscale enclosed shopping malls. She'll wash her hair and underwear in Nordstrom's* ladies' room, dry them under the hand blower, apply makeup from testers at the cosmetic counter downstairs.

She will nibble her way through a supermarket, her cart piled with items useless to a woman with no home in which to use them. While pretending to shop she will munch roast beef, potato logs and salad from the deli counter—then abandon the cart before she checks out with only two apples, which is all she can afford.

You won't know her if you see her. She looks and acts the well-heeled woman. She knows the ropes in an affluent Los Angeles neighborhood. It's where she can survive—someone the census never counts, the regulars never notice. Not even her children, now in college, know she has no home. She will get back on her feet by herself, she says—or die in the attempt.

One recent afternoon, Joanna and Sarah (not their real names) sipped coffee at a Los Angeles cafe. They were invited by Marjorie Bard, who works with the homeless, to meet a reporter who could not quite believe such women exist. Certainly not in such affluent residential areas as Beverly Hills and Malibu.

Everyone knows about the homeless who camp out on the streets. But Bard says there are thousands of hidden homeless—middle-class people who once had fine homes and jobs, who are educated, energetic, capable—but who now have no money for shelter or food.

They are proud, resourceful people, she says, who have already imposed on family and friends as much as they dare. They view their cars as being more dignified, safe and private temporary shelters than anything the social services system could provide.

Bard, who works only with women, found that the hidden homeless survive by staying in the neighborhoods where they used to live and by frequenting familiar places: department stores and markets, libraries and museums. Places that offer food, hygiene facilities or simply the sense of cultural enrichment and well-being to which they were accustomed.

Bard said she has met 1,000 women nationwide and recorded their oral histories. In fact, she said, she used to be one of them herself.

She became an "overnight indigent," she says, when she was forced from her Maryland house by her husband 15 years ago. With no money for necessities, let alone for lawyers to fight for her financial rights, she began looking for a job.

Bard, now in her 50s, had a bachelor's degree and had taught elementary school in Los Angeles before she married. In Maryland, she was a community organizer who taught jewelry making at a college.

"But when I went to look for jobs," she recalled, "they said, 'You're overqualified,' 'You're under-experienced,' 'You don't know the computer,' things like that. They were really saying I didn't fit in anywhere anymore. I couldn't get a decent job."

In desperation, she stashed clothes and jewelry-making tools in her car, which she used as home base for the next three years while selling jewelry to support herself. Then she started the drive west, toward her mother's home in Beverly Hills.

"At first I thought I was alone," she recalls. "But in each city, I spotted women doing the same things I was doing. We had what you might call similar tricks of the trade."

She would, for example, befriend hotel maids, who would let her use just-vacated rooms so she could shower, wash her hair and catch some sleep before the rooms had to be cleaned.

After a month on the road, Bard reached Beverly Hills, moved into the house of her ailing mother and began tracing the hidden homeless population in some of Los Angeles' more pricey neighborhoods. She entered graduate school at the University of California at Los Angeles, supported by grants, and obtained a doctorate in 1988. She did her dissertation on homelessness.

She wrote a book, "Shadow Women" (Sheed & Ward, 1990), which documents stories of women who "mingle with polite society during the day, but sleep in their cars at night; women who may have been wealthy but are suddenly unable to support themselves."

These women don't want handouts or welfare or to sleep in shelters, she says. They want to fend for themselves and are willing to live "in hiding" until they can get back on their feet.

Joanna and Sarah are among these women.

Sarah has not had a home for four years. For 13 years before that, she was married to a lawyer, whom she put through school by "typing dissertations day and night, while caring for two babies." He got his degree and started a practice. They bought a Los Angeles house with walk-in closets and a live-in maid. Sarah left the marriage when she realized her husband would not allow her to have a career.

"I got very little from the sale of the house, which he had highly mortgaged," she says, "and I was advised by his lawyer to take no alimony, only child support.

"I rented a place in the same neighborhood, so the children could continue at school," she recalls. "I established credit for myself and got a job at the school where my children went."

She was proud of herself, and the pride still lingers in her voice as she tells the story. But her job didn't pay enough. Bills piled up—insurance, car payments, rent, all the extras for the kids—and she fell behind.

Soon there wasn't enough extra money even to take the kids out to a movie and a pizza. Her ex-husband, meanwhile, was luring them with his lavish lifestyle.

"My husband thought he would have to fight me for custody of our children. But I told our children, 'I want you to be happy. I want you to be where it will feel best for you.' We all went into therapy. After a year's time, I felt the children knew enough so that they could make a decision. They decided to live with him. I knew he really loved them and would give them what they'd need." And, of course, she thought it would be temporary.

But as soon as he got the children, he sold his practice and moved with them out of the area.

She was determined to change things. She left her job and put all her efforts into finding a better one. But she couldn't. She was "in mourning" for her children. Her savings were dwindling. The rent was too high. She made car payments late, and then not at all. Heartbroken and determined to conserve what little she had left, she put most of her belongings in storage, the rest in her hatchback mini-wagon.

She worked at any jobs she could get, all low-paying. "I was cashier at a delicatessen, among dozens of other things," she says. "But minimum wage was not enough to even begin to get me out of debt. I was educated, willing. But there was no way to get back on my feet. I soon couldn't even pay the monthly storage bills, so I sold my possessions.

"Now, everything I have is in my car, which the repo man is looking for. If he finds me, he'll take the car with everything I own. He won't wait for me to empty it."

She does not sound bitter. Or even sad.

"I do not have sour-grape stories about how the system screwed me," Sarah says. "That is not how I feel. But for a person like me, who fell through the slats because of circumstance, there ought to be a way to get back up. And there doesn't seem to be."

"When I get a good job I will still live in my car, saving to pay it off so that I do not lose the car plus the $6,000 I've already paid for it. I do not want handouts, charity, welfare. I would not sleep in shelters. I do not want you to print my name. I will get out of this, never speak of it again and no one will ever know."

Actually, she admits, some of her best friends do know about her condition. "But if you tell too much, too often, you lose your friends. You 'wear them out.' They don't want to hear this. They love you and it's very sad and they can't help. So they tend to avoid you. And you learn to pretend everything is OK when you talk to them."

Sarah phoned the reporter a few days after their meeting to say that she had landed a job as a domestic companion. The job offered "good living accommodations and relatively low pay. But within a year I can have my car payments up to date."

I. Reading Comprehension Activities

My Title: _____

Main Idea Statement: This story is about _____

_____

_____

Supporting Details / Specific Info / Facts & Details (5W's + H) :

1. _____

2. _____

3. _____

4. _____

5. _____

6. _____

7. _____

8. _____

9. _____

10. _____

Inferences (Educated Guesses/Possibilities/R-B-T-L):

1. _____

2. _____

3. _____

4. _____

5. _____

6. _____

7. _____

8. _____

II. Using Vocabulary In Context

1. Write a complete sentence using 'unknown' word in context: _____

_____

_____

    A. New Word/Unknown Word: _____

    B. Dictionary Definition: _____

    _____

    C. Synonyms: i. _____

                  ii. _____

2. Write a complete sentence using 'unknown' word in context: _____

_____

    A. New Word/Unknown Word: _____

    B. Dictionary Definition: _____

    _____

    C. Synonyms: i. _____

                  ii. _____

3. Write a complete sentence using 'unknown' word in context: _____

_____

    A. New Word/Unknown Word: _____

    B. Dictionary Definition: _____

    _____

    C. Synonyms: i. _____

                  ii. _____

4. Write a complete sentence using 'unknown' word in context: _____

_____

    A. New Word/Unknown Word: _____

    B. Dictionary Definition: _____

    _____

    C. Synonyms: i. _____

                  ii. _____

III. Critical Reading & Thinking, Part One

A. The author's purpose in writing this was to _____

_____

_____

B. I know this because of the following traits included in this reading: _____

_____

C. Of the following tone words, discuss with a partner or in your group which words more appropriately describe the tone of the selection. Support your choices—reasons why you made the choice that you did.

accurate	factual	impartial	truthful	matter-of-fact
calm	angry	direct	dramatic	serious
informal	formal	optimistic	pessimistic	biased
neutral	objective	subjective	emotional	unbiased

D. A graphic organizer is the most effective way to show the visual connection between ideas. The best graphic organizer to use for this selection would be:

_____

_____

Why? _____

_____

E. Complete a graphic organizer, a map, or an outline of main points of selection.

IV. Critical Reading & Thinking, Part Two

Directions: Your instructor will guide you based on which of the sections below students will be working on (individually or in groups). Students are to use the back of this page (Notes Page) to list their information and ideas based on evaluation, analysis, or discussion of the chosen Issues, Readings, or Topics below. This is a teacher-guided activity.

<u>Argument</u> is the ability to exchange ideas, opinions, and conclusions between two or more students based on readings or writings that cover contemporary issues or author's ideas.

Issue #1: _____

Issue #2: _____

Issue #3: _____

Issue #4: _____

<u>Inferences</u> are educated guesses or educated possibilities based on what is already known (past information or background information). These are not assumptions, opinions, or personal points of view.

Reading #1: _____

Reading #2: _____

Reading #3: _____

Reading #4: _____

<u>Points of View</u> are ideas that students come to conclude (draw conclusions) based on their own personal experience or information gained from past knowledge or experiences. These ideas can be personal opinions if they have an educational foundation and are not just personal feelings or beliefs.

Topic #1: _____

Topic #2: _____

Topic #3: _____

Topic #4: _____

V. Summary Page –or– Precis Page

Summary / Precis (Circle One): This story is about _____

_____

_____

_____

_____

_____

_____

_____

_____

_____

_____

_____

_____

_____

_____

_____

_____

_____

_____

_____

_____

_____

_____

_____

_____

Source Information (Citation):

Title of Selection: _____

Author: _____

Publisher: _____

Copyright Date: _____

Notes:

The Lesson

by
Toni Cade Bambara

Image © Robert Adrian Hillman, 2012. Used under license from Shutterstock, Inc.

Back in the days when everyone was old and stupid or young and foolish and me and Sugar were the only ones just right, this lady moved on our block with nappy hair and proper speech and no makeup. And quite naturally we laughed at her, laughed the way we did at the junk man who went about his business like he was some big-time president and his sorry-ass horse his secretary. And we kinda hated her too, hated the way we did the winos who cluttered up our parks and pissed on our handball walls and stank up our hallways and stairs so you couldn't halfway play hide-and-seek without a goddamn gas mask. Miss Moore was her name. The only woman on the block with no first name. And she was black as hell, cept for her feet, which were fish-white and spooky. And she was always planning these boring-ass things for us to do, us being my cousin, mostly, who lived on the block cause we all moved North the same time and to the same apartment then spread out gradual[1] to breathe. And our parents would yank our heads into some kinda shape and crisp up our clothes so we'd be presentable for travel with Miss Moore, who always looked like she was going to church, though she never did. Which is just one of things the grown-ups talked about when they talked behind her back like a dog. But when she came calling with some sachet[2] she'd sewed up or some gingerbread she'd made or some book, why then they'd all be too embarrassed to turn her down and we'd get handed over all spruced up. She'd been to college and said it was only right that she should take responsibility for the young ones' education, and she not even related by marriage or blood. So they'd go for it. Specially Aunt Gretchen. She was the main gofer in the family. You got some ole dumb shit foolishness you want somebody to go for, you send for Aunt Gretchen. She been screwed into the go-along for so long, it's a blood-deep natural thing with her. Which is how she got saddled with me and Sugar and Junior in the first place while our mothers were in a la-de-da apartment up the block having a good ole time.

So this one day Miss Moore rounds us all up at the mailbox and it's puredee hot and she's knockin herself out about arithmetic. And school suppose to let up in summer I heard, but she don't never let

---

[1] little by little
[2] a small cloth bag containing perfumed powder

up. And the starch in my pinafore[3] scratching the shit outta me and I'm really hating this nappy-head bitch and her goddamn college degree. I'd much rather go to the pool or to the show where it's cool. So me and Sugar leaning on the mailbox being surly,[4] which is a Miss Moore word. And Flyboy checking out what everybody brought for lunch. And Fat Butt already wasting his peanut-butter-and-jelly sandwich like the pig he is. And Junebug punchin on Q.T.'s arm for potato chips. And Rosie Giraffe shifting from one hip to the other waiting for somebody to step on her foot or ask her if she from Georgia so she can kick ass, preferably Mercedes'. And Miss Moore asking us do we know what money is, like we a bunch of retards. I mean real money, she say, like it's only poker chips or monopoly papers we lay on the grocer. So right away I'm tired of this and say so. And would much rather snatch Sugar and go to the Sunset and terrorize the West Indian kids and take their hair ribbons and their money too. And Miss Moore files that remark away for next week's lesson on brotherhood, I can tell. And finally I say we oughta get to the subway cause it's cooler and besides we might meet some cute boys. Sugar done swiped her mama's lipstick, so we ready.

So we heading down the street and she's boring us silly about what things cost and what our parents make and how much goes for rent and how money ain't divided up right in this country. And then she gets to the part about we all poor and live in the slums, which I don't feature.[5] And I'm ready to speak on that, but she steps out in the street and hails two cabs just like that. Then she hustles half the crew in with her and hands me a five-dollar bill and tells me to calculate 10 percent tip for the driver. And we're off. Me and Sugar and Junebug and Flyboy hangin out the window and hollering to everybody, putting lipstick on each other cause Flyboy a faggot anyway, and making farts with our sweaty armpits. But I'm mostly trying to figure how to spend this money. But they all fascinated with the meter ticking and Junebug starts laying bets as to how much it'll read when Flyboy can't hold his breath no more. Then Sugar lays bets as to how much it'll be when we get there. So I'm stuck. Don't nobody want to go for my plan, which is to jump out at the next light and run off to the first bar-b-que we can find. Then the driver tells us to get the hell out cause we there already. And the meter reads eighty-five cents. And I'm stalling to figure out the tip and Sugar say give him a dime. And I decide he don't need it bad as I do, so later for him. But then he tries to take off with Junebug foot still in the door so we talk about his mama something ferocious. Then we check out that we on Fifth Avenue and everybody dressed up in stockings. One lady in a fur coat, hot as it is. White folks crazy.

"This is the place," Miss Moore say, presenting it to us in the voice she uses at the museum. "Let's look in the windows before we go in."

"Can we steal?" Sugar asks very serious like she's getting the ground rules squared away before she plays. "I beg your pardon," say Miss Moore, and we fall out. So she leads us around the windows of the toy store and me and Sugar screamin, "This is mine, that's mine, I gotta have that, that was made for me, I was born for that," till Big Butt drowns us out.

"Hey, I'm goin to buy that there."

"That there? You don't even know what it is, stupid."

"I do so," he say punchin on Rosie Giraffe. "It's a microscope."

"Whatcha gonna do with a microscope, fool?"

"Look at things."

---

[3] a sleeveless, apron-like dress
[4] in a disagreeable mood
[5] agree with

"Like what, Ronald?" ask Miss Moore. And Big Butt ain't got the first notion. So here go Miss Moore gabbing about the thousands of bacteria in a drop of water and the somethinorother in a speck of blood and the million and one living things in the air around us is invisible to the naked eye. And what she say that for? Junebug go to town on that "naked" and we rolling. Then Miss Moore ask what it cost. So we all jam into the window smudgin it up and the price tag say $300. So then she ask how long'd take for Big Butt and Junebug to save up their allowances. "Too long," I say. "Yeh," adds Sugar, "outgrown it by that time." And Miss Moore say no, you never outgrow learning instruments. "Why, even medical students and interns and," blah, blah, blah. And we ready to choke Big Butt for bringing it up in the first damn place.

"This here costs four hundred eighty dollars," say Rosie Giraffe. So we pile up all over her to see what she pointin out. My eyes tell me it's a chunk of glass cracked with something heavy, and different-color inks dripped into the splits, then the whole thing put into a oven or something. But for $480 it don't make sense.

"That's a paperweight made of semi-precious stones fused[6] together under tremendous pressure," she explains slowly, with her hands doing the mining and all the factory work.

"So what's a paperweight?" asks Rosie Giraffe.

"To weigh paper with, dumbbell," say Flyboy, the wise man from the East.

"Not exactly," say Miss Moore, which is what she say when you warm or way off too. "It's to weigh paper down so it won't scatter and make your desk untidy." So right away me and Sugar curtsy to each other and then to Mercedes who is more the tidy type.

"We don't keep paper on top of the desk in my class," say Junebug, figuring Miss Moore crazy or lyin one.

"At home, then," she say. "Don't you have a calendar and a pencil case and a blotter and a letter-opener on your desk at home where you do your homework?" And she know damn well what our homes look like cause she nosys around in them every chance she gets.

"I don't even have a desk," say Junebug. "Do we?"

"No. And I don't get no homework neither," say Big Butt.

"And I don't even have a home," say Flyboy like he do at school to keep the white folks off his back and sorry for him. Send this poor kid to camp posters, is his specialty.

"I do," says Mercedes. "I have a box of stationery on my desk and a picture of my cat. My godmother bought the stationery and the desk. There's a big rose on each sheet and the envelopes smell like roses."

"Who wants to know about your smelly-ass stationery," say Rosie Giraffe fore I can get my two cents in.

"It's important to have a work area all your own so that . . ."

"Will you look at this sailboat, please," say Flyboy, cuttin her off and pointin to the thing like it was his. So once again we tumble all over each other to gaze at this magnificent thing in the toy store which is just big enough to maybe sail two kittens across the pond if you strap them to the posts tight. We all start reciting the price tag like we in assembly. "Handcrafted sailboat of fiberglass at one thousand one hundred ninety-five dollars."

---

[6]melted

"Unbelievable," I hear myself say and am really stunned. I read it again for myself just in case the group recitation put me in a trance. Same thing. For some reason this pisses me off. We look at Miss Moore and she lookin at us, waiting for I dunno what.

Who'd pay all that when you can buy a sailboat set for a quarter at Pop's, a tube of glue for a dime, and a ball of string for eight cents? "It must have a motor and a whole lot else besides," I say. "My sailboat cost me about fifty cents."

"But will it take water?" say Mercedes with her smart ass.

"Took mine to Alley Pond Park once," say Flyboy. "String broke. Lost it. Pity."

"Sailed mine in Central Park and it keeled over and sank. Had to ask my father for another dollar."

"And you got the strap," laugh Big Butt. "The jerk didn't even have a string on it. My old man wailed[7] on his behind."

Little Q.T. was staring hard at the sailboat and you could see he wanted it bad. But he too little and somebody'd just take it from him. So what the hell. "This boat for kids, Miss Moore?"

"Parents silly to buy something like that just to get all broke up," say Rosie Giraffe.

"That much money it should last forever," I figure.

"My father'd buy it for me if I wanted it."

"Your father, my ass," say Rosie Giraffe getting a chance to finally push Mercedes.

"Must be rich people shop here," say Q.T.

"You are a very bright boy," say Flyboy. "What was your first clue?" And he rap him on the head with the back of his knuckles, since Q.T. the only one he could get away with. Though Q.T. liable[8] to come up behind you years later and get his licks in when you half expect it.

"What I want to know is," I says to Miss Moore though I never talk to her, I wouldn't give the bitch that satisfaction, "is how much a real boat costs? I figure a thousand'd get you a yacht any day."

"Why don't you check that out," she says, "and report back to the group?" Which really pains my ass. If you gonna mess up a perfectly good swim day least you could do is have some answers. "Let's go in," she say like she got something up her sleeve. Only she don't lead the way. So me and Sugar turn the corner to where the entrance is, but when we get there I kinda hang back. Not that I'm scared, what's there to be afraid of, just a toy store. But I feel funny, shame. But what I got to be shamed about? Got as much right to go in as anybody. But somehow I can't seem to get hold of the door, so I step away for Sugar to lead. But she hangs back too. And I look at her and she looks at me and this is ridiculous. I mean, damn, I have never ever been shy about doing nothing or going nowhere. But then Mercedes steps up and then Rosie Giraffe and Big Butt crowd in behind and shove, and next thing we all stuffed into the doorway with only Mercedes squeezing past us, smoothing out her jumper and walking right down the aisle. Then the rest of us tumble in like a glued-together jigsaw done all wrong. And people lookin at us. And it's like the time me and Sugar crashed into the Catholic church on a dare. But once we got in there and everything so hushed and holy and the candles and the bowin and the handkerchiefs on all the drooping heads, I just couldn't go through with the plan. Which was for me to run up to the altar and do a tap dance while Sugar played the nose flute and messed around in the holy water. And Sugar kept givin me the elbow. Then later teased me so bad I tied her up in the shower and

---

[7]whipped
[8]is likely to

turned it on and locked her in. And she'd be there till this day if Aunt Gretchen hadn't finally figured I was lyin about the boarder takin a shower.

Same thing in the store. We all walkin on tiptoe and hardly touchin the games and puzzles and things. And I watched Miss Moore who is steady watchin us like she waitin for a sign. Like Mama Drewery watches the sky and sniffs the air and takes note of just how much slant is in the bird formation. Then me and Sugar bump smack into each other, so busy gazing at the toys, 'specially the sailboat. But we don't laugh and go into our fat-lady bump-stomach routine. We just stare at that price tag. Then Sugar run a finger over the whole boat. And I'm jealous and want to hit her. Maybe not her, but I sure want to punch somebody in the mouth,

"Watcha bring us here for, Miss Moore?"

"You sound angry, Sylvia. Are you mad about something?" Givin me one of them grins like she tellin a grown-up joke that never turns out to be funny. And she's lookin very closely at me like maybe she plannin to do my portrait from memory. I'm mad, but I won't give her that satisfaction. So I slouch around the store bein very bored and say, "Let's go."

Me and Sugar at the back of the train watchin the tracks whizzin by large then small then gettin gobbled up in the dark. I'm thinkin about this tricky toy I saw in the store. A clown that somersaults on a bar then does chin-ups just cause you yank lightly at his leg. Cost $35. I could see me askin my mother for a $35 birthday clown. "You wanna who that costs what?" she'd say, cocking her head to the side to get a better view of the hole in my head. Thirty-five dollars could buy new bunk beds for Junior and Gretchen's boy. Thirty-five dollars and the whole household could go visit Granddaddy Nelson in the country. Thirty-five dollars would pay for the rent and the piano bill too.

Who are these people that spend that much for performing clowns and $1,000 for toy sailboats? What kinda work they do and how they live and how come we ain't in on it? Where we are is who we are, Miss Moore always pointin out. But it don't necessarily have to be that way, she always adds then waits for somebody to say that poor people have to wake up and demand their share of the pie and don't none of us know what kind of pie she talkin about in the first damn place. But she ain't so smart cause I still got her four dollars from the taxi and she sure ain't gettin it. Messin up my day with this shit. Sugar nudges me in my pocket and winks.

Miss Moore lines us up in front of the mailbox where we started from, seem like years ago, and I got a headache for thinkin so hard. And we lean all over each other so we can hold up under the draggy-ass lecture she always finishes us off with at the end before we thank her for borin us to tears. But she just looks at us like she readin tea leaves. Finally she say, "Well, what did you think of F.A.O. Schwarz?"[9]

Rosie Giraffe mumbles, "White folks crazy."

"I'd like to go there again when I get my birthday money," says Mercedes, and we shove her out the pack so she has to lean on the mailbox by herself.

"I'd like a shower. Tiring day," say Flyboy.

Then Sugar surprises me by sayin, "You know, Miss Moore, I don't think all of us here put together eat in a year what that sailboat costs." And Miss Moore lights up like somebody goosed her. "And?" she say, urging Sugar on. Only I'm standin on her foot so she don't continue.

---

[9] a large toy store in New York City

"Imagine for a minute what kind of society it is in which some people can spend on a toy what it would cost to feed a family of six or seven. What do you think?"

"I think," say Sugar pushing me off her feet like she never done before, cause I whip her ass in a minute, "that this is not much of a democracy if you ask me. Equal chance to pursue happiness means an equal crack at the dough, don't it?" Miss Moore is besides herself and I am disgusted with Sugar's treachery. So I stand on her foot one more time to see if she'll shove me. She shuts up, and Miss Moore looks at me, sorrowfully I'm thinkin. And somethin weird is goin on, I can feel it in my chest.

"Anybody else learn anything today?" lookin dead at me. I walk away and Sugar has to run to catch up and don't even seem to notice when I shrug her arm off my shoulder.

"Well, we got four dollars anyway," she says.

"Uh hunh."

"We could go to Hascombs and get half a chocolate layer and then go to the Sunset and still have plenty money for potato chips and ice-cream sodas."

"Uh hunh."

"Race you to Hascombs," she say.

We start down the block and she gets ahead which is O.K. by me cause I'm goin to the West End and then over to the Drive to think this day through. She can run if she want to and even run faster. But ain't nobody gonna beat me at nuthin.

I. Reading Comprehension Activities

My Title: _____

Main Idea Statement: This story is about _____

_____

_____

Supporting Details / Specific Info / Facts & Details (5W's + H) :

1. _____

2. _____

3. _____

4. _____

5. _____

6. _____

7. _____

8. _____

9. _____

10. _____

Inferences (Educated Guesses/Possibilities/R-B-T-L):

1. _____

2. _____

3. _____

4. _____

5. _____

6. _____

7. _____

8. _____

II. Using Vocabulary In Context

1. Write a complete sentence using 'unknown' word in context: _____

_____

_____

    A. New Word/Unknown Word: _____

    B. Dictionary Definition: _____

_____

    C. Synonyms: i. _____

               ii. _____

2. Write a complete sentence using 'unknown' word in context: _____

_____

    A. New Word/Unknown Word: _____

    B. Dictionary Definition: _____

_____

    C. Synonyms: i. _____

               ii. _____

3. Write a complete sentence using 'unknown' word in context: _____

_____

    A. New Word/Unknown Word: _____

    B. Dictionary Definition: _____

_____

    C. Synonyms: i. _____

               ii. _____

4. Write a complete sentence using 'unknown' word in context: _____

_____

    A. New Word/Unknown Word: _____

    B. Dictionary Definition: _____

_____

    C. Synonyms: i. _____

               ii. _____

III. Critical Reading & Thinking, Part One

A. The author's purpose in writing this was to _____

_____

_____

B. I know this because of the following traits included in this reading: _____

_____

C. Of the following tone words, discuss with a partner or in your group which words more appropriately describe the tone of the selection. Support your choices—reasons why you made the choice that you did.

accurate	factual	impartial	truthful	matter-of-fact
calm	angry	direct	dramatic	serious
informal	formal	optimistic	pessimistic	biased
neutral	objective	subjective	emotional	unbiased

D. A graphic organizer is the most effective way to show the visual connection between ideas. The best graphic organizer to use for this selection would be:

_____

_____

Why? _____

_____

E. Complete a graphic organizer, a map, or an outline of main points of selection.

IV. Critical Reading & Thinking, Part Two

Directions: Your instructor will guide you based on which of the sections below students will be working on (individually or in groups). Students are to use the back of this page (Notes Page) to list their information and ideas based on evaluation, analysis, or discussion of the chosen Issues, Readings, or Topics below. This is a teacher-guided activity.

Argument is the ability to exchange ideas, opinions, and conclusions between two or more students based on readings or writings that cover contemporary issues or author's ideas.

Issue #1: _____

Issue #2: _____

Issue #3: _____

Issue #4: _____

Inferences are educated guesses or educated possibilities based on what is already known (past information or background information). These are not assumptions, opinions, or personal points of view.

Reading #1: _____

Reading #2: _____

Reading #3: _____

Reading #4: _____

Points of View are ideas that students come to conclude (draw conclusions) based on their own personal experience or information gained from past knowledge or experiences. These ideas can be personal opinions if they have an educational foundation and are not just personal feelings or beliefs.

Topic #1: _____

Topic #2: _____

Topic #3: _____

Topic #4: _____

V. Summary Page –or– Precis Page

Summary / Precis (Circle One): This story is about _____

_____

_____

_____

_____

_____

_____

_____

_____

_____

_____

_____

_____

_____

_____

_____

_____

_____

_____

_____

_____

_____

_____

_____

_____

_____

_____

_____

_____

Source Information (Citation):

Title of Selection: _____

Author: _____

Publisher: _____

Copyright Date: _____

Notes:

Of Mice and Men

by
John Steinbeck

Image © vilsow, 2012. Used under license from Shutterstock, Inc.

Although there was evening brightness showing through the windows of the bunkhouse, inside it was dusk. Through the open door came the thuds and occasional clangs of a horseshoe game, and now and then the sound of voices raised in approval or derision.

Slim and George came into the darkening bunk house together. Slim reached up over the card table and turned on the tin-shaded electric light. Instantly the table was brilliant with light, and the cone of the shade threw its brightness straight downward, leaving the corners of the bunkhouse still in dusk. Slim sat down on a box and George took his place opposite.

"It wasn't nothing," said Slim. "I would of had to drowned most of 'em anyways. No need to thank me about that."

George said, "It wasn't much to you, maybe, but it was a hell of alot to him. Jesus Christ, I don't know how we're gonna get him to sleep in here. He'll want to sleep right out in the barn with 'em. We'll have trouble keepin' him from getting right in the box with them pups."

"It wasn't nothing," Slim repeated. "Say, you sure was right about him. Maybe he ain't bright, but I never seen such a worker. He damn near killed his partner buckin' barley. There ain't nobody can keep up with him. God awmighty, I never seen such a strong guy."

George spoke proudly. "Jus' tell Lennie what to do an' he'll do it if it don't take no figuring. He can't think of nothing to do himself, but he sure can take orders."

There was a clang of horseshoe on iron stake outside and a little cheer of voices.

Slim moved back slightly so the light was not on his face. "Funny how you an' him string along together." It was Slim's calm invitation to confidence.

"What's funny about it?" George demanded defensively.

"Oh, I dunno. Hardly none of the guys ever travel together. I hardly never seen two guys travel together. You know how the hands are, they just come in and get their bunk and work a month, and then they quit and go out alone. Never seem to give a damn about nobody. It jus' seems kinda funny a cuckoo like him and a smart little guy like you travelin' together."

"He ain't no cuckoo," said George. "He's dumb as hell, but he ain't crazy. An' I ain't so bright neither, or I wouldn't be buckin' barley for my fifty and found. If I was bright, if I was even a little bit smart, I'd have my own little place, an' I'd be bringin' in my own crops, 'stead of doin' all the work and not getting what comes up outta the ground." George fell silent. He wanted to talk. Slim neither encouraged nor discouraged him. He just sat back quiet and receptive.

"It ain't so funny, him an' me goin' aroun' together," George said at last. "Him and me was both born in Auburn. I knowed his Aunt Clara. She took him when he was a baby and raised him up. When his Aunt Clara died, Lennie just come along with me out workin'. Got kinda used to each other after a little while."

"Umm," said Slim.

George looked over at Slim and saw the calm, Godlike eyes fastened on him. "Funny," said George. "I used to have a hell of a lot of fun with 'im. Used to play jokes on 'im 'cause he was too dumb to take care of 'imself. But he was too dumb even to know he had a joke played on him. I had fun. Made me seem God damn smart alongside of him. Why he'd do any damn thing I tol' him. If I tol' him to walk over a cliff, over he'd go. That wasn't so damn much fun after a while. He never got mad about it, neither. I've beat the hell outta him, and he coulda bust every bone in my body jus' with his han's, but he never lifted a finger against me." George's voice was taking on the tone of confession. "Tell you what made me stop that. One day a bunch of guys was standin' around up on the Sacramento River. I was feelin' pretty smart. I turns to Lennie and says, 'Jump in.' An' he jumps. Couldn't swim a stroke. He damn near drowned before we could get him. An' he was so damn nice to me for pullin' him out. Clean forgot I told him to jump in. Well, I ain't done nothing like that no more."

"He's a nice fella," said Slim. "Guy don't need no sense to be a nice fella. Seems to me sometimes it jus' works the other way around. Take a real smart guy and he ain't hardly ever a nice fella."

George stacked the scattered cards and began to lay out his solitaire hand. The shoes thudded on the ground outside. At the windows the light of the evening still made the window squares bright.

"I ain't got no people," George said. "I seen the guys that go around on the ranches alone. That ain't no good. They don't have no fun. After a long time they get mean. They get wantin' to fight all the time."

"Yeah, they get mean," Slim agreed. "They get so they don't want to talk to nobody."

" 'Course Lennie's a God damn nuisance most of the time," said George. "But you get used to goin' around with a guy an' you can't get rid of him."

"He ain't mean," said Slim. "I can see Lennie ain't a bit mean."

" 'Course he ain't mean. But he gets in trouble alla time because he's so God damn dumb. Like what happened in Weed—" He stopped, stopped in the middle of turning over a card. He looked alarmed and peered over at Slim. "You wouldn't tell nobody?"

"What'd he do in Weed?" Slim asked calmly.

"You wouldn' tell? . . . . No, 'course you wouldn'."

"What'd he do in Weed?" Slim asked again.

"Well, he seen this girl in a red dress. Dumb bastard like he is, he wants to touch ever'thing he likes. Just wants to feel it. So he reaches out to feel this red dress an' the girl lets out a squawk, and that gets Lennie all mixed up, and he holds on 'cause that's the only thing he can think to do. Well, this girl squawks and squawks. I was jus' a little bit off, and I heard all the yellin', so I comes running, an' by that time Lennie's so scared all he can think to do is jus' hold on. I socked him over the head with a fence picket to make him let go. He was so scairt he couldn't let go of that dress. And he's so God damn strong, you know."

Slim's eyes were level and unwinking. He nodded very slowly. "So what happens?"

George carefully built his line of solitaire cards. "Well, that girl rabbits in an' tells the law she been raped. The guys in Weed start a party out to lynch Lennie. So we sit in a irrigation ditch under water all the rest of that day. Got on'y our heads sticking outta water, an' up under the grass that sticks out from the side of the ditch. An' that night we scrammed outta there."

Slim sat in silence for a moment. "Didn't hurt the girl none, huh?" he asked finally.

"Hell, no. He just scared her. I'd be scared too if he grabbed me. But he never hurt her. He jus' wanted to touch that red dress, like he wants to pet them pups all the time."

"He ain't mean," said Slim. "I can tell a mean guy a mile off."

" 'Course he ain't, and he'll do any damn thing I—"

Lennie came in through the door. He wore his blue denim coat over his shoulders like a cape, and he walked hunched way over.

"Hi, Lennie," said George. "How you like the pup now?"

Lennie said breathlessly, "He's brown an' white jus' like I wanted." He went directly to his bunk and lay down and turned his face to the wall and drew up his knees.

George put down his cards very deliberately. "Lennie," he said sharply.

Lennie twisted his neck and looked over his shoulder. "Huh? What you want, George?"

"I tol' you you couldn't bring that pup in here."

"What pup, George? I ain't got no pup."

George went quickly to him, grabbed him by the shoulder and rolled him over. He reached down and picked the tiny puppy from where Lennie had been concealing it against his stomach.

Lennie sat up quickly. "Give 'um to me, George."

George said, "You get right up an' take this pup back to the nest. He's gotta sleep with his mother. You want to kill him? Just born last night an' you take him out of the nest. You take him back or I'll tell Slim not to let you have him."

Lennie held out his hands pleadingly. "Give 'um to me, George. I'll take 'um back. I didn't mean no harm, George. Honest I didn't. I jus' wanted to pet 'um a little."

George handed the pup to him. "Awright. You get him back there quick, and don't you take him out no more. You'll kill him, the first thing you know." Lennie fairly scuttled out of the room.

Slim had not moved. His calm eyes followed Lennie out the door. "Jesus," he said. "He's jus' like a kid, ain't he?"

"Sure he's jes' like a kid. There ain't no more harm in him than a kid neither, except he's so strong. I bet he won't come in here to sleep tonight. He'd sleep right alongside that box in the barn. Well—let 'im. He ain't doin' no harm out there."

It was almost dark outside now. Old Candy, the swamper, came in and went to his bunk, and behind him struggled his old dog. "Hello, Slim. Hello, George. Didn't neither of you play horseshoes?"

"I don't like to play ever' night," said Slim.

Candy went on, "Either you guys got a slug of whisky? I gotta gut ache."

"I ain't," said Slim. "I'd drink it myself if I had, an' I ain't got a gut ache neither."

"Gotta bad gut ache," said Candy. "Them God damn turnips give it to me. I knowed they was going to before I ever eat 'em."

The thick-bodied Carlson came in out of the darkening yard. He walked to the other end of the bunkhouse and turned on the second shaded light. "Darker'n hell in here," he said. "Jesus, how that nigger can pitch shoes."

"He's plenty good," said Slim.

"Damn right he is," said Carlson. "He don't give nobody else a chance to win—" He stopped and sniffed the air, and still sniffing, looked down at the old dog. "God awmighty, that dog stinks. Get him outa here, Candy! I don't know nothing that stinks as bad as an old dog. You gotta get him out."

Candy rolled to the edge of his bunk. He reached over and patted the ancient dog, and he apologized, "I been around him so much I never notice how he stinks."

"Well, I can't stand him in here," said Carlson. "That stink hangs around even after he's gone." He walked over with his heavy-legged stride and looked down at the dog. "Got no teeth," he said. "He's all stiff with rheumatism. He ain't no good to you, Candy. An' he ain't no good to himself. Why'n't you shoot him, Candy?"

The old man squirmed uncomfortably. "Well—hell! I had him so long. Had him since he was a pup. I herded sheep with him." He said proudly, "You wouldn't think it to look at him now, but he was the best damn sheep dog I ever seen."

I. Reading Comprehension Activities

My Title: _____

Main Idea Statement: This story is about _____

_____

_____

Supporting Details / Specific Info / Facts & Details (5W's + H) :

1. _____

2. _____

3. _____

4. _____

5. _____

6. _____

7. _____

8. _____

9. _____

10. _____

Inferences (Educated Guesses/Possibilities/R-B-T-L):

1. _____

2. _____

3. _____

4. _____

5. _____

6. _____

7. _____

8. _____

II. Using Vocabulary In Context

1. Write a complete sentence using 'unknown' word in context: _____

_____

   A. New Word/Unknown Word: _____

   B. Dictionary Definition: _____

   _____

   C. Synonyms: i. _____

               ii. _____

2. Write a complete sentence using 'unknown' word in context: _____

_____

   A. New Word/Unknown Word: _____

   B. Dictionary Definition: _____

   _____

   C. Synonyms: i. _____

               ii. _____

3. Write a complete sentence using 'unknown' word in context: _____

_____

   A. New Word/Unknown Word: _____

   B. Dictionary Definition: _____

   _____

   C. Synonyms: i. _____

               ii. _____

4. Write a complete sentence using 'unknown' word in context: _____

_____

   A. New Word/Unknown Word: _____

   B. Dictionary Definition: _____

   _____

   C. Synonyms: i. _____

               ii. _____

III. Critical Reading & Thinking, Part One

A. The author's purpose in writing this was to _____

_____

_____

B. I know this because of the following traits included in this reading: _____

_____

C. Of the following tone words, discuss with a partner or in your group which words more appropriately describe the tone of the selection. Support your choices—reasons why you made the choice that you did.

accurate	factual	impartial	truthful	matter-of-fact
calm	angry	direct	dramatic	serious
informal	formal	optimistic	pessimistic	biased
neutral	objective	subjective	emotional	unbiased

D. A graphic organizer is the most effective way to show the visual connection between ideas. The best graphic organizer to use for this selection would be:

_____

_____

Why? _____

_____

E. Complete a graphic organizer, a map, or an outline of main points of selection.

IV. Critical Reading & Thinking, Part Two

Directions: Your instructor will guide you based on which of the sections below students will be working on (individually or in groups). Students are to use the back of this page (Notes Page) to list their information and ideas based on evaluation, analysis, or discussion of the chosen Issues, Readings, or Topics below. This is a teacher-guided activity.

Argument is the ability to exchange ideas, opinions, and conclusions between two or more students based on readings or writings that cover contemporary issues or author's ideas.

Issue #1: _____

Issue #2: _____

Issue #3: _____

Issue #4: _____

Inferences are educated guesses or educated possibilities based on what is already known (past information or background information). These are not assumptions, opinions, or personal points of view.

Reading #1: _____

Reading #2: _____

Reading #3: _____

Reading #4: _____

Points of View are ideas that students come to conclude (draw conclusions) based on their own personal experience or information gained from past knowledge or experiences. These ideas can be personal opinions if they have an educational foundation and are not just personal feelings or beliefs.

Topic #1: _____

Topic #2: _____

Topic #3: _____

Topic #4: _____

V. Summary Page –or– Precis Page

Summary / Precis (Circle One): This story is about _____

_____

_____

_____

_____

_____

_____

_____

_____

_____

_____

_____

_____

_____

_____

_____

_____

_____

_____

_____

_____

_____

_____

_____

_____

<u>Source Information (Citation):</u>

    Title of Selection: _____

    Author: _____

    Publisher: _____

    Copyright Date: _____

Notes:

Section Two

Multicultural

Jubilee

by
Margaret Walker

Image © ImageTeam, 2012. Used under license from Shutterstock, Inc.

That morning going back to the plantation everything around her seemed unreal. The fog lifted slowly and through the misty morning she moved steadily toward what she knew would be her punishment. The children were not alarmed, and for that she was glad. Little Jim trotted homeward without a <u>whimper</u> while the baby sleeping in her arms was soundless. Grimes and his men did not speak to her but she knew that they were <u>ruthless</u> and there would be no <u>compassion</u>. It was a well-known fact that if a slave ran away and was caught in the act, flogging was the punishment. She could expect a whipping. She did not let herself think ahead beyond each step. Once she thought about Marse John. Perhaps he would interfere and not let them beat her. But she knew this was not possible because he was never at home whenever anything happened. He had been gone three days and might be gone two or three more; supposedly, he had gone to town on business. Maybe they can put it off until he comes home. No, she also knew better than that. Big Missy would want to get this over with before Marster's return. It was always easier for Missy Salina to explain things later and <u>justify</u> them most after they had occurred. Vyry was not at all surprised, therefore, when Grimes took her children from her on entering Marster's back yard. He led her to the whipping post not far from the wet fields where the field hands were not working this morning because the ground was too wet.

Two of Grimes's men tied her hands together as if she were folding them to pray, and then stretched them high above her head. They tied her to the post so that her feet were tied together and crossed above the ground. It seemed as if she were hanging on the post in mid-air, her feet stretched as far as they could stretch without touching the earth beneath her and her hands stretched as far above her head without reaching beyond the post. Her body was naked to the waist, and she braced herself to bear the lash of the whip upon her naked flesh.

Grimes did not choose to beat her. One of the guards who was generally hired to whip slaves was now ready to flog Vyry.

He took the whip in his hands. It was a raw-hide coach-whip used to <u>spur</u> the horses. He twirled it up high over his head, and when he came down with it he wrapped it all the way around her body and cut neatly into her breast and across her back all at the same time with one motion while the whip was a-singing in the air. It cut the air and her flesh and cried "zing" and Vyry saw stars that were red and black and silver, and there were a thousand of those stars in the midnight sky and her head felt as if it would split open and the whip cut her like a red-hot poke iron or a knife that was razor sharp and cut both ways. The whip burned like fire and cut the blood out of her and stung like red-hot pins sticking in her flesh while her head was reeling and whirling. It hurt so badly she felt as if her flesh were a single <u>molten</u> flame, and before she could catch her breath and brace herself again, he had wrapped the whip around her the second time. When she heard the whip go "zing" the second time and felt the stars rocking in her head, she opened her mouth to scream, but her throat was too dry to holler and she gritted her teeth and smashed her head hard against the post in order to steel herself once more to bear the pain. When he wrapped her all around with the whip the third time she thought she heard a roaring noise like thunder rumbling and a forest of trees falling in a flood. Everything went black; she was caught up in the blackness of a storm. She was whirling around in a cutting, fiery wind while the fire was burning her flesh like a tormenting fever and she kept sinking down in the fire and fighting the blackness until every light went out like a candle and she fainted.

She never did know how many lashes he gave her, whether he cut her the required seventy-five times as he was told to do, or whether he quit short of that number, thinking she was already dead and further beating was useless.

When she came to she heard a buzzing in her ears and everything still looked black though it wasn't yet evening. It must have been afternoon but there was no sunlight. Somebody had cut her loose from the post and left her huddled in a heap on the ground at the bottom of the whipping post. At first she thought it was night because all she could see looked black. She looked at her hands and her arms and she pulled at the shreds of rags on her legs and all her flesh looked black. She was as black as a man's hat and she was black like that all over. She looked around her on the ground and saw blood splattered and clotted around her while something glistened white like salt. Although her mind was still dazed she knew now why her back was still on fire and she felt as if she were lying on a bed of red-hot needles and iron. It was the salt somebody had thrown on her bleeding raw back. She was too weak to move. She wondered why she was still living, because they must have meant to kill her. "Why has God let me live?" *All the black people must be scared to come and get me till it is black dark. Maybe they think I'm dead. Lawd, have mercy, Jesus! Send somebody to get me soon, please Jesus!* The flies were making the buzzing sound and she felt her body throbbing in a rhythm with the flies. Fever <u>parched</u> her lips and eyes and her bruised hands and ran through her <u>brutalized</u> flesh.

After dark the other house servants came and got her and took her to her cabin. Caline and May Liza poured warm oil on her back and washed it free of salt. Then they put her on a soft pallet of rags and let her sleep. When the fever had parched its course through Vyry and the raw bruises began to form healing scars, the cloud in her mind began to lift. She could remember deep waves and complete <u>inundation</u> in the dark waters that threatened to take her under. She could not remember her own children and when they were brought to her she did not know them. Once she thought she saw Marse John standing over her and thought she heard him cursing terrible oaths, but even his face was <u>vague</u> in her memory. Caline and May Liza brought her hot broth to drink and coaxed her to swallow but she did not know them either or remember what they had done. After three days the fever seemed to be leaving her and her mind began to clear. She was too weak to speak above a whisper, and when she was able to examine herself she saw where one of the lashes had left a loose flap of flesh over her breast like a tuck in a dress. It healed that way.

I. Reading Comprehension Activities

My Title: _____

Main Idea Statement: This story is about _____

_____

_____

Supporting Details / Specific Info / Facts & Details (5W's + H) :

1. _____

2. _____

3. _____

4. _____

5. _____

6. _____

7. _____

8. _____

9. _____

10. _____

Inferences (Educated Guesses/Possibilities/R-B-T-L):

1. _____

2. _____

3. _____

4. _____

5. _____

6. _____

7. _____

8. _____

II. Using Vocabulary In Context

1. Write a complete sentence using 'unknown' word in context: _____

_____

_____

   A. New Word/Unknown Word: _____

   B. Dictionary Definition: _____

   _____

   C. Synonyms: i. _____

             ii. _____

2. Write a complete sentence using 'unknown' word in context: _____

_____

   A. New Word/Unknown Word: _____

   B. Dictionary Definition: _____

   _____

   C. Synonyms: i. _____

             ii. _____

3. Write a complete sentence using 'unknown' word in context: _____

_____

   A. New Word/Unknown Word: _____

   B. Dictionary Definition: _____

   _____

   C. Synonyms: i. _____

             ii. _____

4. Write a complete sentence using 'unknown' word in context: _____

_____

   A. New Word/Unknown Word: _____

   B. Dictionary Definition: _____

   _____

   C. Synonyms: i. _____

             ii. _____

III. Critical Reading & Thinking, Part One

A. The author's purpose in writing this was to _____

_____

_____

B. I know this because of the following traits included in this reading: _____

_____

C. Of the following tone words, discuss with a partner or in your group which words more appropriately describe the tone of the selection. Support your choices—reasons why you made the choice that you did.

accurate	factual	impartial	truthful	matter-of-fact
calm	angry	direct	dramatic	serious
informal	formal	optimistic	pessimistic	biased
neutral	objective	subjective	emotional	unbiased

D. A graphic organizer is the most effective way to show the visual connection between ideas. The best graphic organizer to use for this selection would be:

_____

_____

Why? _____

_____

E. Complete a graphic organizer, a map, or an outline of main points of selection.

IV. Critical Reading & Thinking, Part Two

Directions: Your instructor will guide you based on which of the sections below students will be working on (individually or in groups). Students are to use the back of this page (Notes Page) to list their information and ideas based on evaluation, analysis, or discussion of the chosen Issues, Readings, or Topics below. This is a teacher-guided activity.

<u>Argument</u> is the ability to exchange ideas, opinions, and conclusions between two or more students based on readings or writings that cover contemporary issues or author's ideas.

Issue #1: _____

Issue #2: _____

Issue #3: _____

Issue #4: _____

<u>Inferences</u> are educated guesses or educated possibilities based on what is already known (past information or background information). These are not assumptions, opinions, or personal points of view.

Reading #1: _____

Reading #2: _____

Reading #3: _____

Reading #4: _____

<u>Points of View</u> are ideas that students come to conclude (draw conclusions) based on their own personal experience or information gained from past knowledge or experiences. These ideas can be personal opinions if they have an educational foundation and are not just personal feelings or beliefs.

Topic #1: _____

Topic #2: _____

Topic #3: _____

Topic #4: _____

V. Summary Page –or– Precis Page

Summary / Precis (Circle One): This story is about _____

_____

_____

_____

_____

_____

_____

_____

_____

_____

_____

_____

_____

_____

_____

_____

_____

_____

_____

_____

_____

_____

_____

_____

_____

_____

_____

Source Information (Citation):

Title of Selection: _____

Author: _____

Publisher: _____

Copyright Date: _____

Notes:

Then Came the Famous *Kristallnacht*

by
Elise Radell (as told to Joan Morrison and Charlotte Fox Zabusky)

Image © life_is_fantastic, 2012. Used under license from
Shutterstock, Inc.

I was born in 1931 and Hitler came to power in 1933. As a little girl I never noticed anything. We were much <u>integrated</u> into the society. We had friends that were Jewish, that were non-Jewish. There never seemed to be any difference. But by 1937 or 1938, the Brown Shirts came along. All of a sudden, we became very much aware that we were Jews. We didn't know quite what to do with it. I remember going to school one day and somebody said to me, "You're Jewish," and threw a rock at me. I came home and I said to my mom and dad, "What is this being Jewish? Other people are Catholic. There are a lot of Lutherans and there are all kinds of churches, and why are they throwing stones at me?" And my parents said, "Well, that's the way it is." And then they took me out of regular public school and they took a private tutor for me—a young man who used to come to our house every day. I remember sitting in the dining room with him and we studied. I didn't study very well because I liked him more as a friend than as a teacher. I was about seven or eight then.

Excerpt from "Elise Radell from Germany, 1939" from *American Mosaic: The Immigrant Experience in the Words of Those Who Lived it*, by Joan Morrison and Charlotte Fox Zabusky, © 1980. Reprinted by permission of the University of Pittsburg Press.

My grandfather owned a very large apartment house, where we lived. In fact, it was the first apartment house in Ludwigshafen, where I was born, that had glass doors that opened and an elevator. It was on the main street, and I remember the Nazis, on the days when there were parades for the Nazis, coming onto our dining room balcony; because our dining room balcony faced the main street in Ludwigshafen and it had to have a flagpole holder. And they came in every time there was a parade and put up the swastika flag. I didn't like that. I didn't like them and I didn't like that.

Then came the famous *Kristallnacht*.[1] I don't remember the exact date. That morning, Mina, the maid, and I were going to get milk from the milk store. As we opened the door, the SS[2] was there. They pushed us aside and came into the house. "*Guten Morgen*,"[3] they said, "*Guten Morgen,*" I remember. They were very polite and then they went about this utter destruction with axes. They knew exactly how to do it. We had a <u>breakfront</u> in the dining room and it was one piece of teakwood, maybe seven feet long, and they knew just how to wreck it with one ax. Zzaszhh! Just ruined the whole thing. And the china closet was knocked all over and the pictures on the wall, with just one rip in each, and the furniture all just went. They were scientific about it. They had been told exactly how to go about it with the least amount of work. The pillows were ripped and the feathers—at that time there were feathers, you know—they just flew all over the house, and it was total destruction. Just ruined everything. My grandmother locked herself in the bathroom. The rest of us just stood and watched this destruction. Everyone was in shock. There was no fighting back. We were just <u>stunned</u>. Afterward, they took all the Jewish men, put them in jail, and then transported them to Dachau.[4]

My father had been out of town on business and didn't come home until the next day. And then, out of some strange, unbelievable loyalty or honor or whatever the Germans were brought up to believe, when he came home and saw that all the Jewish men were gone, he went to the police station and gave himself up.

Now, I, as a Jew, can't quite understand how the German Jews did this; how my father could come back and turn himself in. But, being raised his whole life as an honorable citizen, to him this was the height of being honorable. And it's very hard for me to accept. I can understand intellectually; I don't understand it emotionally. . . .

After this, all the German Jewish women and children began to live together. I remember a cousin, a neighbor, another neighbor; we all lived in our apartment. We had the largest apartment. The train from Dachau to Ludwigshafen came at 2:10 every morning, and everybody woke up at 2:10 a.m., because you never knew who would come home. We had a distant aunt and her daughter living with us, and one night her husband came home and it was my Uncle Julius. I loved him dearly before that. And he walked into our house and I wouldn't look at him and I said, "How come you didn't bring my daddy?" I just couldn't understand how he came home without my daddy.

Later, much later, <u>eventually</u> my daddy came home. My father was six-foot-one then, and tall and handsome, as a daughter sees her daddy—an eight-year-old daughter. And he had all his hair shaved off and he was down to ninety pounds. He came home and he never spoke about it again. Never mentioned it. It must have been so unbelievably terrible. But he came home. All I remember is his

---

[1] *Kristallnacht*: "crystal night," referring to the broken glass left after a night in November 1938 when organized mobs of Nazis looted, pillaged, and burned Jewish shops, synagogues, and homes
[2] *SS*: abbreviation of *Schutzstaffel* ("elite guard"), a unit of Nazis whose duties included policing and exterminating people deemed undesirable
[3] *Guten Morgen*: "Good morning"
[4] *Dachau*: a city in southwestern Germany that became the site of a concentration camp during Nazi rule

Section Two—Multicultural

shaven head and that he was very skinny. But he hugged me and kissed me and he said hello. "*Guten Tag*,[5] Lisel. Everything's all right."

Those who could got boat tickets then to America, to Shanghai, wherever they could go. You couldn't get a visa to America unless you had relatives there. I think Roosevelt could have tried to open the quota a little bit. Maybe he did try; I don't know. But we had an aunt who had come to the U.S. in 1936, and she did everything she could for us. We had to go to Stuttgart, which was the center where all the visas and passports were given. My mother always took me along because I didn't look Jewish. I had blue eyes and blond hair at the time. We had to go by train, I remember. We finally managed to get the visas and everything, and we got on a boat and landed here in August 1939. The last trip over.

We begged my grandparents to come with us, but my grandfather was a great German nationalist. Not a religious man. He just didn't believe in God, and, therefore, what sense did temple make or religion make? He was an atheist. He was a German. And he said, "No. Nothing will happen to me." He wouldn't go. But now I think back—I have a feeling my grandfather knew my grandmother wouldn't make it through the physical. She was a very sick woman then. So he stayed with her. First they were deported to France, and then they were on one of those trains. The last we ever heard. In fact, we have a picture of them going on one of those trains—stepping up to the car that was going to go to Poland or wherever they went to be gassed. A friend of a friend saw them and took a picture. I have the picture now. I never look at it. . . . Right to the bitter end they were properly dressed. My grandfather had on a tie and a white shirt, and my grandmother had a dress on and a brooch and whatever shoes she had. And they got into that train! That's what I say about the German Jews. Down to the bitter end they had a false dignity. That's what they knew and that's what they were told to do, and they did it in the most elegant and dignified way they knew how. Right down to the gas chamber. And I'm sure that they walked into that gas chamber with their heads held high and that was it. . . . [Breaks down.]

I say, "Why didn't they fight? Why didn't we all fight back?" But if you're raised in a certain milieu, you cannot change. And besides, the fight would have been hopeless. That's something we know. The Poles' fight was hopeless, too, but at least they did it. You know, I'm torn. I always knew, after I got my senses back and was settled, I said, "I never could marry a German Jew," because I don't quite believe in going into the death chamber with your head held high, without somehow, somewhere, fighting back. It might be a terrible thing for me to say. In a way, I feel like a traitor when I think that, and, in another way, I feel, "Well, I'm an individual. I'm a free soul. I can begin to believe the way I would believe—and choose what I would choose." I don't blame my parents, because there were too many who did it the same way. But I don't think I could do it. . . .

---

[5] *Guten Tag*: "Good day"

I. Reading Comprehension Activities

My Title: _____

Main Idea Statement: This story is about _____

_____

_____

Supporting Details / Specific Info / Facts & Details (5W's + H) :

1. _____

2. _____

3. _____

4. _____

5. _____

6. _____

7. _____

8. _____

9. _____

10. _____

Inferences (Educated Guesses/Possibilities/R-B-T-L):

1. _____

2. _____

3. _____

4. _____

5. _____

6. _____

7. _____

8. _____

II. Using Vocabulary In Context

1. Write a complete sentence using 'unknown' word in context: _____

_____

_____

    A. New Word/Unknown Word: _____

    B. Dictionary Definition: _____

_____

    C. Synonyms: i. _____

              ii. _____

2. Write a complete sentence using 'unknown' word in context: _____

_____

    A. New Word/Unknown Word: _____

    B. Dictionary Definition: _____

_____

    C. Synonyms: i. _____

              ii. _____

3. Write a complete sentence using 'unknown' word in context: _____

_____

    A. New Word/Unknown Word: _____

    B. Dictionary Definition: _____

_____

    C. Synonyms: i. _____

              ii. _____

4. Write a complete sentence using 'unknown' word in context: _____

_____

    A. New Word/Unknown Word: _____

    B. Dictionary Definition: _____

_____

    C. Synonyms: i. _____

              ii. _____

III. Critical Reading & Thinking, Part One

A. The author's purpose in writing this was to _____

_____

_____

B. I know this because of the following traits included in this reading: _____

_____

C. Of the following tone words, discuss with a partner or in your group which words more appropriately describe the tone of the selection. Support your choices—reasons why you made the choice that you did.

accurate	factual	impartial	truthful	matter-of-fact
calm	angry	direct	dramatic	serious
informal	formal	optimistic	pessimistic	biased
neutral	objective	subjective	emotional	unbiased

D. A graphic organizer is the most effective way to show the visual connection between ideas. The best graphic organizer to use for this selection would be:

_____

_____

Why? _____

_____

E. Complete a graphic organizer, a map, or an outline of main points of selection.

IV. Critical Reading & Thinking, Part Two

Directions: Your instructor will guide you based on which of the sections below students will be working on (individually or in groups). Students are to use the back of this page (Notes Page) to list their information and ideas based on evaluation, analysis, or discussion of the chosen Issues, Readings, or Topics below. This is a teacher-guided activity.

<u>**Argument**</u> is the ability to exchange ideas, opinions, and conclusions between two or more students based on readings or writings that cover contemporary issues or author's ideas.

Issue #1: _____

Issue #2: _____

Issue #3: _____

Issue #4: _____

<u>**Inferences**</u> are educated guesses or educated possibilities based on what is already known (past information or background information). These are not assumptions, opinions, or personal points of view.

Reading #1: _____

Reading #2: _____

Reading #3: _____

Reading #4: _____

<u>**Points of View**</u> are ideas that students come to conclude (draw conclusions) based on their own personal experience or information gained from past knowledge or experiences. These ideas can be personal opinions if they have an educational foundation and are not just personal feelings or beliefs.

Topic #1: _____

Topic #2: _____

Topic #3: _____

Topic #4: _____

V. Summary Page –or– Precis Page

Summary / Precis (Circle One): This story is about _____

_____

_____

_____

_____

_____

_____

_____

_____

_____

_____

_____

_____

_____

_____

_____

_____

_____

_____

_____

_____

_____

_____

_____

_____

_____

Source Information (Citation):

Title of Selection: _____

Author: _____

Publisher: _____

Copyright Date: _____

Notes:

Black Like Me

by
John Howard Griffin

Image © photobank.ch, 2012. Used under license
from Shutterstock, Inc.

October 28, 1959

For years the idea had haunted me, and that night it returned more insistently than ever.

If a white man became a Negro in the Deep South, what adjustments would he have to make? What is it like to experience discrimination based on skin color, something over which one has no control?

This speculation was sparked again by a report that lay on my desk in the old barn that served as my office. The report mentioned the rise in suicide tendency among Southern Negroes. This did not mean that they killed themselves, but rather that they had reached a stage where they simply no longer cared whether they lived or died.

It was that bad, then, despite the white Southern legislators who insisted that they had a "wonderfully harmonious relationship" with Negroes. I lingered on in my office at my parents'

Mansfield, Texas, farm. My wife and children slept in our home five miles away. I sat there, surrounded by the smells of autumn coming through my open window, unable to leave, unable to sleep.

How else except by becoming a Negro could a white man hope to learn the truth? Though we lived side by side throughout the South, communication between the two races had simply ceased to exist. Neither really knew what went on with those of the other race. The Southern Negro will not tell the white man the truth. He long ago learned that if he speaks a truth unpleasing to the white, the white will make life miserable for him.

The only way I could see to bridge the gap between us was to become a Negro. I decided I would do this.

I prepared to walk into a life that appeared suddenly mysterious and frightening. With my decision to become a Negro I realized that I, a specialist in race issues, really knew nothing of the Negro's real problem.

October 29, 1959

I drove into Fort Worth in the afternoon to discuss the project with my old friend George Levitan. He is the owner of *Sepia*, an internationally distributed Negro magazine with a format similar to that of *Look*. A large, middle-aged man, he long ago won my admiration by offering equal job opportunities to members of any race, choosing according to their qualifications and future potentialities. With an on-the-job training program, he has made *Sepia* a model, edited, printed and distributed from the million-dollar Fort Worth plant.

It was a beautiful autumn day. I drove to his house, arriving there in midafternoon. His door was always open, so I walked in and called him.

An affectionate man, he embraced me, offered me coffee and had me take a seat. Through the glass doors of his den I looked out to see a few dead leaves floating on the water of his swimming pool.

He listened, his cheek buried in his fist as I explained the project.

"It's a crazy idea," he said. "You'll get yourself killed fooling around down there." But he could not hide his enthusiasm.

I told him the South's racial situation was a blot on the whole country, and especially reflected against us overseas; and that the best way to find out if we had second-class citizens and what their plight was would be to become one of them.

"But it'll be terrible," he said. "You'll be making yourself the target of the most ignorant rabble in the country. If they ever caught you, they'd be sure to make an example of you." He gazed out the window, his face puffed with concentration.

"But you know—it is a great idea. I can see right now you're going through with it, so what can I do to help?"

"Pay the tab and I'll give *Sepia* some articles—or let you use some chapters from the book I'll write."

He agreed, but suggested that before I made final plans I discuss it with Mrs. Adelle Jackson, *Sepia's* editorial director. Both of us have a high regard for this extraordinary woman's opinions. She rose from a secretarial position to become one of the country's distinguished editors.

After leaving Mr. Levitan, I called on her. At first she thought the idea was impossible. "You don't know what you'd be getting into, John," she said. She felt that when my book was published, I would be the butt of resentment from all the hate groups, that they would stop at nothing to discredit me, and that many decent whites would be afraid to show me courtesies when others might be watching. And, too, there are the deeper currents among even well-intentioned Southerners, currents that make the idea of a white man's assuming nonwhite identity a somewhat repulsive step down. And other currents that say, "Don't stir up anything. Let's try to keep things peaceful."

And then I went home and told my wife. After she recovered from her astonishment, she unhesitatingly agreed that if I felt I must do this thing then I must. She offered, as her part of the project, her willingness to lead, with our three children, the unsatisfactory family life of a household deprived of husband and father.

I returned at night to my barn office. Outside my open window, frogs and crickets made the silence more profound. A chill breeze rustled dead leaves in the woods. It carried an odor of fresh-turned dirt, drawing my attention to the fields where the tractor had only a few hours ago stopped plowing the earth. I sensed the radiance of it in the stillness, sensed the earthworms that burrowed back into the depths of the furrows, sensed the animals that wandered in the woods in search of nocturnal rut or food. I felt the beginning loneliness, the terrible dread of what I had decided to do.

October 30, 1959

Lunched with Mrs. Jackson, Mr. Levitan, and three FBI men from the Dallas office. Though I knew my project was outside their jurisdiction and that they could not support it in any way, I wanted them to know about it in advance. We discussed it in considerable detail. I decided not to change my name or identity. I would merely change my pigmentation and allow people to draw their own conclusions. If asked who I was or what I was doing, I would answer truthfully.

"Do you suppose they'll treat me as John Howard Griffin, regardless of my color—or will they treat me as some nameless Negro, even though I am still the same man?" I asked.

"You're not serious," one of them said. "They're not going to ask you any questions. As soon as they see you, you'll be a Negro and that's all they'll ever want to know about you."

November 1, 1959,
New Orleans, Louisiana

Arrived by plane as night set in. I checked my bags at the Hotel Monteleone in the French Quarter and began walking.

Strange experience. When I was blind I came here and learned cane-walking in the French Quarter. Now, the most intense excitement filled me as I saw the places I visited while blind. I walked miles, trying to locate everything by sight that I once knew only by smell and sound. The streets were full of sightseers. I wandered among them, entranced by the narrow streets, the iron-grill balconies, the green plants and vines glimpsed in lighted flagstone courtyards. Every view was magical, whether it was a deserted, lamplit street corner or the neon hubbub of Royal Street.

I walked past garish bars where hawkers urged me in to see the "gorgeous girls" do their hip-shaking; and they left the doors open sufficiently to show dim, smoke-blue interiors crossed by long rays of pink spotlights that turned the seminude girls' flesh rose. I strolled on. Jazz blared from the bars. Odors of old stone and Creole cooking and coffee filled the streets.

At Broussard's, I had supper in a superb courtyard under the stars—*huîtres variées*, green salad, white wine and coffee; the same meal I had there in past years. I saw everything—the lanterns, the trees, the candlelit tables, the little fountain, as though I were looking through a fine camera lens. Surrounded by elegant waiters, elegant people and elegant food, I thought of the other parts of town where I would live in the days to come. Was there a place in New Orleans where a Negro could buy *huîtres variées*?

At ten I finished dinner and went to telephone an old friend who lives in New Orleans. He insisted I stay at his house, and I was relieved, for I foresaw all sorts of difficulties staying in a hotel while I turned into a Negro.

November 2, 1959

In the morning I called the medical information service and asked for the names of some prominent dermatologists. They gave me three names. The first one I called gave me an appointment immediately, so I took the streetcar to his office and explained my needs. He had had no experience with such a request, but was willing enough to aid me in my project. After taking my case history, he asked me to wait while he consulted with some of his colleagues by phone as to the best method of darkening my skin.

After some time he stepped back into the room and said they had all agreed we should attempt it with a medication taken orally, followed by exposure to ultraviolet rays. He explained they used it on victims of vitiligo, a disease that causes white spots to appear on the face and body. Until this medication was discovered, the victims of this disease had had to wear pancake make-up when they went out in public. It could be dangerous to use, however. It usually took from six weeks to three months to darken the skin pigmentation. I told him I could not spare that much time and we decided to try accelerated treatments, with constant blood tests to see how my system tolerated the medication.

I got the prescription filled, returned to the house and took the tablets. Two hours later I exposed my entire body to ultraviolet rays from a sun lamp.

My host remained away from the house most of the time. I told him I was on an assignment that I could not discuss and that he should not be surprised if I simply disappeared without saying good-by. I knew that he had no prejudices, but I nevertheless did not want to involve him in any way, since reprisals might be taken against him by bigots or by his associates, who might resent his role as my host once my story became known. He gave me a key to his house and we agreed to maintain our different schedules without worrying about the usual host-guest relationship.

After supper I took the trolley into town and walked through some of the Negro sections in the South Rampart-Dryades Street sections. They are mostly poor sections with cafés, bars and businesses of all sorts alongside cluttered residences. I searched for an opening, a way to enter the world of the Negro, some contact perhaps. As yet, it was a blank to me: My greatest preoccupation was that moment of transition when I would "pass over." Where and how would I do it? To get from the white world into the Negro world is a complex matter. I looked for the chink in the wall through which I might pass unobserved.

November 6

For the past four days, I had spent my time at the doctor's or closed up in my room with cotton pads over my eyes and the sun lamp turned on me. They had made blood tests twice and found no indication of damage to the liver. But the medication produced lassitude and I felt constantly on the verge of nausea.

The doctor, well-disposed, gave me many warnings about the dangers of this project insofar as my contact with Negroes was concerned. Now that he had had time to think, he was beginning to doubt the wisdom of this course, or perhaps he felt strongly his responsibility. In any event, he warned me that I must have some contact in each major city so my family could check on my safety from time to time.

"I believe in the brotherhood of man," he said. "I respect the race. But I can never forget when I was an intern and had to go down on South Rampart Street to patch them up. Three or four would be sitting in a bar or at a friend's house. They were apparently friends one minute and then something would come up and one would get slashed up with a knife. We're willing enough to go all the way for them, but we've got this problem—how can you render the duties of justice to men when you're afraid they'll be so unaware of justice they may destroy you?—especially since their attitude toward their own race is a destructive one." He said this with real sadness. I told him my contacts indicated that Negroes themselves were aware of this dilemma and they were making strong efforts to unify the race, to condemn among themselves any tactic or any violence or injustice that would reflect against the race as a whole.

"I'm glad to hear that," he said, obviously unconvinced.

He also told me things that Negroes had told him—that the lighter the skin the more trustworthy the Negro.

I was astonished to see an intelligent man fall for this cliché, and equally astonished that Negroes would advance it, for in effect it placed the dark Negro in an inferior position and fed the racist idea of judging a man by his color.

When not lying under the lamp, I walked the streets of New Orleans to orient myself. Each day I stopped at a sidewalk shoeshine stand near the French Market. The shine boy was an elderly man, large, keenly intelligent and a good talker. He had lost a leg during World War I. He showed none of the obsequiousness of the Southern Negro, but was polite and easy to know. (Not that I had any illusions that I knew him, for he was too astute to allow any white man that privilege.) I told him I was a writer, touring the Deep South to study living conditions, civil rights, etc., but I did not tell him I would do this as a Negro. Finally, we exchanged names. He was called Sterling Williams. I decided he might be the contact for my entry into the Negro community.

I. Reading Comprehension Activities

My Title: _____

Main Idea Statement: This story is about _____

_____

_____

Supporting Details / Specific Info / Facts & Details (5W's + H) :

1. _____

2. _____

3. _____

4. _____

5. _____

6. _____

7. _____

8. _____

9. _____

10. _____

Inferences (Educated Guesses/Possibilities/R-B-T-L):

1. _____

2. _____

3. _____

4. _____

5. _____

6. _____

7. _____

8. _____

II. Using Vocabulary In Context

1. Write a complete sentence using 'unknown' word in context: _____

_____

   A. New Word/Unknown Word: _____

   B. Dictionary Definition: _____

_____

   C. Synonyms: i. _____

               ii. _____

2. Write a complete sentence using 'unknown' word in context: _____

_____

   A. New Word/Unknown Word: _____

   B. Dictionary Definition: _____

_____

   C. Synonyms: i. _____

               ii. _____

3. Write a complete sentence using 'unknown' word in context: _____

_____

   A. New Word/Unknown Word: _____

   B. Dictionary Definition: _____

_____

   C. Synonyms: i. _____

               ii. _____

4. Write a complete sentence using 'unknown' word in context: _____

_____

   A. New Word/Unknown Word: _____

   B. Dictionary Definition: _____

_____

   C. Synonyms: i. _____

               ii. _____

III. Critical Reading & Thinking, Part One

A. The author's purpose in writing this was to _____

_____

_____

B. I know this because of the following traits included in this reading: _____

_____

C. Of the following tone words, discuss with a partner or in your group which words more appropriately describe the tone of the selection. Support your choices—reasons why you made the choice that you did.

accurate	factual	impartial	truthful	matter-of-fact
calm	angry	direct	dramatic	serious
informal	formal	optimistic	pessimistic	biased
neutral	objective	subjective	emotional	unbiased

D. A graphic organizer is the most effective way to show the visual connection between ideas. The best graphic organizer to use for this selection would be:

_____

_____

Why? _____

_____

E. Complete a graphic organizer, a map, or an outline of main points of selection.

IV. Critical Reading & Thinking, Part Two

Directions: Your instructor will guide you based on which of the sections below students will be working on (individually or in groups). Students are to use the back of this page (Notes Page) to list their information and ideas based on evaluation, analysis, or discussion of the chosen Issues, Readings, or Topics below. This is a teacher-guided activity.

<u>**Argument**</u> is the ability to exchange ideas, opinions, and conclusions between two or more students based on readings or writings that cover contemporary issues or author's ideas.

Issue #1: _____

Issue #2: _____

Issue #3: _____

Issue #4: _____

<u>**Inferences**</u> are educated guesses or educated possibilities based on what is already known (past information or background information). These are not assumptions, opinions, or personal points of view.

Reading #1: _____

Reading #2: _____

Reading #3: _____

Reading #4: _____

<u>**Points of View**</u> are ideas that students come to conclude (draw conclusions) based on their own personal experience or information gained from past knowledge or experiences. These ideas can be personal opinions if they have an educational foundation and are not just personal feelings or beliefs.

Topic #1: _____

Topic #2: _____

Topic #3: _____

Topic #4: _____

V. Summary Page –or– Precis Page

Summary / Precis (Circle One): This story is about _____

_____

_____

_____

_____

_____

_____

_____

_____

_____

_____

_____

_____

_____

_____

_____

_____

_____

_____

_____

_____

_____

_____

_____

_____

_____

Source Information (Citation):

Title of Selection: _____

Author: _____

Publisher: _____

Copyright Date: _____

Notes:

I Know Why the Caged Bird Sings

by
Maya Angelou

Image © file404, 2012. Used under license from Shutterstock, Inc.

During my tenth year, a white woman's kitchen became my finishing school.

Mrs. Viola Cullinan was a plump woman who lived in a three-bedroom house somewhere behind the post office. She was <u>singularly</u> unattractive until she smiled, and then the lines around her eyes and mouth which made her look <u>perpetually</u> dirty disappeared, and her face looked like the mask of an impish elf. She usually rested her smile until late afternoon when her women friends dropped in and Miss Glory, the cook, served them cold drinks on the closed-in porch.

The exactness of her house was inhuman. This glass went here and only here. That cup had its place and it was an act of <u>impudent</u> rebellion to place it anywhere else. At twelve o'clock the table was set. At 12:15 Mrs. Cullinan sat down to dinner (whether her husband had arrived or not). At 12:16 Miss Glory brought out the food.

It took me a week to learn the difference between a salad plate, a bread plate and a dessert plate.

Mrs. Cullinan kept up the tradition of her wealthy parents. She was from Virginia. Miss Glory, who was a descendant of slaves that had worked for the Cullinans, told me her history. She had married beneath her (according to Miss Glory). Her husband's family hadn't had their money very long and what they had "didn't 'mount to much."

As ugly as she was, I thought privately, she was lucky to get a husband above or beneath her station. But Miss Glory wouldn't let me say a thing against her mistress. She was very patient with me, however, over the housework. She explained the dishware, silverware and servants' bells.

The large round bowl in which soup was served wasn't a soup bowl, it was a tureen. There were goblets, sherbet glasses, ice-cream glasses, wine glasses, green glass coffee cups with matching saucers, and water glasses. I had a glass to drink from, and it sat with Miss Glory's on a separate shelf from the others. Soup spoons, gravy boat, butter knives, salad forks and carving platter were additions to my vocabulary and in fact almost represented a new language. I was fascinated with the novelty, with the fluttering Mrs. Cullinan and her Alice-in-Wonderland house.

Her husband remains, in my memory, undefined. I lumped him with all the other white men that I had ever seen and tried not to see.

On our way home one evening, Miss Glory told me that Mrs. Cullinan couldn't have children. She said that she was too delicate-boned. It was hard to imagine bones at all under those layers of fat. Miss Glory went on to say that the doctor had taken out all her lady organs. I reasoned that a pig's organs included the lungs, heart and liver, so if Mrs. Cullinan was walking around without those essentials, it explained why she drank alcohol out of unmarked bottles. She was keeping herself embalmed.

When I spoke to [my brother] Bailey about it, he agreed that I was right, but he also informed me that Mr. Cullinan had two daughters by a colored lady and that I knew them very well. He added that the girls were the spitting image of their father. I was unable to remember what he looked like, although I had just left him a few hours before, but I thought of the Coleman girls. They were very light-skinned and certainly didn't look very much like their mother (no one ever mentioned Mr. Coleman).

My pity for Mrs. Cullinan preceded me the next morning like the Cheshire cat's smile. Those girls, who could have been her daughters, were beautiful. They didn't have to straighten their hair. Even when they were caught in the rain, their braids still hung down straight like tamed snakes. Their mouths were pouty little cupid's bows. Mrs. Cullinan didn't know what she missed. Or maybe she did. Poor Mrs. Cullinan.

For weeks after, I arrived early, left late and tried very hard to make up for her barrenness. If she had had her own children, she wouldn't have had to ask me to run a thousand errands from her back door to the back door of her friends. Poor old Mrs. Cullinan.

Then one evening Miss Glory told me to serve the ladies on the porch. After I set the tray down and turned toward the kitchen, one of the women asked, "What's your name, girl?" It was the speckled-faced one. Mrs. Cullinan said, "She doesn't talk much. Her name's Margaret."

"Is she dumb?"

"No. As I understand it, she can talk when she wants to but she's usually quiet as a little mouse. Aren't you, Margaret?"

I smiled at her. Poor thing. No organs and couldn't even pronounce my name correctly.

"She's a sweet little thing, though."

"Well, that may be, but the name's too long. I'd never bother myself. I'd call her Mary if I was you."

Section Two—Multicultural

I fumed into the kitchen. That horrible woman would never have the chance to call me Mary because if I was starving I'd never work for her. I decided I wouldn't pee on her if her heart was on fire. Giggles drifted in off the porch and into Miss Glory's pots. I wondered what they could be laughing about.

Whitefolks were so strange. Could they be talking about me? Everybody knew that they stuck together better than the Negroes did. It was possible that Mrs. Cullinan had friends in St. Louis who heard about a girl from Stamps being in court and wrote to tell her. Maybe she knew about Mr. Freeman.

My lunch was in my mouth a second time and I went outside and relieved myself on the bed of four-o'clocks. Miss Glory thought I might be coming down with something and told me to go on home, that Momma would give me some herb tea, and she'd explain to her mistress.

I realized how foolish I was being before I reached the pond. Of course Mrs. Cullinan didn't know. Otherwise she wouldn't have given me the two nice dresses that Momma cut down, and she certainly wouldn't have called me a "sweet little thing." My stomach felt fine, and I didn't mention anything to Momma.

That evening I decided to write a poem on being white, fat, old and without children. It was going to be a tragic ballad. I would have to watch her carefully to capture the <u>essence</u> of her loneliness and pain.

The very next day, she called me by the wrong name. Miss Glory and I were washing up the lunch dishes when Mrs. Cullinan came to the doorway. "Mary?"

Miss Glory asked, "Who?"

Mrs. Cullinan, sagging a little, knew and I knew. "I want Mary to go down to Mrs. Randall's and take her some soup. She's not been feeling well for a few days."

Miss Glory's face was a wonder to see. "You mean Margaret, ma'am. Her name's Margaret."

"That's too long. She's Mary from now on. Heat that soup from last night and put it in the china tureen and, Mary, I want you to carry it carefully."

Every person I knew had a hellish horror of being "called out of his name." It was a dangerous practice to call a Negro anything that could be loosely <u>construed</u> as insulting because of the centuries of their having been called niggers, jigs, dinges, blackbirds, crows, boots and spooks.

Miss Glory had a fleeting second of feeling sorry for me. Then as she handed me the hot tureen she said, "Don't mind, don't pay that no mind. Sticks and stones may break your bones, but words. . . You know, I been working for her for twenty years."

She held the back door open for me. "Twenty years. I wasn't much older than you. My name used to be Hallelujah. That's what Ma named me, but my mistress give me 'Glory,' and it stuck. I likes it better too."

I was in the little path that ran behind the houses when Miss Glory shouted, "It's shorter too."

For a few seconds it was a tossup over whether I would laugh (imagine being named Hallelujah) or cry (imagine letting some white woman rename you for her convenience). My anger saved me from either outburst. I had to quit the job, but the problem was going to be how to do it. Momma wouldn't allow me to quit for just any reason.

"She's a peach. That woman is a real peach." Mrs. Randall's maid was talking as she took the soup from me, and I wondered what her name used to be and what she answered to now.

For a week I looked into Mrs. Cullnan's face as she called me Mary. She ignored my coming late and leaving early. Miss Glory was a little annoyed because I had begun to leave egg yolk on the dishes and wasn't putting much heart in polishing the silver. I hoped that she would complain to our boss, but she didn't.

Then Bailey solved my dilemma. He had me describe the contents of the cupboard and the particular plates she liked best. Her favorite piece was a casserole shaped like a fish and the green glass coffee cups. I kept his instructions in mind, so on the next day when Miss Glory was hanging out clothes and I had again been told to serve the old biddies on the porch, I dropped the empty serving tray. When I heard Mrs. Cullinan scream, "Mary!" I picked up the casserole and two of the green glass cups in readiness. As she rounded the kitchen door I let them fall on the tiled floor.

I could never absolutely describe to Bailey what happened next, because each time I got to the part where she fell on the floor and screwed up her ugly face to cry, we burst out laughing. She actually wobbled around on the floor and picked up shards of the cups and cried, "Oh, Momma. Oh, dear Gawd. It's Momma's china from Virginia. Oh, Momma, I sorry."

Miss Glory came running in from the yard and the women from the porch crowded around. Miss Glory was almost as broken up as her mistress. "You mean to say she broke our Virginia dishes? What we gone do?"

Mrs. Cullinan cried louder, "That clumsy nigger. Clumsy little black nigger."

Old speckled-face leaned down and asked, "Who did it, Viola? Was it Mary? Who did it?"

Everything was happening so fast I can't remember whether her action preceded her words, but I know that Mrs. Cullinan said, "Her name's Margaret, goddamn it, her name's Margaret." And she threw a wedge of the broken plate at me. It could have been the hysteria which put her aim off, but the flying crockery caught Miss Glory right over her ear and she started screaming.

I left the front door wide open so all the neighbors could hear.

Mrs. Cullinan was right about one thing. My name wasn't Mary.

I. Reading Comprehension Activities

My Title: _____

Main Idea Statement: This story is about _____

_____

_____

Supporting Details / Specific Info / Facts & Details (5W's + H) :

1. _____

2. _____

3. _____

4. _____

5. _____

6. _____

7. _____

8. _____

9. _____

10. _____

Inferences (Educated Guesses/Possibilities/R-B-T-L):

1. _____

2. _____

3. _____

4. _____

5. _____

6. _____

7. _____

8. _____

II. Using Vocabulary In Context

1. Write a complete sentence using 'unknown' word in context: _____

_____

_____

   A. New Word/Unknown Word: _____

   B. Dictionary Definition: _____

   _____

   C. Synonyms: i. _____

             ii. _____

2. Write a complete sentence using 'unknown' word in context: _____

_____

   A. New Word/Unknown Word: _____

   B. Dictionary Definition: _____

   _____

   C. Synonyms: i. _____

             ii. _____

3. Write a complete sentence using 'unknown' word in context: _____

_____

   A. New Word/Unknown Word: _____

   B. Dictionary Definition: _____

   _____

   C. Synonyms: i. _____

             ii. _____

4. Write a complete sentence using 'unknown' word in context: _____

_____

   A. New Word/Unknown Word: _____

   B. Dictionary Definition: _____

   _____

   C. Synonyms: i. _____

             ii. _____

III. Critical Reading & Thinking, Part One

A. The author's purpose in writing this was to _____

_____

_____

B. I know this because of the following traits included in this reading: _____

_____

C. Of the following tone words, discuss with a partner or in your group which words more appropriately describe the tone of the selection. Support your choices—reasons why you made the choice that you did.

accurate	factual	impartial	truthful	matter-of-fact
calm	angry	direct	dramatic	serious
informal	formal	optimistic	pessimistic	biased
neutral	objective	subjective	emotional	unbiased

D. A graphic organizer is the most effective way to show the visual connection between ideas. The best graphic organizer to use for this selection would be:

_____

_____

Why? _____

_____

E. Complete a graphic organizer, a map, or an outline of main points of selection.

IV. Critical Reading & Thinking, Part Two

Directions: Your instructor will guide you based on which of the sections below students will be working on (individually or in groups). Students are to use the back of this page (Notes Page) to list their information and ideas based on evaluation, analysis, or discussion of the chosen Issues, Readings, or Topics below. This is a teacher-guided activity.

Argument is the ability to exchange ideas, opinions, and conclusions between two or more students based on readings or writings that cover contemporary issues or author's ideas.

Issue #1: _____

Issue #2: _____

Issue #3: _____

Issue #4: _____

Inferences are educated guesses or educated possibilities based on what is already known (past information or background information). These are not assumptions, opinions, or personal points of view.

Reading #1: _____

Reading #2: _____

Reading #3: _____

Reading #4: _____

Points of View are ideas that students come to conclude (draw conclusions) based on their own personal experience or information gained from past knowledge or experiences. These ideas can be personal opinions if they have an educational foundation and are not just personal feelings or beliefs.

Topic #1: _____

Topic #2: _____

Topic #3: _____

Topic #4: _____

V. Summary Page –or– Precis Page

Summary / Precis (Circle One): This story is about _____

_____

_____

_____

_____

_____

_____

_____

_____

_____

_____

_____

_____

_____

_____

_____

_____

_____

_____

_____

_____

_____

_____

_____

_____

_____

_____

Source Information (Citation):

Title of Selection: _____

Author: _____

Publisher: _____

Copyright Date: _____

Notes:

A Tale of Two Proms, One Black, One White

by
Isabel Wilkerson

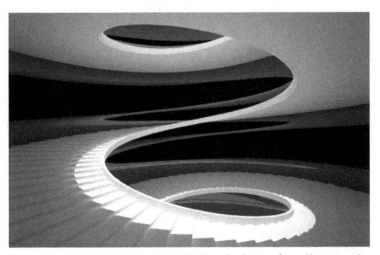

Image © sergeymansurov.ru, 2012. Used under license from Shutterstock, Inc.

The rented limousines carrying young men in tuxedoes and young women in taffeta began arriving at a Gold Coast hotel shortly after dusk on Friday, May 3. It was the official Brother Rice High School prom, and it was virtually all white.

Three miles away at a South Side hotel, about 30 of their classmates—tuxedoed young men in kinte cloth cummerbunds—and their dates dressed in satin alighted from borrowed Cadillacs and BMWs for the school's first all-black prom.

It was a turning point that has torn at the heart of the predominantly white boys' Catholic school here and, sociologists say, is a telling allegory of race relations in this country 20 years after the civil rights movement brought an end to legalized segregation.

"For 20 years we have had a kind of token integration," said Dr. Aldon Morris, an associate professor of sociology at Northwestern University. "Now what we're getting is a real debate. What does integration mean and when has it really occurred? It is one of the most fundamental questions facing America right now."

Sociologists say that as society is forced to redefine integration and the forms it may take, it has become apparent that putting the races under the same roof does not guarantee integration.

Across the country, college campuses that have been desegregated for decades are witnessing growing racial tension and a disenchantment among blacks who have sought out separate cafeterias and dormitories. The situation at Brother Rice appears to be little different.

The college preparatory school is in a virtually all-white, middle-class neighborhood on Chicago's Southwest Side and has 1,330 students, 12 percent of them black, and no black teachers.

And while blacks and whites participate in classes and clubs and sports together, and many consider each other great friends, they sit at separate tables at lunchtime and go their separate ways after school is over.

On a subtler level, black students express a resentment that their culture does not get the attention that white culture does. They say that while they spend the school year learning mostly about the contributions of whites, black culture is relegated to a few seconds each morning during black history month when a student reads a brief sketch about a black inventor or abolitionist over the loudspeaker

"We've been experiencing their culture for four years," said Edward Jones, a black senior. "But they don't seem ready to experience ours."

The prom, with all its ritual and mythic significance, appeared to bring an underlying tension to a head. The trouble began when the prom committee, virtually all white, hired a rock band and a disc jockey and announced that the playlist for the music at the prom would be based on the suggestions of the senior class.

They devised what they saw as an objective means of gauging what the class wanted to hear: Each student would list three favorite songs, and the songs mentioned most would be the ones played.

Black seniors began to complain that their preferences would be effectively shut out, that Marvin Gaye would be squeezed out by Bon Jovi. "For every vote we had, there were eight votes for what they wanted," said Hosea Hill, a black senior.

"If you're paying tuition to the school, you should have some input. But with us being in the minority we're always outvoted. It's as if we don't count."

Music became a metaphor for culture and race, and black students considered the gap too wide to close. "They want to dance to that hard-rocking, bang-your-head-against-the-wall kind of stuff," said Sean Young, a black senior.

And others said that even if they could choose half the songs, which they figured was not going to happen, they would probably still be unhappy. "We would have sat down during their songs and they would have sat down during ours," Jones said.

So the black students decided to put together their own prom, with their own site, menu, theme and decorations. When school administrators got wind of the plans, they called a prom committee meeting to discuss grievances, but black students, figuring they would be outvoted, did not show up.

School administrators have refused to discuss the situation. Several of the black prom organizers, including honor students headed for prestigious universities, said they were threatened with suspension and expulsion if they went ahead with an alternative prom. They did it anyway.

And so while about 200 white couples danced to rock music in two adjoining ballrooms at the Marriott Hotel, about 30 black couples listened to the Isley Brothers and Roy Ayers, danced the Electric Slide and crowned their own prom king and queen, James Warren and Devona Rogers, in Ballroom 15 at the McCormick Hotel.

Several hours into the evening, there were bursts of applause as several of the six black couples who went to the main prom to spend time with their white friends showed up at the black prom.

The organizers for the black prom, who said they had nothing against their white classmates, said that white students were welcome to their prom. But by midnight, none had shown up.

Many of the white students have taken the situation personally. Some said they were hurt and felt rejected. Others were angry and embittered.

"Now you find out what they really think of you," said Jerry Ficaro, a white student at the main prom.

He said the black students should have gone along with the majority. "The majority makes a decision," he said. "That's the way it works."

Mike Kane, another white student, said: "I think the whole thing got out of hand. They should have found some way to compromise. We might as well have separate graduations."

Some said they just missed their friends and felt like the class was not whole without the black students. "It's too bad," said Jack Scott, another white senior, "because it's our senior year, and we should be together."

Brother Rice administrators would not allow reporters into the main prom. They have disavowed the black prom, saying the school has nothing to do with it and barring the black students from using the Brother Rice name in their program, napkins and banner.

The principal, Brother Michael Segvich, told the Chicago Tribune days before the proms, "There is only one prom this year at Brother Rice." The black prom "is something we don't want," he said, adding, "I think it has to do with racism. We felt we went out of our way to accommodate. They seemed to have their minds made up to go along with this other party all along."

Morris, the sociologist, said that the situation is symbolic of the misunderstanding that can occur between a majority and minority culture. "What integration has meant for many whites is that blacks had to interact with them on their terms," Morris said.

"It is a kind of cultural arrogance. Not only do many not want to participate in other cultures, but they feel theirs is the culture, that theirs is very much American and what America is."

For many of the black students, a black prom became something of a crusade, a chance to show that they could do something on their own, that they did not have to rely on whites.

And so Edward Jones, an honor student and one of the main organizers, was beaming as he looked across the small ballroom at his impeccably clad black classmates, helping their dates with their chairs or fetching punch or practicing dance steps to black music.

"I haven't felt this way for four years," Jones said. "We love being black. This makes me proud to be black. If at our 20th year reunion, the white students want to sit and point fingers at us, that's OK. We know we did something meaningful."

I. Reading Comprehension Activities

My Title: _____

Main Idea Statement: This story is about _____

_____

_____

Supporting Details / Specific Info / Facts & Details (5W's + H) :

1. _____

2. _____

3. _____

4. _____

5. _____

6. _____

7. _____

8. _____

9. _____

10. _____

Inferences (Educated Guesses/Possibilities/R-B-T-L):

1. _____

2. _____

3. _____

4. _____

5. _____

6. _____

7. _____

8. _____

II. Using Vocabulary In Context

1. Write a complete sentence using 'unknown' word in context: _____

_____

_____

    A. New Word/Unknown Word: _____

    B. Dictionary Definition: _____

    _____

    C. Synonyms: i. _____

               ii. _____

2. Write a complete sentence using 'unknown' word in context: _____

_____

    A. New Word/Unknown Word: _____

    B. Dictionary Definition: _____

    _____

    C. Synonyms: i. _____

               ii. _____

3. Write a complete sentence using 'unknown' word in context: _____

_____

    A. New Word/Unknown Word: _____

    B. Dictionary Definition: _____

    _____

    C. Synonyms: i. _____

               ii. _____

4. Write a complete sentence using 'unknown' word in context: _____

_____

    A. New Word/Unknown Word: _____

    B. Dictionary Definition: _____

    _____

    C. Synonyms: i. _____

               ii. _____

III. Critical Reading & Thinking, Part One

A. The author's purpose in writing this was to _____

_____

_____

B. I know this because of the following traits included in this reading: _____

_____

C. Of the following tone words, discuss with a partner or in your group which words more appropriately describe the tone of the selection. Support your choices—reasons why you made the choice that you did.

accurate	factual	impartial	truthful	matter-of-fact
calm	angry	direct	dramatic	serious
informal	formal	optimistic	pessimistic	biased
neutral	objective	subjective	emotional	unbiased

D. A graphic organizer is the most effective way to show the visual connection between ideas. The best graphic organizer to use for this selection would be:

_____

_____

Why? _____

_____

E. Complete a graphic organizer, a map, or an outline of main points of selection.

IV. Critical Reading & Thinking, Part Two

Directions: Your instructor will guide you based on which of the sections below students will be working on (individually or in groups). Students are to use the back of this page (Notes Page) to list their information and ideas based on evaluation, analysis, or discussion of the chosen Issues, Readings, or Topics below. This is a teacher-guided activity.

Argument is the ability to exchange ideas, opinions, and conclusions between two or more students based on readings or writings that cover contemporary issues or author's ideas.

Issue #1: _____

Issue #2: _____

Issue #3: _____

Issue #4: _____

Inferences are educated guesses or educated possibilities based on what is already known (past information or background information). These are not assumptions, opinions, or personal points of view.

Reading #1: _____

Reading #2: _____

Reading #3: _____

Reading #4: _____

Points of View are ideas that students come to conclude (draw conclusions) based on their own personal experience or information gained from past knowledge or experiences. These ideas can be personal opinions if they have an educational foundation and are not just personal feelings or beliefs.

Topic #1: _____

Topic #2: _____

Topic #3: _____

Topic #4: _____

V. Summary Page -or- Precis Page

Summary / Precis (Circle One): This story is about _____

_____

_____

_____

_____

_____

_____

_____

_____

_____

_____

_____

_____

_____

_____

_____

_____

_____

_____

_____

_____

_____

_____

_____

_____

<u>Source Information (Citation):</u>

Title of Selection: _____

Author: _____

Publisher: _____

Copyright Date: _____

Notes:

The Boy Who Painted Christ Black

by
John Henrik Clarke

Image © Athanasia Nomikou, 2012. Used under
license from Shutterstock, Inc.

He was the smartest boy in the Muskogee County School—for colored children. Everybody even remotely connected with the school knew this. The teacher always pronounced his name with <u>profound</u> gusto as she pointed him out as the ideal student. Once I heard her say: "If he were white he might, some day, become President." Only Aaron Crawford wasn't white; quite the contrary. His skin was so solid black that it glowed, reflecting an inner virtue that was strange, and beyond my comprehension. . . .

His great variety of talent often startled the teachers. This caused his classmates to look upon him with a mixed feeling of awe and envy.

Before Thanksgiving, he always drew turkeys and pumpkins on the blackboard. On George Washington's birthday, he drew large American flags surrounded by little hatchets. It was these small masterpieces that made him the most talked-about colored boy in Columbus, Georgia. The Negro principal of the Muskogee County School said he would some day be a great painter, like Henry O. Tanner.

For the teacher's birthday, which fell on a day about a week before commencement, Aaron Crawford painted the picture that caused an uproar, and a turning point, at the Muskogee County School. The moment he entered the room that morning, all eyes fell on him. Besides his torn book holder, he was carrying a large-framed concern wrapped in old newspapers. As he went to his seat, the teacher's eyes followed his every motion, a curious wonderment mirrored in them conflicting with the half-smile that wreathed her face.

Aaron put his books down, then smiling broadly, advanced toward the teacher's desk. . . .

Already the teacher sensed that Aaron had a present for her. Still smiling, he placed it on her desk and began to help her unwrap it. As the last piece of paper fell from the large frame, the teacher jerked her hand away from it suddenly, her eyes flickering unbelievingly. Amidst the rigid tension, her heavy breathing was distinct and frightening. Temporarily, there was no other sound in the room. . . .

With a quick, <u>involuntary</u> movement I rose up from my desk. A series of <u>submerged</u> murmurs spread through the room, rising to a distinct monotone. The teacher turned toward the children, staring <u>reproachfully</u>. They did not move their eyes from the present that Aaron had brought her. . . . It was a large picture of Christ—painted black!

Aaron Crawford went back to his seat, a feeling of triumph reflecting in his every movement.

The teacher faced us. . . .

"Aaron," she spoke at last, a slight <u>tinge</u> of uncertainty in her town, "this is a most welcome present. Thanks. I will treasure it." She paused, then went on speaking, a trifle more <u>coherent</u> than before. "Looks like you are going to be quite an artist. . . . Suppose you come forward and tell the class how you came to paint this remarkable picture."

When he rose to speak, to explain about the picture, a hush fell tightly over the room, and the children gave him all of their attention . . . something they rarely did for the teacher. He did not speak at first; he just stood there in front of the room, toying absently with his hands, observing his audience carefully, like a great concert artist.

"It was like this," he said, placing full emphasis on every word. "You see, my uncle who lives in New York teaches classes in Negro History at the Y.M.C.A. When he visited us last year he was telling me about the many great black folks who have made history. He said black folks were once the most powerful people on earth. When I asked him about Christ, he said no one ever proved whether he was black or white. Somehow a feeling came over me that he was a black man, 'cause he was so kind and forgiving, kinder than I have ever seen white people be. So, when I painted his picture I couldn't help but paint it as I thought it was."

After this, the little artist sat down, smiling broadly, as if he had gained entrance to a great storehouse of knowledge that ordinary people could neither acquire nor comprehend.

The teacher, knowing nothing else to do under prevailing circumstances, invited the children to rise from their seats and come forward so they could get a complete view of Aaron's unique piece of art.

When I came close to the picture, I noticed it was painted with the kind of paint you get in the five and ten cent stores. Its shape was blurred slightly, as if someone had jarred the frame before the paint had time to dry. The eyes of Christ were deepset and sad, very much like those of Aaron's father, who was a deacon in the local Baptist Church. This picture of Christ looked much different from the one I saw hanging on the wall when I was in Sunday School. It looked more like a helpless Negro, pleading silently for mercy.

For the next few days, there was much talk about Aaron's picture.

The school term ended the following week and Aaron's picture, along with the best handwork done by the students that year, was on display in the assembly room. Naturally, Aaron's picture graced the place of honor. . . .

In the middle of the day all the children were gathered in the small assembly. On this day we were always favored with a visit from a man whom all the teachers spoke of with mixed <u>esteem</u> and fear. Professor Danual, they called him, and they always pronounced his name with reverence. He was supervisor of all the city schools, including those small and poorly equipped ones set aside for colored children.

The great man arrived almost at the end of our commencement exercises. On seeing him enter the hall, the children rose, bowed courteously, and sat down again, their eyes examining him as if he were a circus freak.

He was a tall white man with solid gray hair that made his lean face seem paler than it actually was. His eyes were the clearest blue I have ever seen. They were the only life-like things about him.

As he made his way to the front of the room the Negro principal, George Du Vaul, was walking ahead of him, cautiously preventing anything from getting in his way. As he passed me, I heard the teachers, frightened, sucking in their breath, felt the tension tightening.

A large chair was in the center of the rostrum. It had been daintily polished and the janitor had laboriously recushioned its bottom. The supervisor went straight to it without being guided, knowing that this pretty splendor was reserved for him.

Presently the Negro principal introduced the distinguished guest and he favored us with a short speech. It wasn't a very important speech. Almost at the end of it, I remember him saying something about he wouldn't be surprised if one of us boys grew up to be a great colored man, like Booker T. Washington.

After he sat down, the school chorus sang two spirituals and the girls in the fourth grade did an Indian folk dance. This brought the commencement program to an end.

After this the supervisor came down from the rostrum, his eyes tinged with curiosity, and began to view the <u>array</u> of handwork on display in front of the chapel. . . .

Suddenly his face underwent a strange <u>rejuvenation</u>. His clear blue eyes flickered in astonishment. He was looking at Aaron Crawford's picture of Christ. Mechanically he moved his stooped form closer to the picture and stood gazing fixedly at it, curious and undecided, as though it were a dangerous animal that would rise any moment and spread destruction.

"Who painted this sacrilegious nonsense?" he demanded sharply.

"I painted it, sir." These were Aaron's words, spoken hesitantly. He wetted his lips timidly and looked up at the supervisor, his eyes voicing a sad plea for understanding.

He spoke again, this time more coherently. "Th' principal said a colored person have jes as much right paintin' Jesus black as a white person have paintin' him white. An he says. . . ." At this point he halted abruptly, as if to search for his next words. A strong tinge of bewilderment dimmed the glow of his solid black face. He stammered out a few more words, then stopped again.

The supervisor strode a few steps toward him. At last color had swelled some of the lifelessness out his lean face.

"Well, go on!" he said, enragedly, ". . . I'm listening."

Aaron moved his lips pathetically but no words passed them. His eyes wandered around the room, resting finally, with an air of hope, on the face of the Negro principal. After a moment, he jerked his face in another direction, regretfully, as if something he had said had betrayed an understanding between him and the principal.

Presently the principal stepped forward to defend the school's prize student.

"I encouraged the boy in painting that picture," he said firmly. "And it was with my permission that he brought the picture into this school. I don't think the boy is so far wrong in painting Christ black. The artists of all other races have painted whatsoever God they worship to resemble themselves. I see no reason why we should be <u>immune</u> from that privilege. After all, Christ was born in that part of the world that had always been predominantly populated by colored people. There is a strong possibility that he could have been a Negro.". . .

The supervisor swallowed dumfoundedly. His face was aglow in silent rage.

"Have you been teaching these children things like that?" he asked the Negro principal, sternly.

"I have been teaching them that their race has produced great kings and queens as well as slaves and serfs," the principal said. "The time is long overdue when we should let the world know that we erected and enjoyed the benefits of a splendid civilization long before the people of Europe had a written language."

The supervisor coughed. His eyes bulged menacingly as he spoke. "You are not being paid to teach such things in this school, and I am demanding your resignation for overstepping your limit as principal."

George Du Vaul did not speak. A strong quiver swept over his sullen face. He revolved himself slowly and walked out of the room towards his office.

The supervisor's eyes followed him until he was out of focus. Then he murmured under his breath: "There'll be a lot of fuss in this world if you start people thinking that Christ was a nigger."

Some of the teachers followed the principal out of the chapel, leaving the crestfallen children restless and in a quandary about what to do next. Finally we started back to our rooms. The supervisor was behind me. I heard him murmur to himself: "Damn, if niggers ain't getting smarter."

A few days later I heard that the principal had accepted a summer job as art instructor of a small high school somewhere in south Georgia and had gotten permission from Aaron's parents to take him along so he could continue to encourage him in his painting.

I was on my way home when I saw him leaving his office. He was carrying a large briefcase and some books tucked under his arm. He had already said good-by to all the teachers. And strangely, he did not look brokenhearted. As he headed for the large front door, he readjusted his horn-rimmed glasses, but did not look back. An air of triumph gave more dignity to his soldierly stride. He had the appearance of a man who had done a great thing, something greater than any ordinary man would do.

Aaron Crawford was waiting outside for him. They walked down the street together. He put his arms around Aaron's shoulder affectionately. He was talking sincerely to Aaron about something, and Aaron was listening, deeply earnest.

I watched them until they were so far down the street that their forms had begun to blur. Even from this distance I could see they were still walking in brisk, dignified strides, like two people who had won some sort of victory.

I. Reading Comprehension Activities

My Title: _____

Main Idea Statement: This story is about _____

_____

_____

Supporting Details / Specific Info / Facts & Details (5W's + H) :

1. _____

2. _____

3. _____

4. _____

5. _____

6. _____

7. _____

8. _____

9. _____

10. _____

Inferences (Educated Guesses/Possibilities/R-B-T-L):

1. _____

2. _____

3. _____

4. _____

5. _____

6. _____

7. _____

8. _____

II. Using Vocabulary In Context

1. Write a complete sentence using 'unknown' word in context: _____

_____

   A. New Word/Unknown Word: _____

   B. Dictionary Definition: _____

_____

   C. Synonyms: i. _____

             ii. _____

2. Write a complete sentence using 'unknown' word in context: _____

_____

   A. New Word/Unknown Word: _____

   B. Dictionary Definition: _____

_____

   C. Synonyms: i. _____

             ii. _____

3. Write a complete sentence using 'unknown' word in context: _____

_____

   A. New Word/Unknown Word: _____

   B. Dictionary Definition: _____

_____

   C. Synonyms: i. _____

             ii. _____

4. Write a complete sentence using 'unknown' word in context: _____

_____

   A. New Word/Unknown Word: _____

   B. Dictionary Definition: _____

_____

   C. Synonyms: i. _____

             ii. _____

III. Critical Reading & Thinking, Part One

A. The author's purpose in writing this was to _____

_____

_____

B. I know this because of the following traits included in this reading: _____

_____

C. Of the following tone words, discuss with a partner or in your group which words more appropriately describe the tone of the selection. Support your choices—reasons why you made the choice that you did.

accurate	factual	impartial	truthful	matter-of-fact
calm	angry	direct	dramatic	serious
informal	formal	optimistic	pessimistic	biased
neutral	objective	subjective	emotional	unbiased

D. A graphic organizer is the most effective way to show the visual connection between ideas. The best graphic organizer to use for this selection would be:

_____

_____

Why? _____

_____

E. Complete a graphic organizer, a map, or an outline of main points of selection.

IV. Critical Reading & Thinking, Part Two

Directions: Your instructor will guide you based on which of the sections below students will be working on (individually or in groups). Students are to use the back of this page (Notes Page) to list their information and ideas based on evaluation, analysis, or discussion of the chosen Issues, Readings, or Topics below. This is a teacher-guided activity.

Argument is the ability to exchange ideas, opinions, and conclusions between two or more students based on readings or writings that cover contemporary issues or author's ideas.

Issue #1: _____

Issue #2: _____

Issue #3: _____

Issue #4: _____

Inferences are educated guesses or educated possibilities based on what is already known (past information or background information). These are not assumptions, opinions, or personal points of view.

Reading #1: _____

Reading #2: _____

Reading #3: _____

Reading #4: _____

Points of View are ideas that students come to conclude (draw conclusions) based on their own personal experience or information gained from past knowledge or experiences. These ideas can be personal opinions if they have an educational foundation and are not just personal feelings or beliefs.

Topic #1: _____

Topic #2: _____

Topic #3: _____

Topic #4: _____

V. Summary Page –or– Precis Page

Summary / Precis (Circle One): This story is about _____

_____

_____

_____

_____

_____

_____

_____

_____

_____

_____

_____

_____

_____

_____

_____

_____

_____

_____

_____

_____

_____

_____

_____

_____

_____

_____

Source Information (Citation):

Title of Selection: _____

Author: _____

Publisher: _____

Copyright Date: _____

Notes:

Section Two—Multicultural

The Autobiography of Malcolm X

by
Alex Haley

Image © Neftali, 2012. Used under license from
Shutterstock, Inc.

Many who today hear me somewhere in person, or on television, or those who read something I've said, will think I went to school far beyond the eighth grade. This impression is due entirely to my prison studies.

It had really begun back in the Charlestown Prison, when Bimbi first made me feel envy of his stock of knowledge. Bimbi had always taken charge of any conversation he was in, and I had tried to emulate him. But every book I picked up had few sentences which didn't contain anywhere from one to nearly all of the words that might as well have been in Chinese. When I just skipped those words, of course, I really ended up with little idea of what the book said. So I had come to the Norfolk Prison Colony still going through only book-reading motions. Pretty soon, I would have quit even these motions, unless I had received the motivation that I did.

I saw that the best thing I could do was get hold of a dictionary—to study, to learn some words. I was lucky enough to reason also that I should try to improve my penmanship. It was sad. I couldn't even write in a straight line. It was both ideas together that moved me to request a dictionary along with some tablets and pencils from the Norfolk Prison Colony school.

I spent two days just riffling uncertainly through the dictionary's pages. I'd never realized so many words existed! I didn't know *which* words I needed to learn. Finally, just to start some kind of action, I began copying.

In my slow, painstaking, ragged handwriting, I copied into my tablet everything printed on that first page, down to the punctuation marks.

I believe it took me a day. Then, aloud, I read back, to myself, everything I'd written on the tablet. Over and over, aloud, to myself, I read my own handwriting.

I woke up the next morning, thinking about those words—immensely proud to realize that not only had I written so much at one time, but I'd written words that I never knew were in the world. Moreover, with a little effort, I also could remember what many of these words meant. I reviewed the words whose meanings I didn't remember. Funny thing, from the dictionary first page right now, that "aardvark" springs to my mind. The dictionary had a picture of it, a long-tailed, long-eared, burrowing African mammal, which lives off termites caught by sticking out its tongue as an anteater does for ants.

I was so fascinated that I went on—I copied the dictionary's next page. And the same experience came when I studied that. With every succeeding page, I also learned of people and places and events from history. Actually the dictionary is like a miniature encyclopedia. Finally the dictionary's A section had filled a whole tablet—and I went on into the B's. That was the way I started copying what eventually became the entire dictionary. It went a lot faster after so much practice helped me to pick up handwriting speed. Between what I wrote in my tablet, and writing letters, during the rest of my time in prison I would guess I wrote a million words.

I suppose it was inevitable that as my word-base broadened, I could for the first time pick up a book and read and now begin to understand what the book was saying. Anyone who has read a great deal can imagine the new world that opened. Let me tell you something: from then until I left that prison, in every free moment I had, if I was not reading in the library, I was reading on my bunk. You couldn't have gotten me out of books with a wedge. Between Mr. Muhammad's teachings, my correspondence, my visitors—usually Ella and Reginald—and my reading of books, months passed without my even thinking about being imprisoned. In fact, up to then, I never had been so truly free in my life.

The Norfolk Prison Colony's library was in the school building. A variety of classes was taught there by instructors who came from such places as Harvard and Boston universities. The weekly debates between inmate teams were also held in the school building. You would be astonished to know how worked up convict debaters and audiences would get over subjects like "Should Babies Be Fed Milk?"

Available on the prison library's shelves were books on just about every general subject. Much of the big private collection that Parkhurst had willed to the prison was still in crates and boxes in the back of the library—thousands of old books. Some of them looked ancient: covers faded, old-time parchment-looking binding. Parkhurst, I've mentioned, seemed to have been principally interested in history and religion. He had the money and the special interest to have a lot of books that you wouldn't have in general circulation. Any college library would have been lucky to get that collection.

As you can imagine, especially in a prison where there was heavy emphasis on rehabilitation, an inmate was smiled upon if he demonstrated an unusually intense interest in books. There was a sizable

Section Two—Multicultural

number of well-read inmates, especially the popular debaters. Some were said by many to be practically walking encyclopedias. They were almost celebrities. No university would ask any student to <u>devour</u> literature as I did when this new world opened to me, of being able to read and *understand*.

I read more in my room than in the library itself. An inmate who was known to read a lot could check out more than the permitted maximum number of books. I preferred reading in the total isolation of my own room.

When I had progressed to really serious reading, every night at about ten p.m., I would be outraged with the "lights out." It always seemed to catch me right in the middle of something <u>engrossing</u>.

Fortunately, right outside my door was a corridor light that cast a glow into my room. The glow was enough to read by, once my eyes adjusted to it. So when "lights out" came, I would sit on the floor where I could continue reading in that glow.

At one-hour intervals the night guards paced past every room. Each time I heard the approaching footsteps, I jumped into bed and <u>feigned</u> sleep. And as soon as the guard passed, I got back out of bed onto the floor area of that light-glow, where I would read for another fifty-eight minutes—until the guard approached again. That went on until three or four every morning. Three or four hours of sleep a night was enough for me. Often in the years in the streets I had slept less than that.

I. Reading Comprehension Activities

My Title: _____

Main Idea Statement: This story is about _____

_____

_____

Supporting Details / Specific Info / Facts & Details (5W's + H) :

1. _____

2. _____

3. _____

4. _____

5. _____

6. _____

7. _____

8. _____

9. _____

10. _____

Inferences (Educated Guesses/Possibilities/R-B-T-L):

1. _____

2. _____

3. _____

4. _____

5. _____

6. _____

7. _____

8. _____

II. Using Vocabulary In Context

1. Write a complete sentence using 'unknown' word in context: _____

_____

_____

   A. New Word/Unknown Word: _____

   B. Dictionary Definition: _____

   _____

   C. Synonyms: i. _____

                 ii. _____

2. Write a complete sentence using 'unknown' word in context: _____

_____

   A. New Word/Unknown Word: _____

   B. Dictionary Definition: _____

   _____

   C. Synonyms: i. _____

                 ii. _____

3. Write a complete sentence using 'unknown' word in context: _____

_____

   A. New Word/Unknown Word: _____

   B. Dictionary Definition: _____

   _____

   C. Synonyms: i. _____

                 ii. _____

4. Write a complete sentence using 'unknown' word in context: _____

_____

   A. New Word/Unknown Word: _____

   B. Dictionary Definition: _____

   _____

   C. Synonyms: i. _____

                 ii. _____

III. Critical Reading & Thinking, Part One

A. The author's purpose in writing this was to _____

_____

_____

B. I know this because of the following traits included in this reading: _____

_____

C. Of the following tone words, discuss with a partner or in your group which words more appropriately describe the tone of the selection. Support your choices—reasons why you made the choice that you did.

accurate	factual	impartial	truthful	matter-of-fact
calm	angry	direct	dramatic	serious
informal	formal	optimistic	pessimistic	biased
neutral	objective	subjective	emotional	unbiased

D. A graphic organizer is the most effective way to show the visual connection between ideas. The best graphic organizer to use for this selection would be:

_____

_____

Why? _____

_____

E. Complete a graphic organizer, a map, or an outline of main points of selection.

IV. Critical Reading & Thinking, Part Two

Directions: Your instructor will guide you based on which of the sections below students will be working on (individually or in groups). Students are to use the back of this page (Notes Page) to list their information and ideas based on evaluation, analysis, or discussion of the chosen Issues, Readings, or Topics below. This is a teacher-guided activity.

Argument is the ability to exchange ideas, opinions, and conclusions between two or more students based on readings or writings that cover contemporary issues or author's ideas.

Issue #1: _____

Issue #2: _____

Issue #3: _____

Issue #4: _____

Inferences are educated guesses or educated possibilities based on what is already known (past information or background information). These are not assumptions, opinions, or personal points of view.

Reading #1: _____

Reading #2: _____

Reading #3: _____

Reading #4: _____

Points of View are ideas that students come to conclude (draw conclusions) based on their own personal experience or information gained from past knowledge or experiences. These ideas can be personal opinions if they have an educational foundation and are not just personal feelings or beliefs.

Topic #1: _____

Topic #2: _____

Topic #3: _____

Topic #4: _____

V. Summary Page –or– Precis Page

Summary / Precis (Circle One): This story is about _____

_____

_____

_____

_____

_____

_____

_____

_____

_____

_____

_____

_____

_____

_____

_____

_____

_____

_____

_____

_____

_____

_____

_____

_____

Source Information (Citation):

Title of Selection: _____

Author: _____

Publisher: _____

Copyright Date: _____

Notes:

La Causa

by
Jessie Lopez De la Cruz

Image © Mary_L, 2012. Used under license from Shutterstock, Inc.

I think I was made an organizer because in the first place I could relate to the farmworkers, being a lifelong farmworker. I was well-known in the small towns around Fresno. Wherever I went to speak to them, they listened. I told them about how we were <u>excluded</u> from the NLRB [National Labor Relations Board] in 1935, how we had no <u>benefits</u>, no minimum wage, nothing out in the fields—no restrooms, nothing. I would talk about how we were paid what the grower wanted to pay us, and how we couldn't set a price on our work. I explained that we could do something about these things by joining a union, by working together. I'd ask people how they felt about these many years they had been working out in the fields, how they had been treated. And then we'd all talk about it. They would say, "I was working for so-and-so, and when I complained about something that happened there, I was fired." I said, "Well! Do you think we should be putting up with this in this modern age? You know, we're not back in the twenties. We can stand up! We can talk back! It's not like when I was a little kid and my grandmother used to say, 'You have to especially respect the Anglos,' 'Yessir,' 'Yes, Ma'am!' That's over. This country is very rich, and we want a share of the money these growers make of our sweat and our work by <u>exploiting</u> us and our children!" I'd have my sign-up book and I'd say, "If anyone wants to become a member of the union, I can make you a member right now." And they'd agree!

So I found out that I could organize them and make members of them. Then I offered to help them, like taking them to the doctor's and translating for them, filling out papers that they needed to fill out, writing their letters for those that couldn't write. A lot of people confided in me. Through the letter-writing, I knew a lot of the problems they were having back home, and they knew they could trust me, that I wouldn't tell anyone else about what I had written or read. So that's why they came to me.

There was a <u>migrant</u> camp in Parlier. And these people, the migrants, were being used as strikebreakers. I had something to do with building that camp. By that time, I had been put on the board of the Fresno County Economic Opportunity Commission, and I was supporting migrant housing for farmworkers. But I had no idea it was going to be turned almost into a concentration camp or prison. The houses were just like matchboxes—square, a room for living, a room for cooking, a bathroom that didn't have a door, just a curtain. The houses are so close together that if one catches fire, the next one does, too, and children have burned in them. It happened in Parlier.

So I went to the camp office and said I wanted to go in and visit. By this time, I was well-known as a <u>radical</u>, an educator, and a troublemaker! The man in the office asked what I wanted to talk about. I just wanted to visit, I said.

"Well, you have to sign your name here." I said, "I also would like to know when I can use the hall for a meeting."

"What kind of meeting?"

"An organizing meeting." You see, when it was built, they told us there was supposed to be a hall built for parties and whatever. I felt we could use it for a meeting to talk to the people. But he said, "We can't authorize you to come in here and talk to the people about a union, but you can write Governor Reagan and ask for permission." I left.

I met a nurse who had to go to this camp. She said, "Why don't you come with me as my translator?" Even though she spoke perfect Spanish! So both of us went in, and she said she was from the Health Department and I was her translator. I got in there and talked to the people and told them about our union meetings, and at our next meeting they were there. I had to do things like that in order to organize.

It was very hard being a woman organizer. Many of our people my age and older were raised with the old customs in Mexico: where the husband rules, he is king of his house. The wife obeys, and the children, too. So when we first started it was very, very hard. Men gave us the most trouble—neighbors there in Parlier! They were for the union, but they were not taking orders from women, they said. . . .

We'd have a union meeting every week. Men, women, and children would come. Women would ask questions and the men would just stand back. I guess they'd say to themselves, "I'll wait for someone to say something before I do." The women were more <u>aggressive</u> than the men. And I'd get up and say, "Let's go on, let's do it!". . .

The women took the lead for picketing, and we would talk to the people. It got to the point that we would have to find them, because the men just wouldn't go and they wouldn't take their wives. So we would say, "We're having our picket line at the Safeway in Fresno, and those that don't show up are going to have to pay a five-dollar fine." We couldn't have four or five come to a picket line and have the rest stay home and watch tv. In the end, we had everybody out there.

One time we were picketing—I think it was the early part of 1972—White River Farms in Delano, for a new contract. To go picket, we had to get up early. See, a lot of these growers were chartering buses, and at four or five o'clock in the morning they'd pick up the scabs. So we would follow these labor bosses who chartered the buses.

At White River Farms one morning very early, we were out there by the hundreds by the road, and these people got down and started working out there in the grapes. We were asking them not to work, telling them that there was a strike going on. The grower had two guards at the entrance, and there was a helicopter above us. At other White River Farm ranches they had the sheriff, the county police, *everybody*. But there were pickets at three different ranches, and where we were picketing there wasn't anybody except these two guards. So I said, "Hey! What about the women getting together and let's rush 'em!" And they said, "Do you think we could do that?" And I said, "Of course we can! Let's go in there. Let's get 'em out of there any way we can." So about fifty of us rushed. We went under the vines. We had our banners, and you could see them bobbing up and down, up and down, and we'd go under those rows on our knees and roll over. When the scabs saw us coming they took off. All of them went and they got on the bus. The guards had guns that they would shoot, and something black like smoke or tear gas would come out. That scared us, but we still kept on. After we saw all those workers get back on the buses, we went back. Instead of running this time, we rolled over and over all the way out. The vines are about four feet tall, and they have wire where you string up the vines. So you can't walk or run across one of these fences. You have to keep going under these wires. So I tripped, and rolled down about three or four rows before I got up. I rolled so they wouldn't get at me when they were shooting. When I got out there on the road they were getting these big, hard dirty clods and throwing them at us. And then the pickets started doing the same thing. When the first police car came, somebody broke the windshield. We don't know if it was the scabs or someone on the picket lines, but the picketers were blamed.

When we women ran into the fields, we knew we'd be arrested if they caught us. But we went in and we told the scabs, "If you're not coming out we're gonna pull you out!" Later I told Arnold, "See? See what women can do? We got all those men out there to come out!"

At another place, in Kern County, we were sprayed with pesticides. They would come out there with their sprayers and spray us on the picket lines. They have these big tanks that are pulled by a tractor with hoses attached, and they spray the trees with this. They are strong like a water hose, but wider. They get it started and spray the vines and the trees. When we were picketing, they came out there to spray the pickets. What could we do? We tried to get as far away as we could, and then we would come back.

They had goons with these big police dogs on leashes. I think they were trying to scare us by letting them loose on us. . . . When the growers realized how strong we were getting and how we had so many members, when our contracts were up for renewal they called the Teamsters in. And even before we bargained for our new contract, the growers signed up with the Teamsters. Then they claimed they already had a union and couldn't recognize ours. That was another way they had of not signing with UFW [United Farm Workers]. They were signing hundreds of what we called "sweetheart contracts."

Another thing the growers did to break our strikes was to bring in "illegal aliens." I would get a list of names of the scabs and give them to the border patrol. At that time, you see, we were pitted against each other, us and the people from Mexico, so it was either us or them. When I went to the border patrol office, I'd go in and say, "Can I come in?" They'd say, "You can't come in. This is a very small office." They kept telling us they were short of men. But every time I went there, there were all of them with their feet up on the desks in their air-conditioned office. They told me they were under orders not to interfere with labor <u>disputes</u>. So I called Bernie Sisk's office and talked to them about it. Then I came home and called a lot of students who'd been helping us, and other people, and the next morning, there we were at the border patrol. I said, "We're paying our tax money, but not for you to sit here while the illegal aliens are being used to break our strike."

I. Reading Comprehension Activities

My Title: _____

Main Idea Statement: This story is about _____

_____

_____

Supporting Details / Specific Info / Facts & Details (5W's + H) :

1. _____

2. _____

3. _____

4. _____

5. _____

6. _____

7. _____

8. _____

9. _____

10. _____

Inferences (Educated Guesses/Possibilities/R-B-T-L):

1. _____

2. _____

3. _____

4. _____

5. _____

6. _____

7. _____

8. _____

II. Using Vocabulary In Context

1. Write a complete sentence using 'unknown' word in context: _____

_____

_____

    A. New Word/Unknown Word: _____

    B. Dictionary Definition: _____

_____

    C. Synonyms: i. _____

                ii. _____

2. Write a complete sentence using 'unknown' word in context: _____

_____

    A. New Word/Unknown Word: _____

    B. Dictionary Definition: _____

_____

    C. Synonyms: i. _____

                ii. _____

3. Write a complete sentence using 'unknown' word in context: _____

_____

    A. New Word/Unknown Word: _____

    B. Dictionary Definition: _____

_____

    C. Synonyms: i. _____

                ii. _____

4. Write a complete sentence using 'unknown' word in context: _____

_____

    A. New Word/Unknown Word: _____

    B. Dictionary Definition: _____

_____

    C. Synonyms: i. _____

                ii. _____

III. Critical Reading & Thinking, Part One

A. The author's purpose in writing this was to _____

_____

_____

B. I know this because of the following traits included in this reading: _____

_____

C. Of the following tone words, discuss with a partner or in your group which words more appropriately describe the tone of the selection. Support your choices—reasons why you made the choice that you did.

accurate	factual	impartial	truthful	matter-of-fact
calm	angry	direct	dramatic	serious
informal	formal	optimistic	pessimistic	biased
neutral	objective	subjective	emotional	unbiased

D. A graphic organizer is the most effective way to show the visual connection between ideas. The best graphic organizer to use for this selection would be:

_____

_____

Why? _____

_____

E. Complete a graphic organizer, a map, or an outline of main points of selection.

IV. Critical Reading & Thinking, Part Two

Directions: Your instructor will guide you based on which of the sections below students will be working on (individually or in groups). Students are to use the back of this page (Notes Page) to list their information and ideas based on evaluation, analysis, or discussion of the chosen Issues, Readings, or Topics below. This is a teacher-guided activity.

<u>Argument</u> is the ability to exchange ideas, opinions, and conclusions between two or more students based on readings or writings that cover contemporary issues or author's ideas.

Issue #1: _____

Issue #2: _____

Issue #3: _____

Issue #4: _____

<u>Inferences</u> are educated guesses or educated possibilities based on what is already known (past information or background information). These are not assumptions, opinions, or personal points of view.

Reading #1: _____

Reading #2: _____

Reading #3: _____

Reading #4: _____

<u>Points of View</u> are ideas that students come to conclude (draw conclusions) based on their own personal experience or information gained from past knowledge or experiences. These ideas can be personal opinions if they have an educational foundation and are not just personal feelings or beliefs.

Topic #1: _____

Topic #2: _____

Topic #3: _____

Topic #4: _____

V. Summary Page –or– Precis Page

Summary / Precis (Circle One): This story is about _____

_____

_____

_____

_____

_____

_____

_____

_____

_____

_____

_____

_____

_____

_____

_____

_____

_____

_____

_____

_____

_____

_____

_____

_____

_____

<u>Source Information (Citation):</u>

Title of Selection: _____

Author: _____

Publisher: _____

Copyright Date: _____

Notes:

La Vida Loca ("The Crazy Life")

Two Generations of Gang Members

by
Luis J. Rodriguez

Image © Febris, 2012. Used under license from Shutterstock, Inc.

Late winter Chicago, 1991: The once-white snow that fell in December has turned into a dark scum, an admixture of salt, car oil and decay; icicles hang from rooftops and window sills like the whiskers of old men. The bone-chilling temperatures force my family to stay inside a one-and-a-half bedroom apartment in a three-flat building in Humboldt Park. My third wife, Trini, our child Ruben and my 15-year-old son Ramiro from a previous marriage huddle around the television set. Tensions build up like a fever.

One evening, words of anger bounce back and forth between the walls of our gray-stone flat. Two-year-old Ruben, confused and afraid, crawls up to my leg and hugs it. Trini and I had jumped on Ramiro's case for coming in late following weeks of trouble: Ramiro had joined the Insane Campbell Boys, a group of Puerto Rican and Mexican youth allied with the Spanish Cobras and Dragons.

Rodriguez, Luis. "La Vida Loca (The Crazy Life)" from *Always Running*. Willimantic: Curbstone Press, 1990. Reprinted by permission of the Northwestern University Press.

Within moments, Ramiro runs out of the house, entering the freezing Chicago night. I go after him, sprinting down the gangway leading to a debris-strewn alley. I see Ramiro's fleeing figure, his breath rising in quickly dissipating clouds.

I follow him toward Division Street, the neighborhood's main drag. People yell out of windows and doorways: "*¿Que pasa, hombre?*"[1] This is not an unfamiliar sight—a father or mother chasing some child down the street.

Watching my son's escape, it is as though he enters the waters of a distant time, back to my youth, back to when I ran, to when I jumped over fences, fleeing *vato locos*,[2] the police or my own shadow, in some drug-induced hysteria.

As Ramiro speeds off, I see my body enter the mouth of darkness, my breath cut the frigid flesh of night—my voice crack open the night sky.

We are a second-generation gang family. I was involved in gangs in Los Angeles in the late 1960s and early 1970s. When I was 2 years old, in 1956, my family emigrated from Mexico to Watts. I spent my teen years in a barrio called Las Lomas, east of Los Angeles.

I was arrested on charges ranging from theft, assaulting an officer to attempted murder. As a teen-ager, I did some time. I began using drugs at age 12—including pills, weed and heroin. I had a near-death experience at 16 from sniffing toxic spray. After being kicked out of three high schools, I dropped out at 15.

By the time I turned 18, some 25 friends had been killed by rival gangs, the police, overdoses, car crashes and suicides.

Three years ago, I brought Ramiro to Chicago to escape the violence. If I barely survived all this, it appeared unlikely my son would make it. But in Chicago, we found kindred conditions.

I had to cut Ramiro's bloodline to the street before it became too late. I had to begin the long intense struggle to save his life from the gathering storm of street violence—some 20 years after I had sneaked out of the hood in the dark of night and removed myself from the death fires of *La Vida Loca*.

What to do with those whom society cannot accommodate? Criminalize them. Outlaw their actions and creations. Declare them the enemy, then wage war. Emphasize the differences—the shade of skin, the accent or manner of clothes. Like the scapegoat of the Bible, place society's ills on them, then "stone them" in absolution. It's convenient. It's logical.

It doesn't work.

Gangs are not alien powers. They begin as unstructured groupings, our children, who desire the same as any young person. Respect. A sense of belonging. Protection. This is no different than the YMCA, Little League or the Boy Scouts. It wasn't any more than what I wanted.

When I entered 109th Street School in Watts, I spoke perfect Spanish, But teachers punished me for speaking it on the playground. I peed in my pants a few times because I was unable to say in English that I had to go. One teacher banished me to a comer, to build blocks for a year. I learned to be silent within the walls of my body.

The older boys who lived on 103rd Street would take my money or food. They chased me through alleys and side streets. Fear compelled my actions.

---

[1]"What's happening, man?"
[2]the crazy guys

The police, I learned years later, had a strategy: They picked up as many 7-year-old boys as they could—for loitering, throwing dirt clods, curfew—whatever. By the time a boy turned 13, and had been popped for something like stealing, he had accumulated a detention record, and was bound for "juvey."

One felt besieged, under intense scrutiny. If you spoke out, dared to resist, you were given a "jacket" of troublemaker; I'd tried many times to take it off, but somebody always put it back on.

Soon after my family moved to South San Gabriel, a local group, Thee Mystics, rampaged through the school. They carried bats, chains, pipes and homemade zip guns. They terrorized teachers and students alike. I was 12.

I froze as the head stomping came dangerously my way. But f was intrigued. I wanted this power. I wanted to be able to bring a whole school to its knees. All my school life until then had been poised against me. I was broken and shy. I wanted what Thee Mystics had. I wanted to hurt somebody.

Police sirens broke the spell. Thee Mystics scattered in all directions. But they had done their damage. They had left their mark on the school—and on me.

Gangs flourish when there's a lack of social recreation, decent education or employment. Today, many young people will never know what it is to work. They can only satisfy their needs through collective strength—against the police, who hold the power of life and death, against poverty, against idleness, against their impotence in society.

Without definitive solutions, it's easy to throw blame. George Bush and Dan Quayle, for example, say the lack of family values is behind our problems.

But "family" is a farce among the propertyless and disenfranchised. Too many families are wrenched apart, as even children are forced to supplement meager incomes. At age 9, my mother walked me to the door and, in effect, told me: Now go forth and work.

People can't just consume; they have to sell something, including their ability to work. If so-called legitimate work is unavailable, people will do the next best thing—sell sex or dope.

You'll find people who don't care about whom they hurt, but nobody I know *wants* to sell death to their children, their neighbors, friends. If there was a viable, productive alternative, they would stop.

At 18, I had grown tired. I felt like a war veteran with a kind of post-traumatic syndrome. I had seen too many dead across the pavement; I'd walk the aisles in the church wakes as if in a daze; I'd often watched my mother's weary face in hospital corridors, outside of courtrooms and cells, refusing, finally, to have anything to do with me.

In addition, I had fallen through the cracks of two languages; unable to communicate well in any.

I wanted the pain to end, the self-consuming hate to wither in the sunlight. With the help of those who saw potential in me, perhaps for some poetry, I got out. No more heroin, spray or pills; no more jails; no more trying to hurt somebody until I stopped hurting—-which never seemed to pass.

There is an aspect of suicide in gang involvement for those whose options have been cut off. They stand on street corners, flash hand signs and invite the bullets. It's life as stance, as bravado. They say "You can't touch this," but "Come kill me!" is the inner cry. It's either *la torcida*[3] or death, a warrior's path, where even self-preservation doesn't make a play. If they murder, the targets are the ones who look like them, walk like them, those closest to who they are—the mirror reflection. They murder and they are killing themselves, over and over.

---

[3]bad luck

Ramiro stayed away for two weeks the day he ran off. When he returned, we entered him into a psychotherapy hospital. After three months, he was back home. Since then, I've had to pull everyone into the battle for my son. I've spent hours with teachers. I've involved therapists, social workers, the police.

We all have some responsibility: Schools, the law, parents. But at the same time, there are factors beyond our control. It's not a simple matter of "good" or "bad" values, or even of choices. If we all had a choice, I'm convinced nobody would choose *la vida loca*, the "insane nation"—to gangbang. But it's going to take collective action and a plan.

Recently, Ramiro got up at a Chicago poetry event and read a piece about being physically abused by a stepfather. It stopped everyone cold. He later read the poem at Chicago's Poetry Festival. Its title: "Running Away."

The best way to deal with your children is to help construct the conditions for free and healthy development of all, but it's also true you can't be for all children if you can't be for your own.

There's a small but intense fire burning in my son. Ramiro has just turned 17; he's made it thus far, but it's day by day. Now I tell him: You have an innate value outside of your job, outside the "jacket" imposed on you since birth. Draw on your expressive powers.

Stop running.

I. Reading Comprehension Activities

My Title: _____

Main Idea Statement: This story is about _____

_____

_____

Supporting Details / Specific Info / Facts & Details (5W's + H) :

1. _____

2. _____

3. _____

4. _____

5. _____

6. _____

7. _____

8. _____

9. _____

10. _____

Inferences (Educated Guesses/Possibilities/R-B-T-L):

1. _____

2. _____

3. _____

4. _____

5. _____

6. _____

7. _____

8. _____

II. Using Vocabulary In Context

1. Write a complete sentence using 'unknown' word in context: _____

_____

_____

   A. New Word/Unknown Word: _____

   B. Dictionary Definition: _____

_____

   C. Synonyms: i. _____

              ii. _____

2. Write a complete sentence using 'unknown' word in context: _____

_____

   A. New Word/Unknown Word: _____

   B. Dictionary Definition: _____

_____

   C. Synonyms: i. _____

              ii. _____

3. Write a complete sentence using 'unknown' word in context: _____

_____

   A. New Word/Unknown Word: _____

   B. Dictionary Definition: _____

_____

   C. Synonyms: i. _____

              ii. _____

4. Write a complete sentence using 'unknown' word in context: _____

_____

   A. New Word/Unknown Word: _____

   B. Dictionary Definition: _____

_____

   C. Synonyms: i. _____

              ii. _____

III. Critical Reading
& Thinking, Part One

A. The author's purpose in writing this was to _____

_____

_____

B. I know this because of the following traits included in this reading: _____

_____

C. Of the following tone words, discuss with a partner or in your group which words more appropriately describe the tone of the selection. Support your choices—reasons why you made the choice that you did.

accurate	factual	impartial	truthful	matter-of-fact
calm	angry	direct	dramatic	serious
informal	formal	optimistic	pessimistic	biased
neutral	objective	subjective	emotional	unbiased

D. A graphic organizer is the most effective way to show the visual connection between ideas. The best graphic organizer to use for this selection would be:

_____

_____

Why? _____

_____

E. Complete a graphic organizer, a map, or an outline of main points of selection.

IV. Critical Reading & Thinking, Part Two

Directions: Your instructor will guide you based on which of the sections below students will be working on (individually or in groups). Students are to use the back of this page (Notes Page) to list their information and ideas based on evaluation, analysis, or discussion of the chosen Issues, Readings, or Topics below. This is a teacher-guided activity.

Argument is the ability to exchange ideas, opinions, and conclusions between two or more students based on readings or writings that cover contemporary issues or author's ideas.

Issue #1: _____

Issue #2: _____

Issue #3: _____

Issue #4: _____

Inferences are educated guesses or educated possibilities based on what is already known (past information or background information). These are not assumptions, opinions, or personal points of view.

Reading #1: _____

Reading #2: _____

Reading #3: _____

Reading #4: _____

Points of View are ideas that students come to conclude (draw conclusions) based on their own personal experience or information gained from past knowledge or experiences. These ideas can be personal opinions if they have an educational foundation and are not just personal feelings or beliefs.

Topic #1: _____

Topic #2: _____

Topic #3: _____

Topic #4: _____

V. Summary Page –or– Precis Page

Summary / Precis (Circle One): This story is about _____

_____

_____

_____

_____

_____

_____

_____

_____

_____

_____

_____

_____

_____

_____

_____

_____

_____

_____

_____

_____

_____

_____

_____

_____

_____

Source Information (Citation):

Title of Selection: _____

Author: _____

Publisher: _____

Copyright Date: _____

Notes:

How the García Girls Lost Their Accents

The Four Girls
Carla, Yolanda, Sandra, Sofia

by
Julia Alvarez

Image © Andresr, 2012. Used under license from Shutterstock, Inc.

The mother still calls them *the four girls* even though the youngest is twenty-six and the oldest will be thirty-one next month. She has always called them *the four girls* for as long as they can remember, and the oldest remembers all the way back to the day the fourth girl was born. Before that, the mother must have called them *the three girls*, and before that *the two girls*, but not even the oldest, who was once the only girl, remembers the mother calling them anything but *the four girls*.

The mother dressed them all alike in diminishing-sized, different color versions of what she wore, so that the husband sometimes joked, calling them *the five girls*. No one really knew if he was secretly displeased in his heart of hearts that he had never had a son, for the father always bragged, "Good bulls sire cows," and the mother patted his arm, and the four girls tumbled and skipped and giggled and raced by in yellow and baby blue and pastel pink and white, and strangers counted them, "One, two, three, four girls! No sons?"

"No," the mother said, apologetically. "Just the four girls."

Each of the four girls had the same party dress, school clothes, underwear, toothbrush, bedspread, nightgown, plastic cup, towel, brush and comb set as the other three, but the first girl brushed in yellow, the second one boarded the school bus in blue, the third one slept in pink, and the baby did everything she pleased in white. As the baby grew older, she cast an envying look at pink. The mother tried to convince the third daughter that white was the best color, and the little one wanted pink because she was a baby and didn't know any better, but the third girl was clever and would not be persuaded. She had always believed that she had gotten the best deal since pink was the color for girls. "You girls are going to drive me crazy!" the mother said, but the girls had gotten used to the mother's rhetorical threats.

The mother had devised the color code to save time. With four girls so close in age, she couldn't indulge identities and hunt down a red cowboy shirt when the third daughter turned tomboy or a Mexican peasant blouse when the oldest discovered her Hispanic roots. As women, the four girls criticized the mother's efficiency. The little one claimed that the whole color system smacked of an assembly-line mentality. The eldest, a child psychologist, admonished the mother in an autobiographical paper, "I Was There Too," by saying that the color system had weakened the four girls' identity differentiation abilities and made them forever unclear about personality boundaries. The eldest also intimated that the mother was a mild anal retentive personality.

The mother did not understand all that psychology talk, but she knew when she was being criticized. The next time the four girls were all together, she took the opportunity of crying a little and saying that she had done the best she could by the four girls. All four girls praised the good job the mother had done in raising four girls so close in age, and they poured more wine into the mother's glass and into the father's glass, and the father patted the mother's arm and said thickly, "Good cows breed cows," and the mother told the story she liked to tell about the oldest, Carla.

For although the mother confused their names or called them all by the generic pet name, "Cuquita," and switched their birthdates and their careers, and sometimes forgot which husband or boyfriend went with which daughter, she had a favorite story she liked to tell about each one as a way of celebrating that daughter on special occasions. The last time she told the story she liked to tell about the eldest was when Carla got married. The mother, tipsy on champagne, seized the mike during the band's break and recounted the story of the red sneakers to the wedding guests. After her good cry at the dinner table, the mother repeated the story. Carla, of course, knew the story well, and had analyzed it for unresolved childhood issues with her analyst husband. But she never tired of hearing it because it was her story, and whenever the mother told it, Carla knew she was the favorite of the moment.

"You know, of course, the story of the red sneakers?" the mother asked the table in general.

"Oh no," the second daughter groaned. "Not again."

Carla glared at her. "Listen to that negativity." She nodded at her husband as if to confirm something they had talked about.

"Listen to that jargon," the second one countered, rolling her eyes.

"Listen to my story." The mother sipped from her wine glass and set it down a little too heavily. Wine spilled on her hand. She looked up at the ceiling as if she had moved back in time to when they were living on the Island. Those downpours! Leaks, leaks—no roof could keep them out during rainy season. "You all know that when we were first married, we were really really poor?" The father nodded, he remembered. "And your sister"—the stories were always told as if the daughter in question were not present—"your sister wanted some new sneakers. She drove me crazy, night and day, she wanted sneakers, she wanted sneakers. Anyhow, we couldn't afford to make any ends, no less start in with sneakers! If you girls only knew what we went through in those days. Words can't describe it. Four—no, three of you, back then—three girls, and no money coming in."

"Well," the father interrupted. "I was working."

"Your father was working." The mother frowned. Once she got started on a story, she did not acknowledge interruptions. "But that measly little paycheck barely covered the rent." The father frowned. "And my father," the mother confided, "was helping us out—"

"It was only a loan," the father explained to his son-in-law. "Paid every penny back."

"It was only a loan," the mother continued. "Anyhow—the point is to make the story short—we did not have money for one little frill like sneakers. Well, she drove me crazy, night and day, I want sneakers, I want sneakers." The mother was a good mimic, and everybody laughed and sipped their wine. Carla's husband rubbed the back of her neck in slow, arousing circles.

"But the good Lord always provides." Although she was not particularly religious, the mother liked to make her plots providential. "It just so happened that a very nice lady who lived down the block with a little girl who was a little older than Carla and much bigger—"

"Much bigger." The father blew out his cheeks and made a monkey face to show how much bigger.

"This little girl's grandmother had sent her some sneakers for her birthday from New York, not knowing she had gotten so much bigger, and the little sneakers wouldn't fit her."

The father kept his cheeks puffed out because the third oldest burst into giggles every time she looked over at him. She never held her liquor well.

The mother waited for her to control herself and gave the father a sobering stare. "So the nice lady offers me the sneakers because she knows how much that Carla has been pestering me that she wants some. And you know what?" The table waited for the mother to enjoy answering her own question. "They were just her size. Always provides," the mother said, nodding.

"But Señorita Miss Carla could not be bothered with white sneakers. She wanted red sneakers, she wanted red sneakers." The mother rolled her eyes the same way that the second daughter had rolled her eyes at her older sister. "Can you believe it?"

"Uh-huh," the second daughter said. "I can believe it."

"Hostile, aren't we?" Carla said. Her husband whispered something in her ear. They laughed.

"Let me finish," the mother said, sensing dissension.

The youngest got up and poured everyone some more wine. The third oldest turned her glass, stem up, and giggled without much enthusiasm when the father puffed out his cheeks again for her benefit. Her own cheeks had gone pale; her lids drooped over her eyes; she held her head up in her hand. But the mother was too absorbed in her story to scold the elbow off the table.

"I told your sister, *It's white sneakers or no sneakers!* And she had some temper, that Carla. She threw them across the room and yelled, *Red sneakers, red sneakers.*"

The four girls shifted in their chairs, anxious to get to the end of the story. Carla's husband fondled her shoulder as if it were a breast.

The mother hurried her story. "So your father, who spoiled you all rotten"—the father grinned from his place at the head of the table—"comes and rescues the sneakers and, behind my back, whispers to

Carlita that she's going to have red sneakers just like she wants them. I find them, the both of them on the floor in the bathroom with my nail polish painting those sneakers red!"

"To Mami," the father said sheepishly, lifting his glass in a toast. "And to the red sneakers," he added.

The room rang with laughter. The daughters raised their glasses. "To the red sneakers."

"That's classic," the analyst said, winking at his wife.

"Red sneakers at that." Carla shook her head, stressing the word *red*.

"Jesus! " the second oldest groaned.

"Always provides," the mother added.

"Red sneakers," the father said, trying to get one more laugh from the table. But everyone was tired, and the third oldest said she was afraid she was going to throw up.

Yolanda, the third of the four girls, became a schoolteacher but not on purpose. For years after graduate school, she wrote down *poet* under profession in questionnaires and income tax forms, and later amended it to *writer*-slash-*teacher*. Finally, acknowledging that she had not written much of anything in years, she announced to her family that she was not a poet anymore.

Secretly, the mother was disappointed because she had always meant for her Yo to be the famous one. The story she told about her third daughter no longer had the charm of a prophetic ending: "And, of course, she became a poet." But the mother tried to convince her daughter that it was better to be a happy nobody than a sad somebody. Yolanda, who was still as clever as when the mother had tried to persuade her that white was a better color than pink, was not convinced.

The mother used to go to all the poetry readings her daughter gave in town and sit in the front row applauding each poem and giving standing ovations. Yolanda was so embarrassed that she tried to keep her readings a secret from her mother, but somehow the mother always found out about them and appeared, first row, center. Even when she behaved herself, the mother threw her daughter off just by her presence. Yolanda often read poems addressed to lovers, sonnets set in bedrooms, and she knew her mother did not believe in sex for girls. But the mother seemed not to notice the subject of the poems, or if she did, to ascribe the love scenes to her Yoyo's great imagination.

"That one has always had a great imagination," the mother confided to whoever sat next to her. At a recent reading the daughter gave after her long silence, the mother's neighbor was the daughter's lover. The mother did not know that the handsome, greying professor at her side knew her daughter at all; she thought he was just someone interested in her poetry. "Of all the four girls," the mother told the lover, "that Yo has always loved poetry."

"That's her nickname, Yo, Yoyo," the mother explained. "She complains she wants her name, but you have to take shortcuts when there's four of them. Four girls, imagine!"

"Really?" the lover said, although Yolanda had already filled him in on her family and her bastardized name—Yo, Joe, Yoyo. He knew better than to take shortcuts. Jo-laahn-dah, she had drilled him. Supposedly, the parents were heavy-duty Old World, but the four daughters sounded pretty wild for all that. There had been several divorces among them, including Yolanda's. The oldest, a child psychologist, had married the analyst she'd been seeing when her first marriage broke up, something of the sort. The second one was doing a lot of drugs to keep her weight down. The youngest had just gone off with a German man when they discovered she was pregnant.

I. Reading Comprehension Activities

My Title: _____

Main Idea Statement: This story is about _____

_____

_____

Supporting Details / Specific Info / Facts & Details (5W's + H) :

1. _____

2. _____

3. _____

4. _____

5. _____

6. _____

7. _____

8. _____

9. _____

10. _____

Inferences (Educated Guesses/Possibilities/R-B-T-L):

1. _____

2. _____

3. _____

4. _____

5. _____

6. _____

7. _____

8. _____

II. Using Vocabulary In Context

1. Write a complete sentence using 'unknown' word in context: _____

_____

_____

   A. New Word/Unknown Word: _____

   B. Dictionary Definition: _____

                                                 _____

   C. Synonyms: i. _____

                    ii. _____

2. Write a complete sentence using 'unknown' word in context: _____

_____

   A. New Word/Unknown Word: _____

   B. Dictionary Definition: _____

                                                   _____

   C. Synonyms: i. _____

                    ii. _____

3. Write a complete sentence using 'unknown' word in context: _____

_____

   A. New Word/Unknown Word: _____

   B. Dictionary Definition: _____

                                                   _____

   C. Synonyms: i. _____

                    ii. _____

4. Write a complete sentence using 'unknown' word in context: _____

_____

   A. New Word/Unknown Word: _____

   B. Dictionary Definition: _____

                                                   _____

   C. Synonyms: i. _____

                    ii. _____

III. Critical Reading & Thinking, Part One

A. The author's purpose in writing this was to _____

_____

_____

B. I know this because of the following traits included in this reading: _____

_____

C. Of the following tone words, discuss with a partner or in your group which words more appropriately describe the tone of the selection. Support your choices—reasons why you made the choice that you did.

accurate	factual	impartial	truthful	matter-of-fact
calm	angry	direct	dramatic	serious
informal	formal	optimistic	pessimistic	biased
neutral	objective	subjective	emotional	unbiased

D. A graphic organizer is the most effective way to show the visual connection between ideas. The best graphic organizer to use for this selection would be:

_____

_____

Why? _____

_____

E. Complete a graphic organizer, a map, or an outline of main points of selection.

IV. Critical Reading & Thinking, Part Two

Directions: Your instructor will guide you based on which of the sections below students will be working on (individually or in groups). Students are to use the back of this page (Notes Page) to list their information and ideas based on evaluation, analysis, or discussion of the chosen Issues, Readings, or Topics below. This is a teacher-guided activity.

<u>Argument</u> is the ability to exchange ideas, opinions, and conclusions between two or more students based on readings or writings that cover contemporary issues or author's ideas.

Issue #1: _____

Issue #2: _____

Issue #3: _____

Issue #4: _____

<u>Inferences</u> are educated guesses or educated possibilities based on what is already known (past information or background information). These are not assumptions, opinions, or personal points of view.

Reading #1: _____

Reading #2: _____

Reading #3: _____

Reading #4: _____

<u>Points of View</u> are ideas that students come to conclude (draw conclusions) based on their own personal experience or information gained from past knowledge or experiences. These ideas can be personal opinions if they have an educational foundation and are not just personal feelings or beliefs.

Topic #1: _____

Topic #2: _____

Topic #3: _____

Topic #4: _____

V. Summary Page –or– Precis Page

Summary / Precis (Circle One): This story is about _____

_____

_____

_____

_____

_____

_____

_____

_____

_____

_____

_____

_____

_____

_____

_____

_____

_____

_____

_____

_____

_____

_____

_____

_____

_____

_____

_____

<u>Source Information (Citation)</u>:

Title of Selection: _____

Author: _____

Publisher: _____

Copyright Date: _____

Notes:

Section Three

Experiential
[Life Lessons]

'A Hoodlum at Harvard'

From the Novel: 'A Hoodlum at Harvard'

by
J. A. Castellano de Garcia

Image © Suzanne Tucker, 2012. Used under license from Shutterstock, Inc.

"You'll never make it 'big' in this world—your goals are very unrealistic especially since you want to go to our university, and you actually believe that you will be successful by going to college. You really need to re-think your plan of going on to Highlands University after graduation. I don't want you to suffer any type of humiliation or **degradation** when you end up failing in college. I want to save you from that embarrassment. You should think about going to our local Vocational-Technical school instead—an automotive or refrigeration certificate is something you might be better suited at, a route you might want to take. Then, if you are able to complete their program and get that certificate, maybe you can settle down, get married, and make a salary, one that's just enough to support a family. I don't see anything more for you at this time. Trust me, you don't belong in college! I'm not going to beat-around-the bush—I am going to be straight with you. You're not smart enough; you're irresponsible; you hang out with a bunch of lowlifes and party too much. Going to the vocational school might be a stretch, too. If you ask me, I honestly believe that you will always be a hoodlum!"

Those words have **haunted** me for years, not because I believed them, but because I wondered how many other kids were told this exact same thing and believed what that idiot advised them—that idiot being my high school counselor!

My upbringing in a very poor family made me feel **sub-par** throughout my young life. Being poor didn't do much for my self-image and self-esteem. However, it was a blessing in disguise—growing up poor actually brought along with it some unexpected things—it gave me traits that I am proud of to this day. Even though we didn't have much, my parents and Grandma were **adamant** about how we would be perceived later in life. So, I was raised to have a strong set of values along with sound moral ethics. It was more important to our family that I become a man of strong character and high integrity than to **compromise** those standards for a quick buck or a big name and grand reputation. "Don't ever give us a bad name" was a phrase that I still live by—it is one that I will always **be true to**. It was important to my family that I grow up with a proper upbringing and go on to live a lifestyle that was above-board and sparkling.

That's not to say that I would never make mistakes or get in some type of trouble along the way, but my family wanted to make sure that others viewed me as an honest and trustworthy person, a person with an exceptional set of standards, a person that would not end up on the streets or in prison someday. That phrase—"don't ever give us a bad name"—was one that Mom and Grandma voiced time and again, almost on a daily basis. It was a phrase that I have kept with me since losing my parents and my grandma a number of years ago. After my little brother was murdered at the age of seventeen, my Grandma passed away shortly thereafter. She was followed not too long afterwards by my mom and also my dad. Each died of a broken heart after losing my little brother even though each of their death certificates indicated 'complications brought about by diabetes.' But, I knew better—Frankie's death sent them spiraling into states of depression and grief that took their lives much too soon.

However, before leaving this earth, I believe that they knew they had **instilled** the kind of standards in me that would make me a man of strong character and exceptional integrity and I would be okay. I know that they knew I would eventually turn out to be the man they always **envisioned**, the man I am today.

After their deaths, I set out to make them proud even though they wouldn't be around to see how I turned out. I believed that they would look down on me from up above and approve of how I have lived my life. I wanted to make them very proud of me; I wanted to live up to what they always wanted me to be, especially my mom. It wasn't so much about success; it was about being the stand-up person others admired—I guess Mom knew I would someday be a good role model and guide others. Mom saw a lot of potential in me, something I didn't see until much later in life—it was 'something' that my high school counselor could not or did not want to see. Regardless of the good advice plus the solid upbringing from Mom, Dad, and Grandma, I always wondered what my life would turn out to be. Mom always said I had two strikes against me: one was being poor and the other was being Hispanic, a minority. "Don't get that third strike, son!" she always urged. I knew the advise I was given wasn't going to get me where I wanted to go—it would not make me successful. It might give me the incentive to keep trying and keep moving onward and upward, but I would have to work diligently to get what I wanted in life. It was going to rest squarely on my shoulders to do the things I would need to do in order to become successful and to live up to the potential that my family saw in me, especially that 'special' thing that Mom recognized years before her passing.

It was difficult to envision myself being something I never imagined—a success! There were many things I wondered about. Would I be poor the rest of my life just like my family was, barely making ends meet and struggling to pay bills and buy food? It was a difficult life. I remember the day-to-day effort it took just to survive. We didn't have an electric or gas range; we had a coal and wood stove. I had to chop wood and bring in buckets of coal so my Grandma could cook. Besides providing for our meals, that old stove also kept our home warm at night. I remember not having regular, full course meals other families ate, families that were well-off and had homes with wall-to-wall carpeting.

We had linoleum floors and one dirt floor that had rotted through. Instead of being able to repair the floor with some of the **meager** saving my parents had, they had to use the money to fix our old truck when the transmission when out. That dirt floor stayed that way for over a year—we would cross into our small living room from the kitchen, passing over the dirt floor in what was called our dining room. It was really just a room with clutter all around—we usually ate in the kitchen at an old, wooden table that rocked if one accidentally bumped into it. We had four chairs and two old stools to sit on when we gathered to eat as a family.

We never had a 'regular' washer—our clothes were washed in an old, outdated washer with rollers instead of a spin cycle. We hung our clothes outdoors on the clothesline to dry. During the freezing cold winter months, when we brought clothes in from the line, much of it was frozen solid and looked like sheets of plywood. We would lay them over our old couch to defrost and dry completely.

We took baths in one small bathtub in the one bathroom we had, a room that was no bigger than the broom closet at our local school—we didn't get our first shower until I was turning fifteen and entering high school.

If my dad and I didn't go hunting that year during hunting season, for deer or elk, we seldom had meat—I thought all families had meat on Sundays only. If we had one chicken, I always ended up with a wing and a tortilla—I would be lucky if I got a second helping. That small baked **poultry** had to feed six people. Our side dishes were always beans, or fried potatoes, or rice—never all three at once. I remember we did have meat by-products—I still make potted meat sandwiches and buy pickled pigs' feet in a jar as well as Spam—it is much more expensive today. I still eat mackerel in place of the more expensive salmon in a can. I still eat Vienna sausages, but today, they are more of a snack with saltine crackers than a full meal like a time long ago.

I always wondered what it would be like to have a career. People who grew up like I did didn't always move into a career. They worked **menial** jobs and did the best they could to survive. Would I ever have a career, or would I have trouble even getting a job? Would I end up on the streets and eventually be one of the many homeless someday? Would I ever amount to much, therefore ending up the 'hoodlum' that my high school counselor **perceived** me to be? Would I ever 'make it' in this world or, as that supposed hoodlum, would I eventually end up like some young men from my old neighborhood, in prison—that is where most 'hoodlums' usually ended up, isn't it? While I had many questions without answers as I tried to make it in the world, I came to **adopt** and carry a set of philosophies with me throughout my lifetime. The one philosophy, at the top of my list, probably brought about by that meeting with my high school counselor: *"Never judge a book by its cover!"* People have done that to me on more than one occasion from the time I was a young teen all the way into **adulthood**. Today, I still get looked at funny at the gym when my tattoos are visible. I have even been asked, "How long have you been out?" Some people actually think I spent time in prison and am out on parole. What a laugh!

To this day, I am **appalled** that we still have a handful of educators and/or counselors who hold positions of authority and, worst of all, get paid for **dispersing** this type of harmful and dream-shattering advice to young men and women who are only trying to achieve some **semblance** of success and venture out into the world to find a career and make an honest living. I have actually witnessed some of these incidents firsthand and have overheard certain authority figures in schools, talking from up on their high pedestals, about certain students who they don't believe have what it takes to 'do' college.

I advise students—do what you think is right, what you have dreamed of doing, what you need to do to achieve your goal. If, by some chance, you aren't able to complete that goal, have another one ready to work on. The worst thing in life is to wake up someday and ask yourself: "I wonder what would've happened if I had tried to become that doctor or lawyer or legal aid or nurse." Don't let anyone squash the dreams that you have. If you end up believing that you cannot do something, you will wake up someday, and it will be too late—all that you will be left with are a bunch of 'what ifs' in life. Given that I am the product of that tarnished gold, I have taken it upon myself to step up, every chance I get, to share my experience with students who were also told they would never make it. Or, maybe the students are made to feel that they aren't good enough to make it. As an educator who truly cares about my students, I feel that it should be a priority in my life! I need to do everything I can to help them achieve their goals, to taste success, to move forward with that success and make something out of nothing. I know what being less than a success means and how much it can take out of a person.

My Dad only had a 2nd grade education—**illiterate** throughout his life—was I destined to end up like him? I couldn't imagine having to help out on a family ranch at the age of seven, not being able to attend school and learn. I loved my Dad—he worked hard to support a family, but I did not want to end up in his position. He worked odd jobs and also worked a small ranch with his eight horses and twelve cows. When he died, he still had those same numbers on that small ranch, a piece of land that was left to him by his family. It was only a few acres, but it was his. With no education, he was never going to work in any department store—he didn't possess any real job skills to work in any type of **blue-collar** business or shop. As a rancher, he would sell the offspring of both the horses and the cows and made a **meager** income doing so, barely enough to feed us. Once a year, he also butchered a calf so we would be able to include meat in our diet. Even though we had a supply of **venison** for the year, it wasn't really that much meat. From one deer, he gave meat to his sister and saved some for his own mom, my other grandmother. So, that meat didn't last too long.

I remember that Dad's highest income amount for a single year was $4,000. That day was a special day. Mom had discovered this amount while calculating their yearly income and doing their income taxes. That evening, she gathered us together, and we celebrated my Dad's minor success—this success was for a hardworking man who could not read or write and only spoke a bit of **broken** English. I never forgot that night—it was an exciting time for our family. Mom wanted to make Dad proud of his accomplishment—she wanted us to show him how much we respected him and were proud of this success. It was a rare occasion when Dad could throw out his chest and feel like a real man—we were all so proud of Dad—I am sure that he felt like some type of superhero, something we actually believed he was. But, I look back and see that it meant the world to him as well as it did to us. That was his only claim to fame—my poor Dad!

Then there was my grandmother (my Mom's mom) who was known as 'Gamma.' She lived at home with us and could never speak English—she only knew Spanish. After my grandfather died of cancer when I was only two years old, Gamma spent the rest of her life living at home with us. She was responsible for helping to raise us as Mom and Dad struggled to support our family. Her only joys in life: were cooking, cleaning, passing on advice that she could only hope we would heed, and finally, reading her prayer book every night.

I remember complaining one day when we were going to eat more beans after having had macaroni for two days and fried potatoes with tortillas for another two days. Wanting more meat and 'regular' food like other folks ate daily, I complained that we should get food stamps like our neighbors—they also had the benefit of government cheese and powdered eggs and fresh milk. We didn't always have eggs; our cheese was always moldy; our milk was either Pet Milk or powdered milk, both made with water. One of our treats was either Kool-Aid to quench our thirst or a pitcher of water with sugar and a few drops of lemon juice mixed in, a weak version of lemonade.

Grandma scolded me for complaining—she said that our life was "rich in so many other ways." Was she kidding? How were we rich? To Gamma, rich consisted of the following: having a safe place to sleep called home, having a vehicle to get to work or school, having food to eat no matter what kind it was, having clean clothes to wear everyday, and having a family who loves and cares for you, your sister, and your little brother.

As a child, I could never understand what she meant by rich—to me, I always considered us in survival **mode**. I wished we had a new car or truck—our vehicle was twelve years old (Mom considered it new). I wanted new clothes not the **hand-me-downs** that our cousins had worn and passed down to us. I wanted 'real' food to eat like meat and eggs and real milk, not beans, chili, macaroni, or potatoes and tortillas with Kool-Aid. I questioned why we couldn't just get food stamps like all our neighbors— they ate 'real' food and had much more than we had. "Hijito, listen carefully! We will *never* get food stamps or go on welfare as long as we have something to put on the table to eat and you are warm each night. If the day comes when we have no food or are at risk of losing our home and living on the street, then we will go seek help! As long as we have something to eat and a place to live, we will not ask for any food stamps or assistance, especially when other families could use it more. "We will not take money away from other families who need it more than we do. That government assistance (food stamps and welfare) needs to go to a needy family who is desperate and who might have *nothing* to feed their kids and are barely surviving. So, I want you to stop your complaining and go chop wood—it's going to be cold tonight! I don't ever want to hear you complain about our living conditions again— your Mom, Dad, and I do the best we can!"

Finally, there was Mom who worked so hard, with little to no reward or self-satisfaction. She worked as a secretary for over thirty-five years just to be able to help support our family and to be able to provide us with the necessities of everyday life. She worked hard all of her adult life—her greatest disappointment was that she had to drop out of college during her second year to help care for my grandpa who was dying of intestinal cancer. She watched as women just out of college with a degree passed her by on their climb to supervisory positions at her job, and they got paid much more than she did. I know it was hard for her to accept that each of these younger women started out making just above her highest income level, especially during their first year on the job. However, that did not **deter** her from doing what she needed to do to help support our family.

Mom was a whiz at crossword puzzles and read almost every monthly issue of *Readers' Digest* that came into the office. She was allowed to take the old issues home. To this day, I am still amazed at her extremely high level of vocabulary—she had the highest level that I have ever witnessed since I got into the field of teaching. Her vocabulary was **phenomenal**! While my grandma taught us Spanish while caring for us during the day, my mom saw to it that she passed on her exceptional English skills and language to us, too. We grew up being **bilingual**—my little brother and I picked up both languages quite easily; our middle sister felt that she didn't need to learn Spanish. As the 'princess' of the family, she could not be bothered with learning Spanish or even believing we were poor. She actually felt she was above all that—but, that was okay. It was just my sister's personality, one that we had become accustomed to.

My childhood has always been a source of pride to me, but this only came to be after I finished my education and moved on to become a successful adult. Then, I could look back on what I now call a very happy and fulfilling childhood. You see, with all the things that should bring a family to its knees, the one thing that kept us together and strong was the love that was abundant in our household. That really made a difference—it didn't make me think twice about being poor, about being Spanish, about the lack of success within our family unit. While I always believed Mom and Dad to be successful, they would never be considered that in today's society—they would be members of the lower class, the **downtrodden**, the hidden class—they would only be considered part of the class of people who were very poor. But, that is not how I viewed them or how they would ever be viewed in my eyes—they did their best, and I will always appreciate them for what they did. I would never view them in any other way except successful at raising a wonderful family and giving us the strength and persistence to go on, do better, make something of ourselves.

"Life is not going to be easy. But, if you set your mind to something and work hard at accomplishing that goal, you WILL SUCCEED! Trust me son—as your Mom, I know what you are made of and what your potential is. While life and reaching your success might be a struggle, just remember, do everything that you can so that you can hold your head high, be proud of what you accomplish. That will also make us proud of you. As you go through life, don't ever give us a bad name." At that time, I did not see what my Mom saw in me, and I wondered if she was just telling me this because I was her first-born. Surely, it had to be a mother's love for her child that guided her to tell me these things, hoping to inspire me. Was it that mother's love that was guiding her to offer those words of encouragement? She seemed to know that I had what it took to be 'special' and to eventually become a success, even though I didn't know what she saw in me. I wondered why Mom didn't see what that counselor saw in me. Couldn't she see that, if I followed my plan and went to our university, I was not only fooling myself, but I was fooling everyone else who saw me as a college student? Maybe the counselor was right—I was just a hoodlum and would always be nothing more than a hoodlum!

As I look back, it's still puzzling to me that I was able to get my B.A. (Bachelor of Arts) degree, in fact, the first of two Bachelor's degrees. That was followed up with my Masters degree in Education from our small-town university in Las Vegas, New Mexico. Even more surprising was that I had the persistence and drive to go further. Immediately after receiving my Master's degree at Highlands, I traveled across the United States to attend another university in a northeastern city (Cambridge, Massachusetts). I had been accepted into a graduate program at Harvard University and was able to complete yet another **milestone**—my Ed.M. (second Master's) and Reading Specialist Degree. Who would have ever imagined that I would someday be a Harvard graduate? And, finally, to finish climbing that educational ladder, I completed my doctoral coursework and oral/written comps several years later.

All these 'successes' had me reflecting on what the high school 'idiot' (oops, I mean counselor), who questioned my **motivation** and intelligence, had told me about what he believed about me. I guess he couldn't see that I had quite a bit of potential and whole lot of future success running through my genes—he was so wrong to label me a failure!

Or, could Mom have been so wrong—could I be nothing more than the irresponsible young man that had his dreams **quashed** by the counselor? Was I nothing more than that 'hoodlum' **masquerading** as a Harvard graduate with several university degrees? A *hoodlum* who had become a teacher, a professor, a motivational speaker, an author? Trust me when I tell you, a *hoodlum* doesn't write a dozen books and have them published unless they're stories about prison life. A hoodlum doesn't have a number of honors hanging from the wall in his living room: ranging from 'Teacher of the Year', to Who's Who among Hispanic Americans, and Honorable Discharge from the U.S. Navy, to Chamber of Commerce Successful Man of the Year. Am I that hoodlum who still considers members of that 'wrong crowd' his friends? Well, at least I could rest in the fact that, no matter what, if I was truly a hoodlum, then I would be the first 'Hoodlum at Harvard'—if he was right all along, I ended up being a very successful and highly esteemed hoodlum! But, he wasn't right—he was dead wrong! He judged me by how I looked, where I lived, who my friends were, and how little we had in terms of wealth (being poor). He judged this book (me) by its cover!

In the end, and in the grand **scheme** of things, none of that mattered. I finished my work, did all of my necessary research, wrote countless papers, graduated from universities, even from Harvard University. I did all that was required of me, and I did it well. I was a success in college—I graduated on more than one occasion! I eventually received several more degrees than that high school counselor would ever get—how **ironic**, huh? That is what really mattered—not what he thought I might be or what he thought I might become! I find it **comical**—I never was a hoodlum, a 'bad seed,' a gang member, or a jailbird. I was just a kid with dreams and goals—he actually believed that I was a hoodlum and would end up a failure! How wrong a person can be for judging another—100% wrong!

Today, the thoughts of Spring Break cross my mind—I fondly remember the many Spring Breaks I lived through. Now, students all over the United States look forward to Spring Break every year—their trips and adventures, or just the opportunity to sleep in all week and watch cartoons. It's the same old routine—students will be going through what we did as college students many years ago.

Wow, it's getting late! That's enough daydreaming for one day—I need to focus on getting to work—I don't want to run late. I have forty-two eager learners waiting for me for my nine o'clock class, waiting to listen to my lecture, a lecture I spent most of last evening planning. They are probably wondering what remarkable activities I have for them as well. Their smiling faces, cocky attitudes, and puzzled grins are what I have become accustomed to from college freshmen. I have to constantly remind them to turn off their cell phones—I don't want any incoming calls or their cell phones buzzing during my class.

It's odd, but at times, when I am looking at my students seated in class, I chuckle—I wonder just how many 'hoodlums' I have in my college class. Would they ever be as successful as I believe they can be—will they achieve well-above their expected potential as I believe they can? Or, will they end up following in the footsteps of their friends, who are probably not in college or were told they didn't belong in college? Would any of my students 'give up' and end up back, living the street life they left to attempt college?

Maybe I can make a difference—I certainly will try to keep them focused on their goals, keep them in college. All I know is that I will constantly and consistently tell them that they 'can' make it—I truly believe in each and every one of them. I also will never give up on them. Their goals and dreams are as important to me as mine were when I was their age. I also wonder what choice they will make when the time comes. All I know for certain is that I will choose one thing for each of them—I will choose not to give up on them. I want them to turn those dreams into actual goals that they can accomplish. My goals are still the same, the same as they have been for the past thirty years as a college/university professor. My goal for each of my students is for each to become successful in whatever they choose. And, I will choose success not failure for each of them—no doubt!

Image © Yuris Schulz Photographer, 2012. Used under license from Shutterstock, Inc.

I. Reading Comprehension Activities

My Title: _____

Main Idea Statement: This story is about _____

_____

_____

Supporting Details / Specific Info / Facts & Details (5W's + H) :

1. _____

2. _____

3. _____

4. _____

5. _____

6. _____

7. _____

8. _____

9. _____

10. _____

Inferences (Educated Guesses/Possibilities/R-B-T-L):

1. _____

2. _____

3. _____

4. _____

5. _____

6. _____

7. _____

8. _____

II. Using Vocabulary In Context

1. Write a complete sentence using 'unknown' word in context: _____

_____

    A. New Word/Unknown Word: _____

    B. Dictionary Definition: _____

    _____

    C. Synonyms: i. _____

                ii. _____

2. Write a complete sentence using 'unknown' word in context: _____

_____

    A. New Word/Unknown Word: _____

    B. Dictionary Definition: _____

    _____

    C. Synonyms: i. _____

                ii. _____

3. Write a complete sentence using 'unknown' word in context: _____

_____

    A. New Word/Unknown Word: _____

    B. Dictionary Definition: _____

    _____

    C. Synonyms: i. _____

                ii. _____

4. Write a complete sentence using 'unknown' word in context: _____

_____

    A. New Word/Unknown Word: _____

    B. Dictionary Definition: _____

    _____

    C. Synonyms: i. _____

                ii. _____

III. Critical Reading & Thinking, Part One

A. The author's purpose in writing this was to _____

_____

_____

B. I know this because of the following traits included in this reading: _____

_____

C. Of the following tone words, discuss with a partner or in your group which words more appropriately describe the tone of the selection. Support your choices—reasons why you made the choice that you did.

accurate	factual	impartial	truthful	matter-of-fact
calm	angry	direct	dramatic	serious
informal	formal	optimistic	pessimistic	biased
neutral	objective	subjective	emotional	unbiased

D. A graphic organizer is the most effective way to show the visual connection between ideas. The best graphic organizer to use for this selection would be:

_____

_____

Why? _____

_____

E. Complete a graphic organizer, a map, or an outline of main points of selection.

IV. Critical Reading & Thinking, Part Two

Directions: Your instructor will guide you based on which of the sections below students will be working on (individually or in groups). Students are to use the back of this page (Notes Page) to list their information and ideas based on evaluation, analysis, or discussion of the chosen Issues, Readings, or Topics below. This is a teacher-guided activity.

Argument is the ability to exchange ideas, opinions, and conclusions between two or more students based on readings or writings that cover contemporary issues or author's ideas.

Issue #1: _____

Issue #2: _____

Issue #3: _____

Issue #4: _____

Inferences are educated guesses or educated possibilities based on what is already known (past information or background information). These are not assumptions, opinions, or personal points of view.

Reading #1: _____

Reading #2: _____

Reading #3: _____

Reading #4: _____

Points of View are ideas that students come to conclude (draw conclusions) based on their own personal experience or information gained from past knowledge or experiences. These ideas can be personal opinions if they have an educational foundation and are not just personal feelings or beliefs.

Topic #1: _____

Topic #2: _____

Topic #3: _____

Topic #4: _____

V. Summary Page –or– Precis Page

Summary / Precis (Circle One): This story is about _____

_____

_____

_____

_____

_____

_____

_____

_____

_____

_____

_____

_____

_____

_____

_____

_____

_____

_____

_____

_____

_____

_____

_____

_____

Source Information (Citation):

Title of Selection: _____

Author: _____

Publisher: _____

Copyright Date: _____

Notes:

Section Three—Experiential [Life Lessons]

Selection 19

'An Unlikely Hero'

From the Novel: 'A Hoodlum at Harvard'

by
J. A. Castellano de Garcia

Image © Christopher Boswell, 2012. Used under license from Shutter-stock, Inc.

She worked hard every day just to support us. She did this for over thirty-five years as a secretary in an office, no promotions and little to no advancement in pay. No reward or job satisfaction. Yet, she still had enough energy each night, after another long day's work, to tuck me into bed and read a story to me. It was probably her love of reading that actually set me on a path that would be my **destiny**—a Reading Specialist.

I remember much of my normal childhood. My best recollection is when I was between six and eight years old. Each night, after I was tucked into bed, I anxiously waited for Mom to find that special book with the story she had chosen to read to me. What would the story be tonight? I hoped it was one of my favorites—or maybe it would be a story I had never listened to before. That thought was really part of my excitement and anticipation for that day. I lay in bed waiting. I was excited, hoping to be transported to another world, a land only found in fairytales. I knew there would be a hero to come alive in my head and later in my dreams, a hero from the story she would read to me. And yet, I don't think that during that time, she actually realized she was my real hero. As I grew older, she became the person I would admire for the rest of my life, the one person who believed in me and knew I would someday be something special, be someone successful. She was my Mom, my real Hero!

Where would the story take me tonight? I waited patiently—maybe I would be visiting the Round Table where King Arthur would be seated as his Knights gathered. I waited to become that special kid with the super strength to take down a hundred **combatants**. Every night was the same, and it never became dull. I was a child who always experienced the same **adrenaline rush**, a rush that would hold me through the night, sometimes making it difficult to fall asleep. I could now take my mind off the bad things that occurred that day—my teacher yelling at me and calling me stupid, the bullies taking another shot at me and taking away my milk money, and then waiting to beat on me after school. Those things didn't bother me now. I was safe. Mom made me feel protected and free from the harm that the outside world seemed to bring my way each day. I could hold my old, tattered teddy bear and wait to listen to Mom's sweet voice as she took me on another journey, an adventure I waited for each night. And I knew that, once I fell asleep, the story would surely carry over into my dreams—the dreams of a child entering a new and unexplored world, a world of fantasy.

After Mom went through her nightly **routine** of tucking me into bed and helping me with my prayers, she would reach for a storybook to begin another spectacular journey into fantasyland. She would smile down at me, preparing to read another story—sometimes she would ask me what story I wanted that night. If I selected the story; I usually chose the same one, my favorite: *Horatio at the Bridge*. If she chose the story, it was one that I was never disappointed with. Rather, it would simply be a surprise—she knew what stories I really enjoyed—the stories that would take my mind away from our situation, the situation that we were very poor. But during this nighttime routine of storytelling, I would simply forget all that.

Each night, I lay there barely able to **contain my excitement** at what story was to come. It didn't matter anymore that we were poor, that I had **hand-me-down** clothes to wear to school the next day, and that my shoes had cardboard cutouts to prevent dirt and gravel from entering the hole in the soles. At times, we really could not afford new shoes. In fact, I now believe the cardboard cutouts Mom placed every day in my shoes were the inspiration for Dr. Scholl's foot pads and insoles. I never thought much about it, but I realized that she never got the credit—she was the genius. We stayed poor—Dr. Scholl got rich!

I quickly forgot the bullies that haunted me during the day on the way to and from school. I joke about it now—I didn't taste chocolate milk until I was twelve years old. Those bullies would take away my milk money. Our elementary school teachers would ask us to bring money for our daily ration of milk. It wasn't very expensive, but in those days, even the few cents it cost was sometimes difficult to come up with. White milk cost five cents, chocolate milk ten cents. While I never snitched on those bullies, I knew I would never get my chocolate milk on the day they cornered me and threw me to the ground, holding me down while one of them stole my milk money. I don't know why I even looked forward to getting chocolate milk—I wasn't going to get it. During my entire time in grade school, I actually never got chocolate milk.

That's one thing I always remembered. I would never forget what those guys did to me; I would forever blame those bullies for that. As a kickboxer later in life, I ended up inviting them to come train with me, to 'teach me' their street skills, just to get them over to the gym. I did end up paying them back for all those days of misery that they put me through—it was quite satisfying getting them into the ring and getting my payback. But, that's a whole different story.

Anyway, if I was fortunate enough to have the ten cents on occasion for chocolate milk, and it was taken from me, it wasn't a problem. Our teacher knew our **family circumstances**—she knew we were poor and probably couldn't afford it. Most of the kids in our grade school came from disadvantaged families, families that were all poor. So, having a dime to buy chocolate milk was rare. On the days I looked forward to getting chocolate milk, I knew I would end up with white milk since I had lost my dime to the bullies during my daily encounter with them. Our teacher would end up buying our milk if we did not have the money—she never made a big deal out of it. I never told my teachers that I did have the money, but now bullies were taking turns drinking chocolate milk that should have been mine. During story time at night, it was not a problem anymore—it was quickly forgotten—Mom's storytelling made me forget everything bad that happened during my day and prepare for my nightly adventure.

While we could never afford a collection of reading books, Mom was able to make sure we had a small library at home. She had collected a set of reading books by exchanging S&H Green Stamps at our local Safeway grocery store. Every time a customer purchased groceries, the store presented the consumer with S&H Green Stamps which were then pasted into a small booklet. Then, folks could exchange those booklets for monthly gifts at the store—there was always a variety of 'gifts' that those stamps could be exchanged for. This was a time when the money paid for groceries always garnered a page of S&H Green Stamps that would go into a booklet. My Grandma kept these booklets in a kitchen drawer that never fully closed, with a handle that was loose and ready to fall off.

Once filled, each booklet could later be exchanged for a number of items at Safeway, such as a set of children's encyclopedias from A to Z; a set of children's fairytale books; books written by The Brothers Grimm, Hans Christen Andersen, or Aesop (fables); or a set of children's booklets that included heroes from times gone by, heroes from Greek **mythology** and the days of the great Roman Empire. Families could also exchange booklets for sets of plates, cups, **saucers**, or silverware. After Mom died, I went through our kitchen and realized that most of the dinnerware and other items that we possessed, had been collected using those S&H Green Stamps from Safeway.

Not realizing how poor we were, I can now see that we were very fortunate to be able to **acquire** a set from each of the gifts available. One of our books that stamps were exchanged for was a three-inch thick book that covered everything from myths and fables to Christmas stories, songs, and poems. While the green stamps could purchase sets of dishware, Mom thought it better to introduce me to the wonders of reading first—this would open up a brand new world simply by using fantasy and adventure. When I think back, I realize that, in a span of two to three years, we had become the proud owners of several sets of these books.

After she set up our small library, both Mom and Grandma started collecting sets of Safeway dishware—dishes, cups, and saucers for a family of four. We were a family of six, so during meals, our dishes never matched. That wasn't so bad; we still had food to eat. This promotion went on for years. Later in my life, most grocers went on to other methods for attracting consumers, leaving the S&H stamps a thing of the past.

"There he stood, bleeding from the wounds of battle, blinded in one eye from the wave of a sword from one of his enemies, waiting for the approaching Greek army. He knew what he had to do—he knew there was no way that he would survive. But, what mattered most was that, in the end, he would save his people." How could I ever forget my favorite story and its hero—*Horatio at the Bridge* or how he ended up saving his **clan**? It was actually a **suicide by army**. Many times, I would play the part of Horatio out back with my cousin, Freddy. We used sticks as swords and cardboard as shields. We made forts out of piles of branches and leaves. It was a magical time until I almost put Freddy's eye out with my 'sword' one day—he just got a scratch under his left eye—it was his grandma that swore that I almost blinded him. Now I understand why parents and grandparents always warned of running with sticks or swinging them at kids. According to them, we could kill a kid with a stick or blind him permanently. Usually, it was just drama among the grandmas!

Well, after that happened, it was the end of playing Horatio and pretending we were fighting Greek soldiers. Didn't they (his grandma and my grandma) realize it really wasn't my fault? It was really Freddy's fault for not defending himself properly. He didn't know what it was to be an expert with a sword (or stick) like I was. I don't think he had ever heard of Horatio or had someone read the story to him. I knew that story so well that it actually made me an expert at warfare, or so I thought. Anyway, Freddy really couldn't handle the skill of a trained Greek soldier that I could. Mom had read that story so many times, at my choosing, that I knew I could easily become a soldier when I grew up, a soldier with a sword, fighting Greek warriors. Freddy was lucky that we were just playing—I was skilled enough to send him to the afterlife if I wanted and if this was real. He could end up in a place called **Valhalla,** a place like heaven for the gods and heroes. There his soul would roam aimlessly with Greek and Roman heroes and gods like Thor, Achilles, Hercules, and Neptune. But, that would never, ever happen to us—we were only playing—it was make-believe!

"Twas the night before Christmas, and all through the house, not a creature was **stirring** not even a mouse. The stockings were hung by the chimney with care, in hopes that St. Nicolas soon would be there." I never forgot how that poem started. I always loved Christmas as a child even if we didn't get many presents. Christmas was always my favorite (and my Mom's) time of the year until Mom died one Christmas when I had already reached adulthood. I never tired of this Christmas classic, even in late April or mid-July. It was especially meaningful when Mom read it to me on Christmas Eve. It softened the blow of being told a month earlier that, this year "Santa Claus is going to be poor." It didn't matter that we weren't getting the toys we dreamed about—a G.I. Joe and a bag of soldiers for me, a Barbie doll and an Easy-Bake oven or tea-cup set for my younger sister, and a Va-rrroom tractor or a large teddy bear for my little brother. Each of us would probably get only one pair of socks each and maybe some Christmas candy and fruit. We might even get a pair of underwear from Santa Claus, if we had been good and were lucky.

The best part of Christmas day was that my family was gathered together. I never thought those wonderful times would end someday and become nothing more than memories. If my parents or grandmother didn't have money for fruit, they would bake homemade bread and some **bizcochitos** (a Southwestern holiday cookie). No matter that we didn't get fruit as well. My aunt and uncle, who ran their own small family grocery store in Santa Fe, always brought treats which included a large fruit basket. They, and their kids, always spent Christmas with us; we spent Thanksgiving with them. Anyway, when they brought all those goodies, it was such a treat. It was the one time I could have plums, pears, apricots, nectarines, bananas, and peaches. All varieties of fruit, all in one day. I knew then how rich people lived, eating anything and everything to their heart's content. This was one day I never thought of the little green apples we stole every summer from the neighbor's apple tree. I had 'real' fruit from the store. And, this fruit surely would not give me 'the runs' like the green apples always did. I could only cross my fingers and hope I would not end up soiling myself. I couldn't afford to ruin the pair of new underwear I received for Christmas that I had already changed into—it was special underwear with cartoon characters on them.

It wasn't just the time Mom took to read to me and instill the value of reading that would eventually bring me a good education and guide me into my career. Besides the educational aspect that reading brought into my world, she was also responsible for a number of other, less academic **pursuits** she introduced me to.

She saved enough money to purchase my first baseball glove at five years of age. She taught me how to catch a baseball, taught me how to field my first grounder and catch my first fly ball. She showed me the proper stance for a batter and the proper throwing motion for a pitcher. It wasn't unusual that my Little League career was a successful one—Mom was responsible for making me a Little League All-Star. I became an exceptional infielder and outfielder, but I was a better pitcher. Mom taught me how to throw a fastball. Her curve ball never quite curved though. She drilled those skills into me—the skill of keeping my eye on the ball as a batter and to time my swing so I could get the best hit possible. As a pitcher and first baseman, in my last year of Little League, I was highlighted in our local newspaper for having hit three homeruns and one triple and pitching a no-hitter in our minor league playoffs. My picture was the only one on our sports page. I still have that picture today. What an accomplishment for a kid—I owed it all to my Mom!

I went on to play baseball, football, and basketball through middle school, high school, and into college. While I gave up basketball in college, I did suit up for football and baseball at our local university. Tragically, I had my nose broken in our first spring practice football game for the upcoming season as a fullback, playing alongside the much older and experienced juniors and seniors. As freshmen, we were just the **scrubs**; we were the practice dummies for the varsity players. But that did not deter me from competing to the best of my ability. Then, since my football days and any hopes of an NFL career (ha-ha-ha) were cut short by the severely damaged broken nose, I stuck to baseball. Since the 'break' had not healed properly, I thought I might stick to baseball. I didn't seek medical attention since my parents did not have medical insurance—I would be okay—it wasn't that bad.

But baseball didn't work out either. The strain put on my facial muscles when running the bases, bending over quickly to field a grounder, or slide into base caused heavy nosebleeds, I had to give up any idea of continuing to play baseball in college. I would never make it to the NFL nor would I make it into Major League Baseball—another joke! Oh well, those are the breaks in life!

After my dream of playing sports in college evaporated, I joined and entered the military after my first year of college. I spent a total of four years on active duty with the Navy as a Medic. I even did a tour with the Marines since they got their Medics from the Navy. That was a whole other adventure. It was during this time in the military that I was introduced to martial arts and eventually trained hard to become a kickboxer (a full contact fighter).

In those early days of kickboxing, we didn't fight in a cage but in a ring. There was no such thing as 'Tap Out'. In my day, it was knock out your opponent or get knocked out. That was the only way a fight could be stopped, barring serious injuries. 'Tap-Out' in those days was similar to calling your daddy or uncle to help you win a fight. But, before becoming a fighter during my **enlistment,** I was able to get a much-needed surgery on my nose.

Since the military covered all medical problems and I worked in a hospital emergency room, I ended up having that surgery (a septoplasty and rhinoplasty) to repair that first fracture and extensive damage done to my nose while playing college football. I took time to heal—it actually took about one and one-half years for the healing process to be completed. It was after this surgery that I took up martial arts and was able to work out, compete, and do almost anything I needed to, in order to become a better than average fighter. That was my goal. I always trained with the thought of those schoolyard bullies crossing my mind every time I entered the ring. Maybe it was that vision of getting beat up so often that made me a good fighter.

Good fighter or not, all the time spent fighting in the ring (eight and one-half years) brought about quite a few more injuries. I ended up having my nose broken two more times as a kickboxer, but each time, I was able to get the surgery needed to repair the damage. I look back now and count the number of injuries that resulted from my kickboxing days, such as torn ACL's, MCL's, and PCL's in both knees, broken fingers and toes, bruised and cracked ribs, and many scars on my body from open wounds. My memories are still fresh today because I still have to resort to ice packs and heating pads several nights a week just to get a good night's sleep. The things we do as young men to prove our worth!

Let's get back to my HERO! Besides being my coach in most sports and a good one if you ask me, my mom took the lead as both mom and dad. Dad wasn't into any organized sports, but he did teach me how to hunt. I killed my first deer, a 10-point buck at the age of fifteen with a .30-.30 my uncle had loaned me. Dad instilled in me a respect for wildlife. He made sure we knew that when we hunted, it was not for sport or for the thrill of the kill as many hunters do, it was for the meat for our family. Being poor, sometimes venison or rabbit or wild turkey were the only types of meat we ate regularly because we were able to hunt these animals and provide for the family. Anything I ever killed was taken home and became part of our diet—we ate everything from the kill and rarely threw out anything that was edible. We also shared it with neighbors in our *barrio* who were just as poor and did not have meat very often.

While I learned how to hunt from my dad and uncle, my mom taught me many other sports and hobbies. She taught me how to play tennis; she taught me how to become a skilled archer by borrowing equipment from the university coaches. She was friends with two wives of coaches at our local university—she had attended school with them as a young girl. I was able to go out into an empty lot and practice my archery without any distractions. Mom and I would go out to the city courts and play tennis at least one or two times a week during spring and summer.

In addition, she bought me my first fishing rod at a yard sale, a cheap rod designed for a kid. With a hook and worms, she was there when I caught my first fish at Harris Lake, just outside our hometown of Las Vegas, New Mexico. She was a tireless mom—she took me fishing at least two or three times per month, regardless of sunshine, rain or snow. It didn't take much gas since my favorite fishing place was Harris Lake (actually a pond) about five minutes from where we lived on the **outskirts** of town, in the barrio. She taught me how to use different lures that my uncle had given me, how to ice fish, how to use a fly in a stream, and how to clean the fish I caught. Our family had trout as often as I went fishing. We may not have had much meat, but we did have plenty of fish.

As an adult, I wondered how she was so good at so many activities. After she passed away, I discovered her secret of success in so many sports and hobbies. I found a collection of outdated sports and hobby magazines that she had been given, each one with guides on how to learn certain sports or take up a variety of hobbies. She even taught me how to build my first kite from scratch. I am thankful she took the time to learn all these skills on her own and then pass them on to her first-born son, something a regular father would have done, had my Dad been into any of those activities.

I don't blame him though—he worked outside from sunup to sunset, and it was strenuous, back-breaking work. So, I don't have the right to cast blame on him for not taking the time to spend teaching his son a variety of things—he was always worn out and did not have the time to teach me extra-curricular activities. He was too busy trying to make an honest dollar to support our family, and since he didn't like sports or was interested in any hobbies (old-school dad), he never took time to create a quality experience for me. I didn't mind; I knew his priority was working to make money to support the family. When I found out that his greatest yearly income had been $4,000.00 to support a family of six, I understood why he did not have the time. I missed learning from Dad.

It was years later when I was already a full-grown man and as I stood over Mom as she lay dying in her hospital bed, I realize what she had done for me—the sacrifices she made and the time and effort she put into giving me a normal childhood, full of adventure and sport. I could only imagine what wonderful memories she was leaving me. I could never forget the stories, the trips she took me on, our first camping trip sleeping in the back (flatbed) of our truck under the stars and having a meager breakfast cooked over an open fire the next morning, and the many glorious adventures I lived through, from her reading to me. Mom had been in a coma for a month—she actually spent four months in the hospital before dying. On her final day, I remember wiping away tears as she spoke to me in the same sweet voice she used when reading to me. "Son, you will be alright—you're a man now—just make sure to take care of your sister. She is too scatterbrained and fiery—she acts first and thinks later. Just know

Section Three—Experiential [Life Lessons]

that I love you—I will miss our birthday." Another thing we shared was our birthday—I was born on her birthday years ago.

Now, her words seemed to finalize the life of struggle to support a family, the life she lived knowing she was never able to achieve her dreams or lived up to her potential. I wonder if she considered the fact that, when I was born on her birthday, that would the last thought to cross her mind, the last words to leave her lips as she lay dying, leaving a son behind whose successes would carry on the family name. Or, maybe she just wanted to comfort me before leaving—she must have seen that little kid standing over her, tears streaming down my face. I bent down and kissed her on her cheek as I held her hand. My parting words: "I love you so very much, Mom! Thanks for my life—and, thanks for reading to me every night! I am going to miss you so much!"

The sound of her **flat-lining** seemed to drown out all other sounds in ICU at St. Vincent's Hospital in Santa Fe on that cold December evening. While everyone was planning their Christmas holiday, I would be planning for Mom's funeral services. I faintly heard the EKG machine going crazy—it was all like a dream. Before I knew it, she was gone as quickly as she had been here—her life now only a fading memory! Who knows where she will go?

As Catholics, we believe in Heaven, but maybe she now roams the plains of Valhalla with Greek and Roman heroes—I wonder if she is encountering all the heroes I still dream about. Maybe she is in a fantasyland **spinning gold** from her hair for Rumplestiltskin or taking on the **persona** of Sleeping Beauty. Or, could she be chasing that rabbit down the hole with Alice in a place called Wonderland? I want to think that she is waking up in another place as a Princess surrounded by a handsome Prince Charming. Knowing Mom, she will want to read to those heroes, to those people living in fantasyland, in the mythological heaven called Valhalla. She would tell them stories of my growing up, of our family in the barrio, or of our life and adventures in our small hometown. Who knows where she is at—I look up each day, look at the tattoo on my arm that I got for her after her death, and say a small prayer as I talk to her.

She lives in me and around me everyday. Her advice still echoes in my head. Her smile and sweet voice cross my mind—her patience remembered as she taught me new things that all kids yearn to know. I thank her for a wonderful life; I thank her for all she did to make my life perfect. She will always be in my heart! Goodbye, Mom—wherever you're at, please know that YOU were always my REAL HERO, not the Greek or Roman heroes that you told me about in the stories you read to me! They could never be the HERO you turned out to be—tell them that when you see them!

Image © Kakigori Studio, 2012. Used under license from Shutterstock, Inc.

I. Reading Comprehension Activities

My Title: _____

Main Idea Statement: This story is about _____

_____

_____

Supporting Details / Specific Info / Facts & Details (5W's + H) :

1. _____

2. _____

3. _____

4. _____

5. _____

6. _____

7. _____

8. _____

9. _____

10. _____

Inferences (Educated Guesses/Possibilities/R-B-T-L):

1. _____

2. _____

3. _____

4. _____

5. _____

6. _____

7. _____

8. _____

II. Using Vocabulary In Context

1. Write a complete sentence using 'unknown' word in context: _____

_____

   A. New Word/Unknown Word: _____

   B. Dictionary Definition: _____

   _____

   C. Synonyms: i. _____

               ii. _____

2. Write a complete sentence using 'unknown' word in context: _____

_____

   A. New Word/Unknown Word: _____

   B. Dictionary Definition: _____

   _____

   C. Synonyms: i. _____

               ii. _____

3. Write a complete sentence using 'unknown' word in context: _____

_____

   A. New Word/Unknown Word: _____

   B. Dictionary Definition: _____

   _____

   C. Synonyms: i. _____

               ii. _____

4. Write a complete sentence using 'unknown' word in context: _____

_____

   A. New Word/Unknown Word: _____

   B. Dictionary Definition: _____

   _____

   C. Synonyms: i. _____

               ii. _____

III. Critical Reading & Thinking, Part One

A. The author's purpose in writing this was to _____

_____

_____

B. I know this because of the following traits included in this reading: _____

_____

C. Of the following tone words, discuss with a partner or in your group which words more appropriately describe the tone of the selection. Support your choices—reasons why you made the choice that you did.

accurate	factual	impartial	truthful	matter-of-fact
calm	angry	direct	dramatic	serious
informal	formal	optimistic	pessimistic	biased
neutral	objective	subjective	emotional	unbiased

D. A graphic organizer is the most effective way to show the visual connection between ideas. The best graphic organizer to use for this selection would be:

_____

_____

Why? _____

_____

E. Complete a graphic organizer, a map, or an outline of main points of selection.

IV. Critical Reading & Thinking, Part Two

Directions: Your instructor will guide you based on which of the sections below students will be working on (individually or in groups). Students are to use the back of this page (Notes Page) to list their information and ideas based on evaluation, analysis, or discussion of the chosen Issues, Readings, or Topics below. This is a teacher-guided activity.

Argument is the ability to exchange ideas, opinions, and conclusions between two or more students based on readings or writings that cover contemporary issues or author's ideas.

Issue #1: _____

Issue #2: _____

Issue #3: _____

Issue #4: _____

Inferences are educated guesses or educated possibilities based on what is already known (past information or background information). These are not assumptions, opinions, or personal points of view.

Reading #1: _____

Reading #2: _____

Reading #3: _____

Reading #4: _____

Points of View are ideas that students come to conclude (draw conclusions) based on their own personal experience or information gained from past knowledge or experiences. These ideas can be personal opinions if they have an educational foundation and are not just personal feelings or beliefs.

Topic #1: _____

Topic #2: _____

Topic #3: _____

Topic #4: _____

V. Summary Page –or– Precis Page

Summary / Precis (Circle One): This story is about _____

_____

_____

_____

_____

_____

_____

_____

_____

_____

_____

_____

_____

_____

_____

_____

_____

_____

_____

_____

_____

_____

_____

_____

_____

<u>Source Information (Citation):</u>

   Title of Selection: _____

   Author: _____

   Publisher: _____

   Copyright Date: _____

Notes:

'The Fatal Daydream'

From the Novel: 'A Hoodlum at Harvard'

by
J. A. Castellano de Garcia

Image © SFerdon, 2012. Used under license from Shutterstock, Inc.

"Please, John, lend Frankie your car to take me to work," Bonny yelled **frantically**. "I'm going to be late to my job!" I was still half asleep and tossed Frankie the keys, warning them both of the consequences if they dared to put a scratch or dent on my car, a beautiful Trans Am, which had recently been sprayed metallic-black with a pearl overlay, almost **Picasso-like**.

This was how his English paper had started that Sunday night as he was trying to fulfill the assignment for his English class the next day. He started out his paper with him **running** Bonny to work so that she would not be late. He wrote that I lent him my car which was not unusual since he cared for it sometimes better than I did.

Whenever he did borrow it, I made it clear that it would cost them plenty and nothing short of hell to pay if something happened. They scoffed knowing that I was just kidding. I might get upset, but it was just a material possession. While I always let them use my car, they knew I expected them to care for it as I always had. My threats were **idle**, both of them knowing my **'bark was worse than my bite'** which was a phrase I took from Mom.

Bonny hollered a quick "thank you" and I heard her tell Frankie, "I'll treat you later at Dairy Queen." She coaxed!

"I'll put gas in your car, John," she promised, as always. I knew that wasn't going to happen—just an empty promise from my princess sister. We never really quite understood why she always thought she had to pay us for anything—she was our only sister, the 'princess of the family' and we were always doing her favors without ever seeking payment of any kind. She knew we both loved her dearly, and as the only girl, she played the princess part to the **hilt**—she would take advantage of her position in the family on more than one occasion. Among the family, the running joke was that, even though she was treated as a princess (and thought she actually deserved that special treatment), she was actually a very sly, fiery young girl that always got her way, many times after throwing a **tantrum**—this was something she had carried forward with her since childhood. Her **modus operandi** was to promise something and then not follow through—her history of throwing out promises was a common practice. When she didn't fulfill any of her promises, she seemed to always have a quick excuse to cover her tracks. But, to us, it did not matter—we knew that it was just Bonny being Bonny!

The English paper had been assigned to Frankie's class by Mrs. Lancaster on Wednesday, February 8th and was due on the following Monday, the 13th. Students were given several days to come up with a plan to write their paper. The topic was one that is quite common in many English classes: *My Greatest Fear!*

The following is *Frankie's paper,* written in his own words:

The day started out as all others. Another new week is upon us. It's Monday, another regular school day, the daily **grind** once again. And, as usual, my sister Bonny is running late for work. I guess it's my duty and left up to me to give my sister another ride to work since her car is inoperable, again—I don't know what was wrong with her car. It was usually one of the following: no gas, a bad battery, or maybe even a blown engine, ha-ha! She needs to learn how to take care of a car—she thinks that just starting it and 'going' is all that is important. I really don't mind taking her to work since I'll get to use John's Trans Am again (oh boy). My plan this morning is to drop Bonny off at work and then take my time driving back home so that I can enjoy the ride in my brother's car. I will probably be the only one cruising through town in a hot car at eight o'clock in the morning. Maybe I'll see some girls walking to school and they will see me in the Trans Am—how cool is that? I just need to be back home in time for John to take me to school—he usually has a nine o'clock class at the university on Mondays.

The car is warm now—February is always the coldest month of the year in New Mexico. I honk and honk, and finally, Bonny slowly exits our home, taking **measured** steps in her high heels, her usual princess-like walk to the car, I yell out, "Hurry up, you're late. And, you're going to make me late!" As she jumps into the bucket seat and quickly reaches for the visor so she can check her makeup in the mirror (again) for probably the eighth time this morning, I let her know that John will probably let me take his car to school. Then, I would pick her up at six p.m. when she gets out. She asks if I there was any way I can also pick her up at noon to take her to lunch, her treat—another promise. Not today—I have plans I tell her. This is a day I will probably hang out in John's car with my friends at school—the Trans Am just might bring girls to us as we lean up against it during lunch. I know I lied to Bonny and told her I had homework to do in the library, but I don't always get to take a Trans Am to school—John usually drops me off because it is too far to walk. Bonny responds as she continues checking her face, "No problemo!" Her Spanish isn't the greatest, but we deal with it (and tease her about it, too).

Driving her to work, with the music blaring and Bonny focusing on her makeup, is usually an **opportune** time to spend ten minutes or so daydreaming about the day or about my future. The daydream starts out just like always—I am now the cool one driving the Trans Am. But, something seems different now. When I speed off to take Bonny to work, I **inadvertently** step down too far on the gas—I didn't mean to floor it—the car backfires loudly. The backfire of the engine now carries me deep into a daydream—sometimes I like daydreaming during the day when I am bored. In this daydream, caused by the car backfiring, I have been **transported** onto a battlefield. I'm not sure if the **intermittent** backfire of the engine continues. But, I know that the sound I hear is more than just backfire from an engine. I can hear the gunfire, blasts that are expected and normal on a battlefield. Wow, this is weird. My daydream has taken me into a war zone, into a battle, a nightmare! The sound of **artillery** now echoes in my ears. There's smoke, and bright flashes, and I recognize the smell of death in the air. The other loud noises that I hear are blasts of artillery—there are sounds of whizzing and buzzing all around me—it sounds like a **swarm** of bees. Or, could it be that my hearing has now become **impaired** due to all the blasting around us? In this daydream, I am in the military, just like my brother had been—I am fighting on a battlefield with my friends. The gunfire increases and the whizzing of bullets flying by get closer and closer. I also wonder if there are any land mines as I move forward with my friends. Where are we? How did we get here? What happened to high school and the life I know?

Then, the actual horror begins! My friends, who have joined me in battle, are dropping all around me—what's going on? I don't understand what's happening. The distinct sound of 'metal tearing through flesh' is all I can hear—a series of horrible thuds. Those bullets are taking my friends away from me—they are falling around me. I've never heard it before, but the sound of metal piercing flesh is **undeniable**—I am terrified! I have never seen or heard anything like this before except in movies. Could this be what I think it is? My friends are all dying, being shot dead by an enemy we can't see. I now know what lies ahead—one of those bullets is for me—the whizzing sound draws closer and closer—will I be next? I am so scared! Oh, God! I don't want to die! It's only a matter of time before my time comes—I know it. One of those bullets is meant for me—that bullet will find its target, and I am the target. I know one bullet is meant for me. Please, God—don't let me die like this. I don't want to get shot—I don't want to die like this—I am so, so scared! I'm supposed to have a bright future—I can't die like this! Then I hear it—the final shot—the loudest of them all—this bullet's the one, the one with my name on it! It won't be long now—I'm hit—I feel warm all over. I'm dying!

I was wrong. The sound was only the sound of the car backfiring again—is this real now? I'm back—it was only a daydream. But, it felt so real, so intense—the sounds, the smells, the actual visions of death, the feeling of getting shot and dying. But, I am back now—I could jump out of the car and kiss the ground. Thank God—no actual war, no bullets whizzing through the still air, no death, no friends falling before my feet, no bullet meant for me, not my time! That was close. Oh, so close—I've got to stop this daydreaming! Boy, that was so weird—I'm even sweating!

Just then, Bonny interrupted my thoughts: "Let me out in front of Penney's—I am going to have to sneak in—I'm five minutes late. Don't forget to pick me up at six this evening—at six not six-thirty—okay? Call me if John doesn't lend you his car. Then, I can call Eddie to pick me up. And, don't be late—I hate to be picked up late and have to waste my time waiting for you to get here, Frankie! Remember, I'll take us to the Dairy Queen—my treat!" I assure her that I'll be there to pick her up at six p.m.—I have nothing better to do, and besides, I'll get to drive the Trans Am again, treat or no treat! After dropping her off at work, I head to school. I want to get there a bit early so I can hang out in the parking lot as planned, next to the Trans Am. I hope that it's not too freezing outside. I wonder if we're going to get snow this week. Anyway, the fading memory of that daydream still haunts me as I pull into the parking lot at school. I'm back in the real world now, having just barely survived my greatest fear ever—*Getting Shot to Death!*

On the way back home to get John's car to him, after that horrific daydream, I decide not to take the long way. I just want to get home—I don't even bother to notice if there are any girls walking to school. My mind is somewhere else, still bothered by that daydream. That daydream still has me sort of spooked. But, I need to realize that it was just a daydream—nothing real, nothing to **fret** about!

After that daydream, I couldn't imagine my day would get better, but it did—John surprised me by telling me he was giving me his car as an early graduation present. He wanted me to enjoy it the last

Section Three—Experiential [Life Lessons]

months of high school. And, it would start today—he asked me to drop him off at the university and take the car. This is absolutely the greatest day ever! The daydream now has become a thing of the past, something I'm not going to dwell on—I am driving my dream car to school. What will my friends say? What will the girls think? I never expected John to give me his car yet—this is the greatest day of my life! I love my life!

I am so glad that it was just a daydream. I really am afraid to die—I wonder why I am even thinking of dying. I am too young to die. But, if I die, I hope it isn't by getting shot—that is my greatest fear. I shouldn't worry about such a ridiculous thing—we live in a small town. I don't ever remember someone getting shot in our town. Anyway, it was just a daydream—those types of dreams don't really come true! I don't know what my life will turn out to be, but I feel that it is already looking bright. My sister and my brother are helping the family out with money from her work and his school money from the military. We are actually living better than ever before—we're not as poor as we once were! I can thank God for all that has happened to me. I can't stop saying it—I honestly love my life and will not worry about my greatest fear—*getting shot to death*—I now know that will never happen! It's silly to think that I was afraid of something that won't ever happen. And, if I am afraid of getting shot and dying by such an event, I can always prevent it. I just won't go into the military like my brother—problem solved. I have nothing to worry about now except finishing school. Just three months until graduation. *The End!*

Frankie finished writing his paper on Sunday night, February 11th. Coincidentally, I loaned him my car the next day—he said he thought it was weird because he had had a dream that I let him have the Trans Am to use. This was very weird but we didn't give it a second thought. Yeah, right—I told him not to be so dramatic.

On the following day, Monday, February 13th, I had a full day of classes at the university followed by training for an upcoming fight the following month in Colorado. I was fighting a kickboxer from Denver—I didn't know too much about him though. Since I couldn't pick Frankie up after school due to my training schedule, and it was too cold for him to risk not getting a ride with friends, I figured it would be easier for him to take my car instead of having to walk home from school. I would just walk to the gym after my last class that day—the gym was only two blocks away from the university. I chose to let Frankie use my car instead of picking him up at school—my training session was my priority on that **fateful** day! Not picking up my little brother at school on that day is a regret that I have had to live with ever since!

On that late Monday afternoon, after turning in his English paper to his teacher that morning in his English class, Frankie was shot and killed, driving my car on the way home from school. Had I picked him up, I would have taken him to the gym with me, and he never would have traveled that route home that evening. An errant bullet, resulting from a fight in a parking lot, at a local bar, found its mark.

Frankie stayed late at school to attend an assembly. He left school and as he approached one of the streets leading to our home, he turned right at the corner, just across from one of our small city parks. The bar was located on the other side of the park. The bullet that killed him traveled across the park and directly into the back window of the car, hitting him in the back of the neck. Not too long after slowing to a stop because of the gunshot, Frankie died alone on the side of the road. Witnesses that he didn't even know tried to help stop his bleeding. They recalled his final words: "Where's my Mom; please call my brother, John!"

What followed in the next couple of years was truly a nightmare. I not only lost my little brother and best friend, but I ended up losing most of my close-knit family. Frankie's fear was realized on that cold February afternoon; his daydream actually did come true.

Our family didn't know about his English paper until his teacher called our home and told us about it after the funeral services. It was quite **eerie** and difficult to **fathom**. She later asked Mom if she had her permission to send his paper to a magazine and get the paper, along with the newspaper account of what happened on that fateful day, published in the magazine. Mom gave her permission after talking to Dad, Grandma, my sister, and me. We didn't have a problem with her request. The teacher sent Frankie's paper, along with the story of the tragedy that occurred, to a high school publication. I still have his paper in a portfolio with the many clippings of his murder. I sometimes go through those papers—I don't know why—it doesn't do any good but to bring me a renewed sadness.

I don't think I will ever get over what happened to my little brother. Every year, as Valentine's Day approaches, instead of preparing for that day of love, I sit and ponder what could have been. I find a bit of solace remembering what a great kid he was and how much he missed in life. It was all taken away in a flash—there were no answers as to 'why' this happened to such a good and caring kid. One thing is for sure: his fatal daydream eventually became my nightmare!

Closing Note: To this day, I consider Frankie's death a killing, a murder! Within a couple of years, our family experienced what is known as the **'domino effect.'** *Grandma, Mom, and Dad tragically passed away before their time, each the result of what I believe was a 'broken heart' not what the death certificates read, 'complications due to diabetes.' I saw them wither away right before my eyes as they slowly lost their will to live. Frankie had been the baby of the family, the miracle baby not expected to survive at birth In an instant, he was taken away from us.*

I still 'daydream' every chance I get, of happier times and of all the adventures that we shared. I daydream of what could have been. A few days after Frankie's funeral, I got a 'special tattoo for him—my only brother, my baby brother (a black cross with a black rose draped across it). I wanted to have a reminder, for me and for others who might have forgotten what happened on that cold February afternoon, the most horrific day our lives. I did not want Frankie to ever be forgotten! And, I never forgot that his greatest fear was what came to pass!

Image © blojfo, 2012. Used under license from Shutterstock, Inc.

I. Reading Comprehension Activities

My Title: _____

Main Idea Statement: This story is about _____

_____

_____

Supporting Details / Specific Info / Facts & Details (5W's + H) :

1. _____

2. _____

3. _____

4. _____

5. _____

6. _____

7. _____

8. _____

9. _____

10. _____

Inferences (Educated Guesses/Possibilities/R-B-T-L):

1. _____

2. _____

3. _____

4. _____

5. _____

6. _____

7. _____

8. _____

II. Using Vocabulary In Context

1. Write a complete sentence using 'unknown' word in context: _____

_____

_____

    A. New Word/Unknown Word: _____

    B. Dictionary Definition: _____

_____

    C. Synonyms: i. _____

               ii. _____

2. Write a complete sentence using 'unknown' word in context: _____

_____

    A. New Word/Unknown Word: _____

    B. Dictionary Definition: _____

_____

    C. Synonyms: i. _____

               ii. _____

3. Write a complete sentence using 'unknown' word in context: _____

_____

    A. New Word/Unknown Word: _____

    B. Dictionary Definition: _____

_____

    C. Synonyms: i. _____

               ii. _____

4. Write a complete sentence using 'unknown' word in context: _____

_____

    A. New Word/Unknown Word: _____

    B. Dictionary Definition: _____

_____

    C. Synonyms: i. _____

               ii. _____

III. Critical Reading & Thinking, Part One

A. The author's purpose in writing this was to _____

_____

_____

B. I know this because of the following traits included in this reading: _____

_____

C. Of the following tone words, discuss with a partner or in your group which words more appropriately describe the tone of the selection. Support your choices—reasons why you made the choice that you did.

accurate	factual	impartial	truthful	matter-of-fact
calm	angry	direct	dramatic	serious
informal	formal	optimistic	pessimistic	biased
neutral	objective	subjective	emotional	unbiased

D. A graphic organizer is the most effective way to show the visual connection between ideas. The best graphic organizer to use for this selection would be:

_____

_____

Why? _____

_____

E. Complete a graphic organizer, a map, or an outline of main points of selection.

IV. Critical Reading & Thinking, Part Two

Directions: Your instructor will guide you based on which of the sections below students will be working on (individually or in groups). Students are to use the back of this page (Notes Page) to list their information and ideas based on evaluation, analysis, or discussion of the chosen Issues, Readings, or Topics below. This is a teacher-guided activity.

Argument is the ability to exchange ideas, opinions, and conclusions between two or more students based on readings or writings that cover contemporary issues or author's ideas.

Issue #1: _____

Issue #2: _____

Issue #3: _____

Issue #4: _____

Inferences are educated guesses or educated possibilities based on what is already known (past information or background information). These are not assumptions, opinions, or personal points of view.

Reading #1: _____

Reading #2: _____

Reading #3: _____

Reading #4: _____

Points of View are ideas that students come to conclude (draw conclusions) based on their own personal experience or information gained from past knowledge or experiences. These ideas can be personal opinions if they have an educational foundation and are not just personal feelings or beliefs.

Topic #1: _____

Topic #2: _____

Topic #3: _____

Topic #4: _____

V. Summary Page –or– Precis Page

Summary / Precis (Circle One): This story is about _____

_____

_____

_____

_____

_____

_____

_____

_____

_____

_____

_____

_____

_____

_____

_____

_____

_____

_____

_____

_____

_____

_____

_____

_____

_____

<u>Source Information (Citation):</u>

Title of Selection: _____

Author: _____

Publisher: _____

Copyright Date: _____

Notes: _____

Section Three—Experiential [Life Lessons]

'Nine Lives'

From the Novel: 'A Hoodlum at Harvard'

by
J. A. Castellano de Garcia

Image © STILLFX, 2012. Used under
license from Shutterstock, Inc.

COMMON KNOWLEDGE ABOUT CATS

There are two things I know (or have heard) about cats—they always land on all fours no matter how many twists and turns they take while traveling through the air, and they have an unusual life span, one that has them escaping **peril** as many as nine times while alive. It is said that a cat has 'nine lives' and will escape death nine different times throughout their lifetime.

It is also common knowledge that there exists a number of people who go through and survive many ordeals that have brought them close to death. Sometimes there is no explanation of why they are still alive, they just are. They are survivors! Those folks could be considered to have the same **fortune** as a cat—they have nine lives. In my case, I think I have actually used up my nine lives and have been **'walking a thin line'** since the last time I eluded death. I'm afraid the next time I face a dangerous, near-death situation or encounter, it will be the last time I will cheat death.

Remember the movie where a group of young men and women cheated death? They spent their remaining days trying to stay alive, watching over their shoulder for that figure clad in black with his sickle to rear up and take them to the afterlife. Each one was slowly stalked and set-up to die a horrible death for having fooled the 'Grim Reaper' and eluded their own death. Maybe the same holds true for us! One thing is for sure—we will eventually be faced with our own **demise**, maybe today or maybe next week or next year. Two things are for sure: we were born and we will die! One thing that I am not so sure of—does a cat live through his full nine lives or is the eighth life his last? Do I have one more life to live, or is this my last life of the nine lives I figure I have been given?

In my case, there have been a number of close calls—some folks might **characterize** them as **brushes with death,** but I see them as nothing more than situations where I got lucky! These situations have followed me for a number of years, ever since I was a child. One thing I do know for sure is that my luck will run out eventually—I will not be able to cheat death again! While I was a normal kid, there were times when things occurred which landed me in the hospital or on my knees saying a prayer and thanking the 'man upstairs' for giving me another chance. I guess you could say that I was glad that I didn't die during any of those given situations.

Now, as an adult that has lived a great and adventurous life (I look at those situations as adventures or challenges that I faced), I look back and wonder why I am still here, why I still walk the earth on a daily basis doing what most folks do—working to pay rent, buying groceries, filling up my car with gas, attending church, going to my job teaching classes, and sleeping. Then, I start all over again each day, doing the same things as the day before. While there is some variation to my daily routine, it is usually the same and will continue being that until I win the lottery and am able to travel around the world helping those **less fortunate**, my goal after I retire. At times, I look back at my life and realize that there were many times (nine to be exact) where I should have actually taken my last breath and then, shortly thereafter, placed **'six feet under,'** where I would lie in eternal peace! I now actually believe that I might have some cat's blood running through my veins; however, I have run out of lives—I have **expended** my nine lives and am living close to the edge from day to day!

DEATH AT MY DOORSTEP

It was a Friday night and I had been clubbing with friends until the bar closed down. After last call, I passed the word that there would be an 'after-party' at my house. I had had quite a few of these, which always turned out being a great time for all who attended. Usually word got around the club and quite a few folks would show up at my home—I always had an entourage of former kickboxer friends, and since most folks attending knew this, we rarely had any trouble. People just attended to have fun and finish off their night by partying until the wee hours of the morning. We were never ready to call it a night when the club closed—it was too early. The parties at my home always carried on until early morning, sometimes even until sunrise. Many times, groups of friends would end up at Denny's for breakfast before going home and sleeping most of the day, only to wake in the early evening for another night at one of the many clubs in town. Then the scene was usually repeated once again.

The party on that Friday night was attended by a number of people that I knew—sometimes they brought friends that had never attended but all were welcome. It was better when several people had planned ahead and bought beer or other forms of alcohol before going to the club for the evening, knowing that there were usually several after-hours parties that would spring up once the club closed. On that night, a number of people showed up at my home after the club had closed. One of those in attendance was a young man, and casual acquaintance, who had been at the club. His name was David Montoya (not his actual name).

While everyone was having fun as the night wore on, he slowly drank himself into **oblivion** and became quite obnoxious and threatening. He was a bit menacing, having showed up with a large Bowie knife in a sheath, strapped to his leg. I ended up in a fist fight with him outside my back door on the patio. Where we began to **tussle** and the fists were flying. During the brief physical **altercation,** he pulled the knife (a knife that had a blade approximately 8–10 inches long), and lunged at me, leaving a small cut on my right arm from barely having caught me with the tip of the blade. Friends and I later **surmised** that he not only wanted to hurt me but probably intended to kill me for having ruined his night of partying. I was very lucky that two friends intervened when they saw the blade in his hand—it was quickly taken away from him by one of those friends as the other put a full-Nelson wrestling lock on him. It was quite a awhile later when I realized that I had been poked with the tip of his blade—my date noticed that the sleeve of my black shirt was wet—I didn't even know I was bleeding much less that my shirt had been punctured. I still look back and know that I was very fortunate that this fight did not escalate into something deadly, but I will always have a scar to remind me of that night.

Anyway, I was forced to throw him out of the party—the fight started when he refused to stop harassing some of the young women there—he was very, very drunk and made sexual innuendos that were not going to be tolerated in my home. After the fight, I told him to leave and not to return—he was no longer welcome. He was escorted to the end of the cul-de-sac where my home was. I threatened him with law enforcement, thinking that this threat would deter him from coming back. I thought that that was the reason he never returned—I actually was naïve enough to believe that he had been afraid of getting arrested and jailed, and that's why he left for good. He must have just passed out somewhere—we will never know what he did later that night after leaving my home. His actions the following days proved he was not afraid of cops or even of going to jail—he simply did not care—he was the type of person who enjoyed defying authority. No one was going to bully him or make him do anything he wasn't prepared to do.

But, what he did the next evening ran a chill up my spine and still makes me cringe to think of what I avoided that night at my home. The next night, after leaving a local club, he followed a young woman on the way home from the club, running her off the road with his vehicle, in a sparsely populated area on the **outskirts** of the city. He ran up on her vehicle as she tried to gather herself from this unexpected ordeal and pulled her out, dragging her further into the woods. He then raped her and stabbed her several times—her screams brought folks out from the few homes that surrounded the wooded area. One couple, a man and his wife, who had heard her screams, called 911 and then went out to investigate, figuring they could assist the woman in distress. They did not realize what awaited them in the woods surrounding the home they had lived in for twelve years. They came upon the young girl being assaulted by Mr. Montoya. The husband tried to intervene and jumped Montoya from behind—the husband, a local dentist in the city, was flipped onto his back and quickly stabbed. As his wife screamed for help and tried to help her husband, Mr. Montoya pulled a pistol and shot her dead. Both husband and wife died trying to help the young woman. Having made the 911 call, a sheriff's deputy responding to the call, came upon the scene which was just off the side of the road. As he exited his cruiser, Mr. Montoya ran out of the brush. Before he knew what happened, Mr. Montoya shot and killed him without giving him a chance to pull his service revolver or call for backup. The young woman, who Montoya had raped and stabbed, survived to testify at his trial later that year.

After this stabbing and shooting **rampage**, Montoya eluded law enforcement—there was a statewide manhunt that ensued. He ended up breaking into a home the following afternoon about four and one-half miles from the site of the killings, where he raped another young girl who had just arrived home from her part-time job. No one knows why he left her alive after the brutal rape. Montoya then went 'on the run' and eluded police for eleven days. Bulletins went out throughout the Southwest and West Coast for this killer. After receiving a tip from a man in a suburb in southern California (Mr. Montoya's acts of brutality had gone national with the story of what occurred, and his face had been plastered on the news in several states for the horrific acts that were attributed to him), police with the help of a SWAT team eventually captured him after a shootout in the neighborhood of an average community in southern California—Montoya was wounded in the shootout with law enforcement, but he survived to face trial for murder back in his home state. He now sits on death row for having murdered three citizens, one being a police officer, and for brutally raping two women. I wonder what would have happened had my friends not disarmed him that night when we fought in my yard. Apparently, this man, who I had had in my home on a few occasions, was not afraid to pull a weapon and kill someone. That someone could have easily been me on that Friday night!

My life has been great; however, as I look back, I still wonder how I survived the situations that I had been encountered with. I still wonder how I was able to make it through a stabbing by a girlfriend who had been taking drugs with friends and wanted my bankcard. When I declined to give it to her (no extra money in account), I ended up with a dagger in my chest—she was the only fatal attraction of my life.

There was the time I was run off the road on Easter Sunday by what I believe was a drunk driver. I was traveling back to my home in Santa Fe after spending the day with my sister and her family. It was late at night when I was run off the highway, and my new truck ran through a bridge, flipping seven times before coming to rest, partially submerged in the Pecos River. Had it not been for two Albertson's truck drivers the next morning who found me unconscious and trapped in the vehicle, I might have been swept down river or died from internal bleeding.

Then, there was the time I was with a date at a dinner club. After we had a wonderful dinner, we settled in to listen and dance to the house band. An ex-boyfriend of hers had followed us there, and when he jumped me from behind with two friends, I knew I would probably not escape with my life, especially when he pulled a knife and caught me unaware of how dangerous the situation had become. Had it not been for three other guys, who saw I was in need, I might have perished right there on the dance floor. Those guys, who later became good friends, jumped in to disarm the guy with a knife and proceeded to beat on his friends—I remember them yelling out: "Now, it's a fair fight!"

Finally, there was the wedding at the Marriott Resort where my close friend was shot in the chest by a **parolee** because he was being ejected from the wedding reception. He was enraged that security guards were throwing him out for not having an invitation—he saw us entering and pulled a pistol from his waistband (which had been covered by a loose shirt). My friend got the worst of this—he ended up fighting for his life and in a coma for a month, a bullet having entered his chest. While I only ended up with a scar from **shrapnel** that had **ricocheted** off the pavement from one of the three shots he was able to get off before being subdued, I felt fortunate that I didn't get shot or worse, that none of my other two friends died that night. Only one was shot directly and was hospitalized for several months, coming close to losing his life.

Have I run out of luck or lives? Besides the times I have included here, there are others that have me scratching my head with amazement at having avoided the afterlife. There was another major event in my life that has left quite an **indelible impression**, one I call the 'Perfect Storm' where I came within seconds of drowning had it not been for a couple of fishermen who **plucked** me out of the center of a lake after I had been in the water for a couple of hours.

Then, as a child, I was trapped in a burning shed, a shed that I was responsible for setting ablaze—I had accidentally caused the fire at my neighbors home when I was six years old trying to burn ants while playing with my tiny, plastic soldiers—the fire burned their shed and carport to the ground. I was rescued by the neighbor before being overcome by smoke or burning to death.

There was the time I got injured on a merry-go-round at the city park one summer. I ended up spending a couple of nights in ICU at the local hospital after suffering a major head injury from a bar that hit me directly upside my head and caused me to get over a dozen stitches—I was only eight years old and staying the summer at my auntie and uncle's home—my summer ended abruptly while I spent several months recovering.

I'm not even counting the time in the military that I came within a few seconds of getting hit (and killed) by an AmTrack train as I was headed to church one Sunday morning. This came after a night of wild partying just outside San Diego (actually in Encinitas, CA.). I was following the tracks to the church—I was trying to maintain my upbringing of attending church every week. I was walking on the tracks on the side of the interstate and left the tracks once I saw the path leading to the church. Because of the interstate noise caused by mid-morning traffic, I never heard the train, which passed over the same tracks within a matter of seconds after I had stepped off of them and onto the path. I do not count this narrow escape since I suffered no apparent injuries—I was just quite shaken after realizing what I had just avoided—I was actually shaking a bit as the train whizzed by me, about ten yards away. A friend later commented (idiotic comment): "See what could happen when you go to church—you should have stayed home and had a 'breakfast beer' with us!"

Anyway, since my last dangerous situation or encounter, I have become very cautious about all that I do now; however, I can honestly say that I never became **paranoid**. I figured that it was just part of life, adventures that just come your way. I have to look at them as adventures or end up 'freaked out' and being overly cautious, waiting for that Grim Reaper to come by again and this time take me away for good! But, he better know that I won't go easy or without a fight—you can bet your life on that!

Image © wectomart, 2012. Used under license from Shutterstock, Inc.

I. Reading Comprehension Activities

My Title: _____

Main Idea Statement: This story is about _____

_____

_____

Supporting Details / Specific Info / Facts & Details (5W's + H) :

1. _____

2. _____

3. _____

4. _____

5. _____

6. _____

7. _____

8. _____

9. _____

10. _____

Inferences (Educated Guesses/Possibilities/R-B-T-L):

1. _____

2. _____

3. _____

4. _____

5. _____

6. _____

7. _____

8. _____

II. Using Vocabulary In Context

1. Write a complete sentence using 'unknown' word in context: _____

_____

_____

    A. New Word/Unknown Word: _____

    B. Dictionary Definition: _____

    _____

    C. Synonyms: i. _____

               ii. _____

2. Write a complete sentence using 'unknown' word in context: _____

_____

    A. New Word/Unknown Word: _____

    B. Dictionary Definition: _____

    _____

    C. Synonyms: i. _____

               ii. _____

3. Write a complete sentence using 'unknown' word in context: _____

_____

    A. New Word/Unknown Word: _____

    B. Dictionary Definition: _____

    _____

    C. Synonyms: i. _____

               ii. _____

4. Write a complete sentence using 'unknown' word in context: _____

_____

    A. New Word/Unknown Word: _____

    B. Dictionary Definition: _____

    _____

    C. Synonyms: i. _____

               ii. _____

III. Critical Reading & Thinking, Part One

A. The author's purpose in writing this was to _____

_____

_____

B. I know this because of the following traits included in this reading: _____

_____

C. Of the following tone words, discuss with a partner or in your group which words more appropriately describe the tone of the selection. Support your choices—reasons why you made the choice that you did.

accurate	factual	impartial	truthful	matter-of-fact
calm	angry	direct	dramatic	serious
informal	formal	optimistic	pessimistic	biased
neutral	objective	subjective	emotional	unbiased

D. A graphic organizer is the most effective way to show the visual connection between ideas. The best graphic organizer to use for this selection would be:

_____

_____

Why? _____

_____

E. Complete a graphic organizer, a map, or an outline of main points of selection.

IV. Critical Reading & Thinking, Part Two

Directions: Your instructor will guide you based on which of the sections below students will be working on (individually or in groups). Students are to use the back of this page (Notes Page) to list their information and ideas based on evaluation, analysis, or discussion of the chosen Issues, Readings, or Topics below. This is a teacher-guided activity.

Argument is the ability to exchange ideas, opinions, and conclusions between two or more students based on readings or writings that cover contemporary issues or author's ideas.

Issue #1: _____

Issue #2: _____

Issue #3: _____

Issue #4: _____

Inferences are educated guesses or educated possibilities based on what is already known (past information or background information). These are not assumptions, opinions, or personal points of view.

Reading #1: _____

Reading #2: _____

Reading #3: _____

Reading #4: _____

Points of View are ideas that students come to conclude (draw conclusions) based on their own personal experience or information gained from past knowledge or experiences. These ideas can be personal opinions if they have an educational foundation and are not just personal feelings or beliefs.

Topic #1: _____

Topic #2: _____

Topic #3: _____

Topic #4: _____

V. Summary Page –or– Precis Page

Summary / Precis (Circle One): This story is about _____

_____

_____

_____

_____

_____

_____

_____

_____

_____

_____

_____

_____

_____

_____

_____

_____

_____

_____

_____

_____

_____

_____

_____

_____

Source Information (Citation):

   Title of Selection: _____

   Author: _____

   Publisher: _____

   Copyright Date: _____

Notes:

Black Is Black

A Real Man's Love Story

From the Novel: 'A Hoodlum at Harvard'

by
J. A. Castellano de Garcia

Image © ssuaphotos, 2012. Used under license from Shutterstock, Inc.

I've recently come to realize that when I **reminisce** about my past and my love life, I am overwhelmed with sadness. At the same time, I quickly come to realize that it is quite devastating as well. Some close friends recently pointed out to me that it was not only eerie but heartbreaking that I have lost both of the great loves in my life—my first, and my last, both to an untimely death! I actually lost my first love to a heroine overdose when I was back in high school, and just recently, I lost my last love, my former wife, to suicide. While I had not anticipated anything like these events ever happening, they are part of life. It's sad that two young women, who undoubtedly had many dreams left in life, will no longer be able to realize those dreams, or live their lives hoping to experience many more adventures. However, in my case, I know that they have left me memories to last my lifetime.

A question that bothers me is: did they ever get to **live their dash** to its fullest? The dash is a person's entire life. It is the space or dash that one finds on every person's tombstone, the dash between their birth date and their date of passing. It is called living the dash! That dash, between the birth date and date of death on the tombstone, actually represents a person's entire life, i.e., their dreams, their adventures, their failures and accomplishments, their sad and happy times, and finally, the loves they encountered!

Throughout my life, I have actually matched up my relationships to songs on the radio (an old school listening device) or to songs that I have on a CD or have downloaded for me to listen to and remind me of days gone by. I know many of you, who are reading this now, can relate to this: a certain song either reminds you of someone special in your life at the present time, or it will help you recall someone that was special during some point in your life, events that occurred as you lived your dash! Many times, I use songs to keep me tied to those memories—usually they are all good memories because I choose them to be good. I do not walk around with any type of **animosity** against anyone because a relationship did not end the way I wanted it to or because it just didn't work out and go as expected.

"I WANT TO HOLD YOUR HAND"

Jackie was like a swan gliding across the water. The first time I saw her at recess, I couldn't do anything but stand there with my mouth open, **gawking** at the way she moved across the playground like a ballerina, or as she glided into the cafeteria like a princess entering the dining hall of her castle, all eyes upon her. I thought she was the most beautiful girl I had ever seen in my entire life—a life that was still quite young and immature. I was a scrawny, **naïve** eight-year-old entering fourth grade at our local Catholic school.

From that first day that I saw her entering her fifth grade home room, I became **enthralled** with her looks and decided I wanted to be around her every chance I got. During the day, I couldn't concentrate on math or spelling—I thought about her constantly. I think my grades might have suffered because I couldn't concentrate on academics, especially when I knew Jackie was just next door. As the year went by, one day stood out more than the rest

It was the day that I remember volunteering to participate in our school's annual talent show. I only volunteered because it would have me up on stage with Jackie. That is how I knew her, even though teachers used her more mature-sounding name, Jacqueline. Later in life, I thought that she had been named after Jacqueline Kennedy, the wife of President John F. Kennedy. While they lived their life in the White House during a time known as **Camelot**, I chose to live my own Camelot with Jackie as my princess. But, at recess and around the playground, she was known to all us kids as Jackie.

Let me rephrase something: I actually didn't volunteer for the talent show—I was selected by Jackie and her cousin, Martha. Their idea was to lip-sync two songs as we **mimicked** the Beatles. It was Jackie's idea. She had coaxed her cousin Martha, their best friend Dorothy, and me to join her in preparing for our **parochial** school talent show. I still don't know why they asked me to be part of their group—there are some things we can never explain in life—this was one of them. Maybe it was because I was always staring at her and acting goofy on the playground at recess. Who knows? She never told me why she selected me instead of choosing the much older and more **refined** fifth graders in her class. Could it be that she really liked me? That thought actually never entered my mind, in my eyes she seemed to be way **out of my league**. Could she actually like me as much as I liked her, without me even realizing it? Did she hold that same **infatuation** of me that I had of her—a condition usually referred to as 'Puppy Love' for kids our age. By the way, that was a song made popular by a teen idol named Donny Osmond back in the day.

How lucky could a little guy in fourth grade get? Her plan for the program was to pretend that we were the Beatles, a British group from Liverpool, who were up and coming on the music charts in those days, the days of peace and love, back in the 1960's. Our group of four was going to have to spend time practicing (actually lip-synching) two songs by the Beatles. We were going to have to practice every day after school. For the program, we planned to dress like the Beatles in black pants, white shirts, Beatle boots, and even wear our hair down in bangs just like they did. I don't know how I ever convinced my parents to let my hair grow long and then to comb it like one of the Beatles. I saved every penny I earned doing lawns and delivering our local newspaper so I could buy the things I needed to outfit myself like a Beatle. For the talent show, we would have to prance around the stage like 'real' rock stars while someone played their two records we had chosen. A kid would play them on the record player that the nun, in charge of the talent show, loaned us for our **skit**. Sometime later in life, I wondered if the kid, who chose to 'spin those Beatles songs' on the record player ever became a DJ as an adult. Who knows? At the time, I was so preoccupied with thoughts of being close to Jackie that I can't even remember the name of the kid who played the records.

When it was our turn to perform, I would be the one **emulating** John Lennon; Jackie would be Paul McCartney. I forget who was supposed to be George Harrison and who was playing the drummer, Ringo Starr—I just know that Martha and Dorothy played those parts. However, it didn't really matter, Jackie and I would be the lead singers of the group. We would both get a chance to be the actual Beatles, singing to the audience of screaming fans. Actually the screaming fans were a few third and fourth graders. The first and second graders were too busy doing what they do, which was usually not sitting still or paying attention while a few kicked each other and giggled, or picked their nose while no one was watching. We really didn't care—we still had a few screaming fans on the Friday afternoon the talent show was scheduled for. In fact, we might have even been the first 'lip-synchers' in music history, long before Milli Vanilli got caught faking their songs and even winning a Grammy for one of their hits.

The two songs we chose to carry us through the talent program on that day: **"I Want To Hold Your Hand"** and **"When I Saw Her Standing There."** These two classic rock-n-roll songs were popularized by the Fab Four—The Beatles—and were two of their top hits of that era. Those songs became *our* songs! I still recall that time in our young lives every time I hear them playing on an FM Oldies radio program today. I knew that after we performed those songs in the talent show, and after practicing them over and over again, I would someday get to 'hold her hand in mine,' and I never forgot when I first 'saw her standing there' (actually playing on the playground swings)—what a memory for a fourth grader to carry through life, huh?

After that talent program (we didn't win anything), I didn't know if I would ever get the opportunity to spend that many hours around her again. Only because of this program, and the practice time we had to put in after school each day for three or four weeks, was I able to be around her, and close to her, for an extra hour and a half every afternoon in our auditorium. However, once the program was over, there was nothing to keep us in close **proximity** to each other. I would only have recess to gaze at her across the playground as she played with her classmates. You see, being in the fourth grade while she was in the fifth grade meant that I could only gaze upon her beauty during recess since we were both in different classrooms. And, being from a poor family, I didn't get to eat in the cafeteria with her across the room from me. Those kids who brought lunch to school had to eat it in one of the classrooms and not in the cafeteria. Now I find it funny that she was actually the first older woman in my life, older by two years since I had started kindergarten at the age of four years old. She would be the first girl in my life, my first love, to **mesmerize** me and keep me walking around in a complete daze from day to day! At that time, I probably could've run head first into a tree while thinking of her. I probably would've felt nothing at all—I was in love!

Then, much to my amazement, there came another *special* day in my life, a day that would forever be etched in my mind. It also occurred during that school year, not long after we had acted like foolish kids in the talent show. On that day, her best friend, Dorothy, ran across the playground in my direction. All the while, Jackie and Martha giggled while leaning on the playground fence. I wondered what was going on—it still puzzles me that she made the first move—I later liked that she was very **assertive**. Dorothy brought over a handwritten note from Jacqueline. It read: "I like you—do you like me?" Can you believe it—she liked me! It was simple and to the point. I loved that about her—no beating around the bush. She wasn't afraid to go after what she wanted. And, apparently (much to my surprise), she wanted me!

Our love affair (puppy love) carried on for a little over two years. To date, it is one of the longest relationships in my life! Jackie never argued with me; I never argued with her. We wrote each other love notes, and we never forgot our two special Beatle songs. I wrote our initials in my notebook as a sign of our love—JR + JG. I even carved those initials on the fence in our backyard. We were like two peas in a pod—we were meant for each other! We were **destined** to be together forever! Or, so I thought.

The most physical we ever got was holding hands. It was a magical time. We never even kissed, but that didn't matter. We first held hands one Sunday afternoon at the weekly matinee, a James Bond thriller, at our local theater. In those days, my mom would drive me and drop me off at the movies, and her parents would do the same for her. We would meet inside and sit together. We even stepped up our relationship one Sunday by sharing popcorn and a box of Junior Mints, the next step after holding hands had become the **pinnacle** of our love.

During the next couple of years, we spent many Sundays together. We spent time at one another's homes. We went ice skating and snow sledding together. We walked around our local pond on many occasions, skipping rocks off the water. I actually taught her how to do this—it was a skill that I was proud of. I even saved her one time from a garden snake that was about eight inches long and had **slithered** across her sweater as we played by the pond. She was terrified as I grabbed it by the head and tossed it into the grass. It never bit her (non-poisonous, just scary to a girl). I was her hero. We were young; we wanted to be around each other as much as we could (without causing gossip). I thought what we had was 'true love'—what else could it be at our young age! These were simple and wonderful times!

And then, as quickly as it had begun, it was over. It happened so quickly: another day at recess, another note. "I like someone else," she wrote. "I can't talk to you—he won't let me. And, I can't be your girlfriend anymore." I was shocked, devastated, destroyed. What was I going to do? The love of my life no longer wanted me, no longer loved me—she was out of my life! Now what I had been drawn to, I hated—her assertiveness. Did she **seduce** this 'other guy' with her smile on the playground as she had done with me? What was I to think? How could she do this to me? Where did our love go, a love that had once been? It reminds me of another song, **"Where Did Our Love Go"** by The Supremes. Even today, I think of little Jackie when I hear the Black Eyed Peas sing **"Where Is The Love?"** It's not difficult to remember her—she was my first love!

Time went by quickly. She ended up transferring to another school in another city after her parents moved the family away to Albuquerque. But, I never forgot her. I remembered her through my remaining grade school years, through my junior high years, and even thought of her on occasion while in high school. What was she doing? How much more beautiful had she become? What guy was calling her his girlfriend now? I had many questions, but like any normal young kid who has had his heart broken, I decided not to **pine** over someone I could not have or would never have in my life again. So, I moved on—painful as it was!

Mom answered the phone that night. It was the end of my junior year in high school. I would be graduating next year, and that took up most of my time—I was living my dash! As time went on, I really had not thought much about Jackie or how she had devastated my life and broke my heart into a million pieces. Instead, I had concentrated my efforts and energy on sports, probably to take my mind off of her. I played football, basketball, baseball, and ran track. That night, Mom came into the next room where I was listening to some tapes—my music sometimes took my mind off the daily routine. Mom sat next to me and asked me to turn off the music. She told me that she had some very bad news—she told me she was so very sorry for having to tell me this news. I didn't understand where she was going with this. She relayed what had happened—it was devastating. My heart sank and broke into a million pieces again as she told me the news she had received.

Jackie's parents had called—they thought I would want to know. It turns out that Jackie had become involved with the wrong crowd during her senior year in high school in Albuquerque. After her graduation (that past weekend), she had gone to a class party. That night her parents suffered the ultimate tragedy—they were notified that their 'little Jackie,' who was now a young woman, had died suddenly. She had died of a fatal drug overdose—she was given heroin by some friends, and she overdosed. I was shocked by the news. Mom told me she was very sorry again and hugged me. She said she would always be available if I wanted to talk. I didn't need to talk—it had been so long since our break-up. I don't even know what Jackie looked like as a teenager—we never kept in touch. I was sorry, but I chalked it up to life, to things that happen to people as they go about their daily lives.

After Mom walked out of the room, I lay on the bed and thought about Jackie. Why would she ever take drugs? What kind of friends were these—idiots who would give her heroin? I even wondered if her new boyfriend was somewhat to blame for her death. Why didn't he protect her if he truly loved her like I had? I certainly would have protected her. And then, I wondered why we didn't stay together—she would still be alive; we would still be together; we were meant for each other! That night, as I remembered our young love, I cried myself to sleep—and cried myself to sleep several other nights afterwards. No one ever knew how much I had missed her or that I cried for her. That pain never went away—the pain in my heart at having lost my first love—she was now gone for good!

We might have been very young when we shared what people would probably call puppy love, but to us, it was real—it was special—it was a magical ride! Wow, this is getting rather ridiculous—another song to help mend a broken heart: **"Magic Carpet Ride"** by Steppenwolf! And yet this is followed by another, **"How Can You Mend A Broken Heart"** by the Bee Gees.

"BLACK IS BLACK"

And then there was Ashley—my last love! I still remember the song to beat all songs—**"Black Is Black"** by Los Bravos. It still reminds me of her and the love we shared. This was the song that made me think about her the most, the song that brought that same pain back into my chest, the pain of a broken heart. This time it was much worse than the pain that Jackie had caused. I could now differentiate the puppy love I had with Jackie to the real love I had with Ashley. Sad to say, I adopted this song shortly after our divorce. You see, I ended up falling head over heels for Ashley, after she had made the first move to get to know me—sounds familiar, huh? It was very similar to the **circumstances** that occurred with my first love, but this time we weren't on the playground; we were too old for recess. We were young adults and way beyond that puppy love stage. We were professionals, well into our careers. We could take our love and build it into something really special, a love we thought would last forever!

Even the name of the group, Los Bravos, had a certain **machismo** to it. Our love was destined to be—Ashley had her little **quirks**, I had mine. However, we were both so much alike. But like most guys, when we grow up, we never admit some things when it comes to women. We will convince ourselves that she wants us, and she wants us badly—we get this from a simple smile. Why not—we are bad; we could part the waves in the ocean; we could tangle with the biggest grizzly, we could take on an entire gang of hoodlums and come out **unscathed**, or so we think. Nothing can beat us; nothing can ever get under our skin. Gentlemen, you know the truth—we are not as 'bad' as we think we are!

When we 'fall' for that special woman, we fall hard. She is the woman that takes our breath away— we end up really walking into trees, tripping over ourselves, falling down stairs, stuttering our words, drooling like newborn babies, and even, and pay attention to this, trying to convince ourselves (which is really a lie), that there is no place for love in the life of a 'bad boy' like us. Gentlemen, we are just fooling ourselves! I have actually seen a guy crossing the street, unaware of the oncoming traffic, as he glances back to see if 'she' is watching him cross the street. The next thing you know, yes, you guessed it—a trip to the emergency room after being hit or run over by an unsuspecting motorist, who never expected an idiot to cross from between parked cars as he hummed **"Bad To The Bone"** by George Thorogood & the Destroyers in his mind. Yes, she probably *was* watching him cross the street and then had to hold in the laughter after she witnessed this idiot barely escape death. What a story this will be to her friends, huh? That story will make its way through the next several party nights with friends.

Well, Ashley made me realize that I was not that bad—she brought butterflies to my stomach—she built me up and developed my larger-than-life ego, a self-esteem I never had before or ever imagined I would have. She was the one, the light of my life—my true love! I still thought I was 'bad' and maybe I still was. Several friends told me that she was out of my league—they couldn't believe how I ended up with such a 'looker,' a part-time model. I still don't know how that happened either. I wonder if it was my **charisma**—yeah right! But, I told my friends that it was just me, a bad boy—and, she loved bad boys! I soon gave up trying to be a bad boy—I didn't need to anymore. In the end, I had gotten the girl! I could see other guys wished they were me. They could look all they wanted—she would go home with me! Things were different when I was around her. She made me a better man—we were made for each other.

We decided we belonged together forever. So, as our love grew, we decided to get married. Since we had met on Valentine's Day, we decided that would forever be our day. We got engaged on Valentine's day a couple of years later, and then we finally set a date and planned to marry the next Valentine's Day. It was like a love story, one you see in a Hollywood flick. In fact, I still wonder why a movie wasn't made about our love! I'm still waiting for Hollywood to come calling, ha-ha-ha!

Today, I still remember the times we laughed, the special times we shared, and even the times we held and consoled each other during sad times. I remember those times we sat silently, gazing longingly into one another's eyes, knowing what the other was thinking. I remember the walks in the park, the picnics in the forest, the trips to Los Angeles just for fun, the trip to New York City for New Year's Eve, the trip to New Orleans for Mardi Gras, and our 'special' honeymoon in Las Vegas at the Mirage. So many wonderful memories of days gone by.

We went to clubs together; we partied with other friends; she even talked me into participating in some of her activities like bike riding the trails of the Santa Fe Ski Basin, learning how to two-step to country music even though I refused to wear a cowboy hat and boots. I couldn't go that far—dressing like a **drugstore cowboy**. But hell, if she had insisted, I just might've taken that chance—I'm glad she never insisted. I recall those lazy Saturdays when she helped me wash and wax my black Corvette. She supported me when I fought—I was a full-contact kickboxer, a sport she didn't actually agree with. She thought it was too violent, but she still stood by me while I got my brains bashed in (and did some bashing myself). She was there to celebrate the wins, to console me whenever I lost, especially whenever I got knocked out. Luckily my bad boy image wasn't **tarnished** since I won more fights in the ring than I lost. And, oddly enough, she only did it because of her love for me. I knew that she actually hated any type of violence, but she wasn't out to change me.

We did many other things together—she learned to camp, fish, and hunt—some of my activities. I learned to enjoy traveling every chance we got and to spend time shopping with her. But, most of all, she appreciated that I sat and listened intently to her stories. We actually shared each other's passions and excitement for life. Last of all, she grieved with me when my mom died suddenly. Mom's death, as tragic as it was, made me realize that now I had to be a 'real' man—I could now plan my future with the new woman in my life. Knowing that Mom had approved of Ashley, and even thought we were great together, I knew the next step was to marry her. And I did just that!

Our wedding was one for the ages—we 'did it up' just the way she wanted. Mom's advice just before her death: "When you decide to get married, you need to give your bride-to-be the wedding she wants, regardless of the cost. You pay for it—do not let her dad pay for the wedding—it is your responsibility as a real man. Take her wherever she wants to go for your honeymoon. You also need to plan ahead and make sure that, once the honeymoon is over, you can provide her with everything that she expects. You will need to be sure you are financially secure and that you can provide her a home, transportation, and all the things a princess deserves." Mom's advice was followed to a tee. I believe Mom guided me in this way since she had had a rough life and did not live her life as she had envisioned. She resigned herself to the fact that she married a poor man and that their love would have to carry them through life, without all the **amenities** she would have liked to have had. So, when Ashley accepted my proposal with such happiness and joy, I knew she really loved me. And, I really loved her!

I spent over $12,000 for our wedding and reception (a lot of money in those days)—we had over 100 guests, a sit-down dinner with exceptional food, and a rock band that played until the wee hours of the morning. We decided not to leave the party early—we stayed for the entire reception. It was a fantastic night—we had held the reception at a resort in Santa Fe, New Mexico. Ashley got all the things she dreamed of, all the things she wanted, all the things she deserved.

Once we settled into our married life, I contracted to have the house of her dreams built, plus I surprised her with a new sports car, the one she always wanted and dreamed about. I did it the right way. I showed her how much she meant to me. I was going to do everything in my power to make her happy and provide us with the life we wanted and the life that she deserved. That sounds good now, but since life takes many unknown twists, it turns out that all good things must eventually come to an end!

And, as life would have it, even as we 'lived our dash,' I finally came to believe that nothing lasts forever. I believe that now more than ever! Even though Ashley and I eventually drifted apart during our marriage, I probably should have done things differently. I realized that money doesn't buy happiness! One reason we drifted apart is that I did not make enough quality time to spend with her. Instead, I thought that making more money would buy us things that would keep both of us happy. It certainly didn't buy our happiness. I worked two jobs and wrote books to benefit from future **royalties**. I should not have taken those steps to make more money, which kept me away from her more and more, especially when I decided to spend more time traveling during the breaks when I wasn't teaching. I started up my own educational consulting business. Our eventual downfall—a lack of communication **coupled** with having no quality time to spend together. So, when we finally decided to split up, it was another devastating blow. As hard as it was, I decided that if she could not be happy with me, she should have the opportunity to be happy with another man who could make her happier than I ever had. The thought that hurt the most—my true love with another man! How would I ever deal with that?

At the end of our marriage, maybe we should have reminded ourselves of how we met, what fun we had, what we once meant to each other. Why didn't we make a special effort to try and go back to the beginning and start fresh? Then, who knows, we might have still been together—which might not have led to that fateful night in her life—the night she decided her life was no longer worth living. Could I have done anything to prevent this tragedy? But, we didn't think things through. We both agreed to the divorce and the end of our relationship, but apparently it was not the end of our love. As I **reminisce** about days gone by, about memories of our life together, I have concluded that we should have never split up. We should've fought for the love we had, for that everlasting love that brought us together and kept us happy for many years.

She ended up back with her 'ex' for awhile after our divorce—he ended up leaving her as he had before. What a man. When she wanted 'us' to get back together and be a family, after he had abandoned her for a second time, my strong ego would not allow me to cross into that **realm** or even think of that possibility. Remember, I once was that bad boy who wasn't supposed to fall in love. After our divorce, I went back to being that 'bad boy.' Bad boys don't step back in life and go back to relationships; we move on. We develop the attitude that there are many more fish in the sea, so why go back to something that didn't work out in the first place? Why go back into the fire once we have been burnt? I lied to myself! Now I know better, but now it is too late. Maybe it's a hard lesson that I finally learned about life. That is something I regret to this day—letting my ego control the decisions that could have made me happy again. I should have lost that bad boy attitude—I was an idiot!

I think now that things could have been so different had we stayed together as we had once promised in our wedding vows. Maybe we could have started over, and things would've been different. Maybe we could've learned what it would take to keep our love alive. But, like I said, I refused to give it a chance. There is no bringing back that feeling we once shared, no turning back the pages, no turning back the hands of time—yet another song, **"Turn Back The Hands of Time"** by R. Kelly. I always had a fantasy of both of us running into one another sometime in the future and then discovering there was still a spark between us. A thought still haunts me to this day: Could we have taken up where we left off? I'll never know. That's the sad part of living the dash—sometimes we'll never know what could've been!

I thought that there was always that possibility of ending up together again until today, when my world came crashing down around me. My dream of reuniting, my fantasy of still being able to live happily ever after, the thought of falling in love all over again (even though I can actually admit that I never stopped loving her)—all that was now gone for good!

It was late morning when I received a message at the college that she had passed away the night before—her totally unexpected death due to a suicide—a painful and slow death that was brought about by (what I was later told) loneliness. As her closest friends shared with me after her death, she actually had the same dream that I had—that we would someday end up together again. She had shared a boxful of Hallmark cards I had given her throughout our relationship, special cards acknowledging my love for her. She had saved each card and read them while sharing a bottle of wine with friends two weeks before her untimely death. I never knew this until it was too late to do anything about it. Why hadn't she sought me out, shared her true feelings, the same feelings I carried with me all this time? This hurts the most, knowing that we both missed each other immensely since our divorce, knowing that we both thought about one another frequently, all these years later. Had I known what she was feeling, what I meant to her, I would have climbed the highest mountain and swam the deepest ocean just to find her again! I don't know why we didn't make our reunion happen, make our love come alive one more time. Why did we take each other for granted so long ago?

There are many other songs that we listened to together, songs that now bring tears to my eyes when I hear them playing. I sometimes hear Journey sing one of her favorite songs, **"Don't Stop Believing,"** and I realize that I will never 'run' into her again, that we will never rekindle our love affair. I can now actually stop believing, stop dreaming—it's really over! I will now only have those wonderful memories, a mental picture of the day that I married my 'princess' so long ago, the day she walked down the aisle to become my bride! What a beautiful sight it was—she was my dream come true!

The moment I found out about Ashley's untimely passing, I actually had to sit down—it caught me by surprise and threw me into a state of shock. I had just finished teaching one of my classes, the week before spring break in 2012. I couldn't believe that, after 25 years, I would take this news so hard—the tears came easily as I sat in my office that morning reading the e-mail of her passing over and over. At home, I spent countless hours listening to the voice mail from her dad again and again, hoping that what I had heard was not possible or true, knowing that I would never get the opportunity to look into her deep blue eyes again, to swipe her blonde hair from her face, to see her beautiful smile and hear her laughter—we would never rekindle our love, the love of a lifetime. Worst of all, in the message that I will save forever, he told me she actually thought of me often and that I was truly the love of her life. Now, my dreams of reuniting with her were taken from me as quickly as my marriage to her ended years ago—it was as if I was getting my heart broken all over again! But, this time, it would probably never heal!

I have listened to that song, **"Black Is Black"** quite often, listened to the same lyrics that I had listened to dozens of times since our divorce. The lyrics mention wanting my baby back—that will never happen. The sixties group Los Bravos must have written that song for a love like ours, a love that we thought would never end. And now, she is gone for good—did she know I also thought of her often, dreamed of her again and again? One thing I do know—we will never get back the days we shared, the love that possessed us, and the dream of living happily ever after. My days are now dreary, my future black and cold, my dreams empty and dark. My love life can actually be **summed** up by Barry White's song **"You're the First, The Last, My Everything!"**

Today, a number of songs remind me of the two special loves that I had, the two loves that I lost, and the two loves that I will never experience again. I know I don't sound very **optimistic** about my future and ever finding that special one again. How **ironic** that I was the bad boy, fortunate enough to have not one but two special loves in my lifetime, only to end up alone, with no love to look forward to, no love to make me a better man. I now know I will probably live my life 'Happily Never After!' But, I can deal with it—I will try to move on. I guess that is how bad boys are supposed to live their life, mourning what once was and will never be. I guess I must now continue to live the dash and see what my future holds and what's in store for me—I wonder what's around the next corner? Maybe it's just a date at the end of my dash. Each of my loves, the first and the last, lived their dash as best they could. In the end, a date is all that comes after their dash, two dates showing their once beautiful and glorious lives are over. It's sad to say and hard to **fathom** that I, just like them, will someday travel deep into the **abyss** where **"Black Is Really Black!"**

Image © Nixx Photography, 2012. Used under license from Shutterstock, Inc.

I. Reading Comprehension Activities

My Title: _____

Main Idea Statement: This story is about _____

_____

_____

Supporting Details / Specific Info / Facts & Details (5W's + H) :

1. _____

2. _____

3. _____

4. _____

5. _____

6. _____

7. _____

8. _____

9. _____

10. _____

Inferences (Educated Guesses/Possibilities/R-B-T-L):

1. _____

2. _____

3. _____

4. _____

5. _____

6. _____

7. _____

8. _____

II. Using Vocabulary In Context

1. Write a complete sentence using 'unknown' word in context: _____

_____

_____

    A. New Word/Unknown Word: _____

    B. Dictionary Definition: _____

    _____

    C. Synonyms: i. _____

               ii. _____

2. Write a complete sentence using 'unknown' word in context: _____

_____

    A. New Word/Unknown Word: _____

    B. Dictionary Definition: _____

    _____

    C. Synonyms: i. _____

               ii. _____

3. Write a complete sentence using 'unknown' word in context: _____

_____

    A. New Word/Unknown Word: _____

    B. Dictionary Definition: _____

    _____

    C. Synonyms: i. _____

               ii. _____

4. Write a complete sentence using 'unknown' word in context: _____

_____

    A. New Word/Unknown Word: _____

    B. Dictionary Definition: _____

    _____

    C. Synonyms: i. _____

               ii. _____

III. Critical Reading & Thinking, Part One

A. The author's purpose in writing this was to _____

_____

_____

B. I know this because of the following traits included in this reading: _____

_____

C. Of the following tone words, discuss with a partner or in your group which words more appropriately describe the tone of the selection. Support your choices—reasons why you made the choice that you did.

accurate	factual	impartial	truthful	matter-of-fact
calm	angry	direct	dramatic	serious
informal	formal	optimistic	pessimistic	biased
neutral	objective	subjective	emotional	unbiased

D. A graphic organizer is the most effective way to show the visual connection between ideas. The best graphic organizer to use for this selection would be:

_____

_____

Why? _____

_____

E. Complete a graphic organizer, a map, or an outline of main points of selection.

IV. Critical Reading & Thinking, Part Two

Directions: Your instructor will guide you based on which of the sections below students will be working on (individually or in groups). Students are to use the back of this page (Notes Page) to list their information and ideas based on evaluation, analysis, or discussion of the chosen Issues, Readings, or Topics below. This is a teacher-guided activity.

Argument is the ability to exchange ideas, opinions, and conclusions between two or more students based on readings or writings that cover contemporary issues or author's ideas.

Issue #1: _____

Issue #2: _____

Issue #3: _____

Issue #4: _____

Inferences are educated guesses or educated possibilities based on what is already known (past information or background information). These are not assumptions, opinions, or personal points of view.

Reading #1: _____

Reading #2: _____

Reading #3: _____

Reading #4: _____

Points of View are ideas that students come to conclude (draw conclusions) based on their own personal experience or information gained from past knowledge or experiences. These ideas can be personal opinions if they have an educational foundation and are not just personal feelings or beliefs.

Topic #1: _____

Topic #2: _____

Topic #3: _____

Topic #4: _____

V. Summary Page –or– Precis Page

Summary / Precis (Circle One): This story is about _____

_____

_____

_____

_____

_____

_____

_____

_____

_____

_____

_____

_____

_____

_____

_____

_____

_____

_____

_____

_____

_____

_____

_____

_____

_____

Source Information (Citation):

Title of Selection: _____

Author: _____

Publisher: _____

Copyright Date: _____

Notes: _____

_____

_____

_____

_____

_____

_____

_____

_____

_____

_____

_____

_____

_____

_____

_____

_____

_____

_____

_____

_____

_____

_____

_____

_____

_____

_____

_____

_____

_____

_____

_____

_____

Aunt Sister Gets Married

by
Loretta Rodgers

Image © Viacheslav V. Fedrov, 2012. Used under
license from Shutterstock, Inc.

I could tell you about the time my brother, Jug and I, wiped our muddy hands on Aunt Sister's fresh laundry hanging on the line in her back yard. And how she spanked us so hard, it resulted in our sleeping so long, my mother thought we had died from the spanking. But I won't tell you about that.

Or I could tell you about how when Jug and I would come from school, Aunt Sister sometimes baby sat us . As we listened to *Dick Tracy* mystery stories on the radio, she would serve us Fig Newtons and milk. I didn't know anyone else who bought or ate Fig Newtons except Aunt Sister. But I won't tell you about that either.

I could tell you how one of Aunt Sister's boyfriends, Fat Mack, would buy popsicles for all the children playing in the yard. Fat Mack came by to visit Aunt Sister every Wednesday afternoon about two-thirty and Sunday afternoon about four. Regardless of the season or weather, Aunt Sister never allowed Fat Mack into her house. Fat Mack drove a big green and white 1955 Buick with white walled tires. Curious, Aunt Sister never went for a drive in that big beautiful car. It was one of the nicest cars we had ever seen a Black man drive. So, why did I believe he was her boyfriend? But I'm not going to tell you about that either.

PREPARATIONS FOR THE WEDDING

What I will tell you about is one of the most exciting, most memorable events—when Aunt Sister married Uncle Jim. Only Aunt Sister, Daddy, and Mother had met Uncle Jim prior to the wedding. Aunt Sister was Daddy's older sister by five years. She lived next door to us our entire lives. My dad's mother, Grandmother Nina, had owned both houses and when she died had left one to Dad and one to Aunt Sister. Grandmother Nina had actually owned several "shotgun" houses on our block before she passed on to Glory. They were called shotgun houses because it was said if a person would open all of the doors of the rooms and shot a shotgun, the pellets would fly cleanly from one end of the house to the other. The way Grandmother had come to have money to purchase these houses was she was an entrepreneur of sorts. She sold "boot leg" whiskey in her kitchen. But I digress from the marriage. The wedding between Aunt Sister and Uncle Jim was the first one I had ever attended. We were all so very excited. The ceremony took place in our living room, which we called the front room. We were all excited for days before the wedding. My mother had Jug and me thoroughly scrub and wax the linoleum floors and the baseboards, with emphasis on the corners. My mother always said she could tell if a room was really clean by checking the corners and the baseboards. My mother and Aunt Sister and Ms. Jimmie from across the street cleaned and shined all the windows and washed and ironed all of the curtains in the house. I was responsible for polishing the old oak coffee table and end tables that had been passed down to us from Grandmother Nina. I freshened up the huge blue velveteen Chesterfield sofa by rubbing it down with an old cloth diaper that had been soaked in lemon water. The best part of all, for Jug and me, was the honor of writing up the invitations and delivering them from door to door to everyone in the neighborhood.

The wedding took place on a perfectly beautiful Saturday evening. Mrs. Margie Green, who was the head cook of the elementary school cafeteria, was in our kitchen about six o'clock that morning overseeing the food preparations. Cousin Margie from "the country," Ms. Jimmy, my mother, and the bride to be, Aunt Sister cooked all the same kinds of foods that were reserved for Thanksgiving and Christmas: turkey and dressing, turnip greens, collard greens, green beans, corn on the cob, sweet potato pudding, potato salad, homemade rolls, corn bread, three different kinds of cakes, three sweet potato pies, and a huge apple cobbler. Dad was out back barbecuing some ribs and chicken. He was also icing down some cans of beer in a tin tub back in the shed where he thought no one could see it. Everything smelled sooo good. My special contribution was to mix the lemonade punch with lots of fresh lemons and extra sugar.

My mother had me and Jug to take our baths early and put on our Sunday clothes. We were to greet and entertain the minister and the early guests. Jug was also in charge of playing the music on the record player. Daddy had a special collection of vinyl records—75's and some 45's. Everybody was dressed up, smelled good, and feeling happy. We were happy just thinking about how happy Aunt Sister was going to be being a married lady.

Finally, everyone was excitedly standing around and ready for the ceremony. Daddy, very handsome in his blue Sunday suit and shiny shoes, escorted the lovely bride, Aunt Sister, into the room wearing a beautiful silk white suite, with a bouquet of white gardenias from a bush in our front yard that had been planted by Grandmother Nina. Oh, I forgot to tell you. We hardly noticed when they came in, because we were still staring at the groom. It was the first time most of us had met Uncle Jim. Why were we staring? Shockingly, the groom was White and a Dwarf! Marrying our Aunt Sister?

I. Reading Comprehension Activities

My Title: _____

Main Idea Statement: This story is about _____

_____

_____

Supporting Details / Specific Info / Facts & Details (5W's + H) :

1. _____

2. _____

3. _____

4. _____

5. _____

6. _____

7. _____

8. _____

9. _____

10. _____

Inferences (Educated Guesses/Possibilities/R-B-T-L):

1. _____

2. _____

3. _____

4. _____

5. _____

6. _____

7. _____

8. _____

II. Using Vocabulary In Context

1. Write a complete sentence using 'unknown' word in context: _____

_____

_____

    A. New Word/Unknown Word: _____

    B. Dictionary Definition: _____

    _____

    C. Synonyms: i. _____

                ii. _____

2. Write a complete sentence using 'unknown' word in context: _____

_____

    A. New Word/Unknown Word: _____

    B. Dictionary Definition: _____

    _____

    C. Synonyms: i. _____

                ii. _____

3. Write a complete sentence using 'unknown' word in context: _____

_____

    A. New Word/Unknown Word: _____

    B. Dictionary Definition: _____

    _____

    C. Synonyms: i. _____

                ii. _____

4. Write a complete sentence using 'unknown' word in context: _____

_____

    A. New Word/Unknown Word: _____

    B. Dictionary Definition: _____

    _____

    C. Synonyms: i. _____

                ii. _____

III. Critical Reading & Thinking, Part One

A. The author's purpose in writing this was to _____

_____

_____

B. I know this because of the following traits included in this reading: _____

_____

C. Of the following tone words, discuss with a partner or in your group which words more appropriately describe the tone of the selection. Support your choices—reasons why you made the choice that you did.

accurate	factual	impartial	truthful	matter-of-fact
calm	angry	direct	dramatic	serious
informal	formal	optimistic	pessimistic	biased
neutral	objective	subjective	emotional	unbiased

D. A graphic organizer is the most effective way to show the visual connection between ideas. The best graphic organizer to use for this selection would be:

_____

_____

Why? _____

_____

E. Complete a graphic organizer, a map, or an outline of main points of selection.

IV. Critical Reading & Thinking, Part Two

Directions: Your instructor will guide you based on which of the sections below students will be working on (individually or in groups). Students are to use the back of this page (Notes Page) to list their information and ideas based on evaluation, analysis, or discussion of the chosen Issues, Readings, or Topics below. This is a teacher-guided activity.

Argument is the ability to exchange ideas, opinions, and conclusions between two or more students based on readings or writings that cover contemporary issues or author's ideas.

Issue #1: _____

Issue #2: _____

Issue #3: _____

Issue #4: _____

Inferences are educated guesses or educated possibilities based on what is already known (past information or background information). These are not assumptions, opinions, or personal points of view.

Reading #1: _____

Reading #2: _____

Reading #3: _____

Reading #4: _____

Points of View are ideas that students come to conclude (draw conclusions) based on their own personal experience or information gained from past knowledge or experiences. These ideas can be personal opinions if they have an educational foundation and are not just personal feelings or beliefs.

Topic #1: _____

Topic #2: _____

Topic #3: _____

Topic #4: _____

V. Summary Page –or– Precis Page

Summary / Precis (Circle One): This story is about _____

_____

_____

_____

_____

_____

_____

_____

_____

_____

_____

_____

_____

_____

_____

_____

_____

_____

_____

_____

_____

_____

_____

_____

_____

Source Information (Citation):

Title of Selection: _____

Author: _____

Publisher: _____

Copyright Date: _____

Notes:

On the Edge of Village Creek

by
Loretta Rodgers

Image © Nagel Photography, 2012. Used under license from Shutterstock, Inc.

Steel City, Alabama—1952

Raw sewage emptied into Village Creek.

Village Creek ran through the "colored" community of Steel City, Alabama. When it rained heavily, the creek, with all of the feces and urine, spilled over into the yards and onto the front porches of the people who lived in the neighborhood. The odd thing is, no one ever complained about this horrendous health hazard. Once, a boy named Jimmy from New York City came down and swam naked in Village Creek. We laughed about that for years.

Village Ball Park was adjacent to the creek with a huge mound near the edge of the park. Behind the mound, at the edge of the creek, lived a family: Ragman, the father; Leah, the mother; a deaf-mute, whom we wrongly assumed to be retarded because of her disabilities; and Mart Jr., the son, about eighteen years old, who was referred to as "the Village Idiot." He never went to school and could not read or write. He helped Ragman collect rags. He was a hard worker and often did odd jobs for widows in the community.

The Ragman family home, a hovel, was constructed of cardboard boxes covered with scrap sheets of tin to keep it dry, sticks, and rags. Around their home were several hogs and two dogs named Muni and Boo. The awful stench surrounding this hovel and these three people was overwhelming. When my brother Jug and I felt adventurous, we would hold our noses, sneak up the mound, and peak over and watch this family. We were curious to know how Ragman and Mart Jr. communicated with Leah. She made unintelligible high-pitched sounds and seemed to signal frantically with her hands. Her husband and son had no problems understanding her.

How did they survive? It was said that Ragman sold the rags he collected to a paper company. He also sold cabbages and green onions, which he grew near their home, to people in the community. Our mother and grandmother would never buy them. Can you imagine how those vegetables were fertilized? Hmmm.

One late summer evening when Jug and I were bored and spying, we saw a very odd happening. Ragman used a magnificent gold-handled dagger to slit the throat of a tiny, pink piglet and caught the blood in a majestic silver goblet. The squealing sound of that poor little pig haunted me for days. Ragman, Leah, and Mart Jr., all dressed in beautiful, long white gowns tied at the waist with strips of gold cloth, knelt around a pyramid of white stones and sipped the blood from the goblet. Ragman poured the remainder of the blood over the pyramid of stones. The stones immediately began to blaze. The family danced around the blazing stones with strangely exaggerated movements of their hips and shoulders. Their heads bobbed up and down as though there were no bones or muscles in their necks! Leah began to make loud, owl-like sounds as they danced. Two very tall and extremely thin young women, completely covered in pink rose petals, emerged from the shelter. One carried a plate of bread and the other a plate of huge chunks of raw fish. These two women hand-fed the family. When all of the food was consumed, the family fell asleep and the two women dissolved into two pools of sparkling pink water!

When Jug and I told our mother what we had seen, she said we had made it all up. When we told Grandma Cici, she said she had heard of strange rituals like this being performed for specific things a family might want, and she believed our story.

Exactly six months after we observed this bizarre ritual, Ragman, Leah, and Mart Jr. came and sat on Grandma Cici's porch. A young woman we had never seen before was with them. They introduced her as Mart Jr.'s wife, Aleah Rose. She was exotic, with long golden braids and dark chocolate skin. She was very tall and very pregnant. When Grandma Cici asked how Mart Jr. and Aleah Rose came to know each other, Ragman said she was a special gift to Mart Jr. and the family from Village Creek.

Well, it turned out that Aleah Rose really was a very special gift to Ragman's family. She gave birth to healthy twin boys, Monty and Mark. The brothers learned easily in school, were tremendous athletes, got scholarships, and became famous Olympic swimmers. They built luxurious homes in Steel City, Alabama for their family who had once lived on the edge of Village Creek.

I. Reading Comprehension Activities

My Title: _____

Main Idea Statement: This story is about _____

_____

_____

Supporting Details / Specific Info / Facts & Details (5W's + H) :

1. _____

2. _____

3. _____

4. _____

5. _____

6. _____

7. _____

8. _____

9. _____

10. _____

Inferences (Educated Guesses/Possibilities/R-B-T-L):

1. _____

2. _____

3. _____

4. _____

5. _____

6. _____

7. _____

8. _____

II. Using Vocabulary In Context

1. Write a complete sentence using 'unknown' word in context: _____

_____

_____

    A. New Word/Unknown Word: _____

    B. Dictionary Definition: _____

    _____

    C. Synonyms: i. _____

              ii. _____

2. Write a complete sentence using 'unknown' word in context: _____

_____

    A. New Word/Unknown Word: _____

    B. Dictionary Definition: _____

    _____

    C. Synonyms: i. _____

              ii. _____

3. Write a complete sentence using 'unknown' word in context: _____

_____

    A. New Word/Unknown Word: _____

    B. Dictionary Definition: _____

    _____

    C. Synonyms: i. _____

              ii. _____

4. Write a complete sentence using 'unknown' word in context: _____

_____

    A. New Word/Unknown Word: _____

    B. Dictionary Definition: _____

    _____

    C. Synonyms: i. _____

              ii. _____

III. Critical Reading & Thinking, Part One

A. The author's purpose in writing this was to _____

_____

_____

B. I know this because of the following traits included in this reading: _____

_____

C. Of the following tone words, discuss with a partner or in your group which words more appropriately describe the tone of the selection. Support your choices—reasons why you made the choice that you did.

accurate	factual	impartial	truthful	matter-of-fact
calm	angry	direct	dramatic	serious
informal	formal	optimistic	pessimistic	biased
neutral	objective	subjective	emotional	unbiased

D. A graphic organizer is the most effective way to show the visual connection between ideas. The best graphic organizer to use for this selection would be:

_____

_____

Why? _____

_____

E. Complete a graphic organizer, a map, or an outline of main points of selection.

IV. Critical Reading & Thinking, Part Two

Directions: Your instructor will guide you based on which of the sections below students will be working on (individually or in groups). Students are to use the back of this page (Notes Page) to list their information and ideas based on evaluation, analysis, or discussion of the chosen Issues, Readings, or Topics below. This is a teacher-guided activity.

Argument is the ability to exchange ideas, opinions, and conclusions between two or more students based on readings or writings that cover contemporary issues or author's ideas.

Issue #1: _____

Issue #2: _____

Issue #3: _____

Issue #4: _____

Inferences are educated guesses or educated possibilities based on what is already known (past information or background information). These are not assumptions, opinions, or personal points of view.

Reading #1: _____

Reading #2: _____

Reading #3: _____

Reading #4: _____

Points of View are ideas that students come to conclude (draw conclusions) based on their own personal experience or information gained from past knowledge or experiences. These ideas can be personal opinions if they have an educational foundation and are not just personal feelings or beliefs.

Topic #1: _____

Topic #2: _____

Topic #3: _____

Topic #4: _____

V. Summary Page –or– Precis Page

Summary / Precis (Circle One): This story is about _____

_____

_____

_____

_____

_____

_____

_____

_____

_____

_____

_____

_____

_____

_____

_____

_____

_____

_____

_____

_____

_____

_____

_____

_____

_____

Source Information (Citation):

Title of Selection: _____

Author: _____

Publisher: _____

Copyright Date: _____

Notes: _____

_____

_____

_____

_____

_____

_____

_____

_____

_____

_____

_____

_____

_____

_____

_____

_____

_____

_____

_____

_____

_____

_____

_____

_____

_____

_____

_____

_____

Selection 24: On the Edge of Village Creek

The Perfect Girl

by
Loretta Rodgers

Image © ostill, 2012. Used under license from Shutter-stock, Inc.

I live in Oak Cliff, Texas. One afternoon, while shelling peas on the front porch with my neighbor, Mrs. Miranda Palmer, she told me this amazing story that happened to her handsome, intelligent, 21-year-old son, Sam.

Sam's father bought him a computer when he was only three years old. He wanted Sam to be able to learn basic math and reading before enrolling in school. Sam, a rather precocious child, learned very fast. He was curious and capable. Sam also had an endearing, loving, trusting spirit. As the years passed, Sam, as did his peers, branched off into social networks. He enjoyed connecting with others on Myspace and, of course, later on Facebook.

In the spring of last year, Sam befriended Jenna, of El Paso, Texas, on Facebook. After chatting with her for about three weeks, they exchanged pictures. Sam shared the pictures with his mother, Mrs. Palmer, and told her how perfect Jenna was. Jenna was a dark-haired beauty who could have been a model. Mrs. Palmer even spoke with her on the phone and agreed that she impressed her as a loving, polite, kind young woman. A few weeks later, Sam had Mrs. Palmer say hello to Jenna's sister, Aurelia on the phone. Mrs. Palmer and Sam both thought the likeness in the voices of Jenna and Aurelia was remarkable. But after consideration, Mrs. Palmer offered, "You know Sam, on the phone, you and your dad sound very much alike." So they agreed that family member's voices often sound the same. Secretly, however, Mrs. Palmer had an unexplainable, eerie feeling about the uncanny similarity between the girls' voices.

Jenna told Sam how she and her sister, Aurelia, both twenty-three, had the same birthday and yet were not twins. "How could this be?" Sam asked.

Jenna explained, "My sister and I were both born on July 4th. Aurelia was born in the morning and I was born in the evening. How is that possible? We have the same father but different mothers. When Aurelia was two years old, her mother was killed on a country road by a drunk driver as she was riding on the back of a motorcycle. My father brought Aurelia home, my mother accepted her as her daughter, and we have lived together as sisters ever since. Aurelia and I are very close."

Sam and Jenna talked on the phone every day for hours at a time. They talked about Sam's dreams to own his own recording studio and Jenna's goal of becoming a fashion designer. They confessed that they had fallen in love. Sam said Jenna was the perfect girl. She was a good listener, insightful, intelligent, and loving. Mrs. Palmer was perplexed as to how her son could be in love with someone he had never actually met, had never touched, had never kissed.

In late summer, Jenna, Aurelia, and Sam agreed that the girls would move to the Dallas area and the three of them would get an apartment together. Soon, through a family friend, both girls had acquired jobs at the Dallas Fort Worth Airport as security personnel. That was really great news because so many other people were losing jobs during that time.

Jenna told Sam "Go ahead and find a two bedroom apartment so we'll already have a place to live when we get there. Aurelia and I will pay seventy-five percent of the rent. It will be great fun getting to know each other."

Mrs. Palmer drove Sam to look at several apartments before he finally decided on a suitable one located about thirty minutes from the airport, convenient for the girl's jobs and his at the post office. Sam was ecstatic. He was deeply in love. Everything was in place for Sam's new life with Jenna.

On a late summer evening, Mrs. Palmer was relaxing, reading her bible in bed, when Sam ran into her room with this unbelievable expression of a mixture of shock and sadness on his face. Aurelia had called and said Jenna had been killed in a car accident on a corner at the end of their block. Sam fell on his knees and cried from deep within his soul. His perfect girl was gone too soon before he could even hold her or see her face-to-face. Mrs. Palmer tried to sooth him as best she could. Sam's pain was severe. His eyes were red and swollen. His heart was indeed broken beyond repair.

The doberman dog began to bark furiously. Mrs. Palmer said "Jenna's spirit is passing over our house. She came to say good-by to Sam."

Because the funeral was to be in two days, Sam arranged to fly to El Paso to pay his respects to Jenna's family. Aurelia made a reservation for him at a hotel.

After dropping Sam off at the Dallas Fort Worth airport, Mrs. Palmer decided to call and offer her sympathy to Jenna's family. When Mrs. Palmer asked to speak to the mother of Jenna, the mother said she did not have a daughter named Jenna. She had one daughter by the name of Aurelia. She further informed her that her daughter Aurelia had some mental issues, manic depression, and had told her that she, Aurelia, was soon going to be engaged to Sam. This news, of course, sent Mrs. Palmer into panic mode. Aurelia appeared to be very unstable and possibly dangerous. Mrs. Palmer immediately called Sam on his phone and asked him where he was.

He said he was in the hotel room with Aurelia. She had told him they couldn't go to see the family just yet, they were all too emotional. When Mrs. Palmer told him what she had learned, that Jenna never existed, Sam remained calm. He said he expected as much when Aurelia called him on Jenna's cell phone when he arrived at the airport in El Paso. Aurelia could not explain how she had Jenna's phone.

Sam asked Aurelia to show him a picture of Jenna on her cell phone. She did not have one. Aurelia finally confessed the truth. Aurelia had deceived Sam because she had been desperate for a male companion. She was 27-years-old and had never had a boyfriend. Aurelia was horribly obese and half of her face was marked by old burn scars.

The pictures Aurelia had sent of "Jenna" were actually of a girl Aurelia hardly knew who sang in the choir with her at The Rising Star Christian Church.

Mrs. Palmer called Sam several times, frantically urging him to "Get out of that room now, I am afraid she might hurt you."

Moral of the story: _____

I. Reading Comprehension Activities

My Title: _____

Main Idea Statement: This story is about _____

_____

_____

Supporting Details / Specific Info / Facts & Details (5W's + H) :

1. _____

2. _____

3. _____

4. _____

5. _____

6. _____

7. _____

8. _____

9. _____

10. _____

Inferences (Educated Guesses/Possibilities/R-B-T-L):

1. _____

2. _____

3. _____

4. _____

5. _____

6. _____

7. _____

8. _____

II. Using Vocabulary In Context

1. Write a complete sentence using 'unknown' word in context: _____

_____

    A. New Word/Unknown Word: _____

    B. Dictionary Definition: _____

    _____

    C. Synonyms: i. _____

               ii. _____

2. Write a complete sentence using 'unknown' word in context: _____

_____

    A. New Word/Unknown Word: _____

    B. Dictionary Definition: _____

    _____

    C. Synonyms: i. _____

               ii. _____

3. Write a complete sentence using 'unknown' word in context: _____

_____

    A. New Word/Unknown Word: _____

    B. Dictionary Definition: _____

    _____

    C. Synonyms: i. _____

               ii. _____

4. Write a complete sentence using 'unknown' word in context: _____

_____

    A. New Word/Unknown Word: _____

    B. Dictionary Definition: _____

    _____

    C. Synonyms: i. _____

               ii. _____

III. Critical Reading & Thinking, Part One

A. The author's purpose in writing this was to _____

_____

_____

B. I know this because of the following traits included in this reading: _____

_____

C. Of the following tone words, discuss with a partner or in your group which words more appropriately describe the tone of the selection. Support your choices—reasons why you made the choice that you did.

accurate	factual	impartial	truthful	matter-of-fact
calm	angry	direct	dramatic	serious
informal	formal	optimistic	pessimistic	biased
neutral	objective	subjective	emotional	unbiased

D. A graphic organizer is the most effective way to show the visual connection between ideas. The best graphic organizer to use for this selection would be:

_____

_____

Why? _____

_____

E. Complete a graphic organizer, a map, or an outline of main points of selection.

IV. Critical Reading
& Thinking, Part Two

Directions: Your instructor will guide you based on which of the sections below students will be working on (individually or in groups). Students are to use the back of this page (Notes Page) to list their information and ideas based on evaluation, analysis, or discussion of the chosen Issues, Readings, or Topics below. This is a teacher-guided activity.

<u>**Argument**</u> is the ability to exchange ideas, opinions, and conclusions between two or more students based on readings or writings that cover contemporary issues or author's ideas.

Issue #1: _____

Issue #2: _____

Issue #3: _____

Issue #4: _____

<u>**Inferences**</u> are educated guesses or educated possibilities based on what is already known (past information or background information). These are not assumptions, opinions, or personal points of view.

Reading #1: _____

Reading #2: _____

Reading #3: _____

Reading #4: _____

<u>**Points of View**</u> are ideas that students come to conclude (draw conclusions) based on their own personal experience or information gained from past knowledge or experiences. These ideas can be personal opinions if they have an educational foundation and are not just personal feelings or beliefs.

Topic #1: _____

Topic #2: _____

Topic #3: _____

Topic #4: _____

V. Summary Page –or– Precis Page

Summary / Precis (Circle One): This story is about _____

_____

_____

_____

_____

_____

_____

_____

_____

_____

_____

_____

_____

_____

_____

_____

_____

_____

_____

_____

_____

_____

_____

_____

_____

_____

<u>Source Information (Citation):</u>

Title of Selection: _____

Author: _____

Publisher: _____

Copyright Date: _____

Notes:

Section Three—Experiential [Life Lessons]

Section Four

Content-Area

Maslow's Hierarchy of Needs

by
Stephen Davis and Joseph Palmer

PYRAMID OF NEEDS

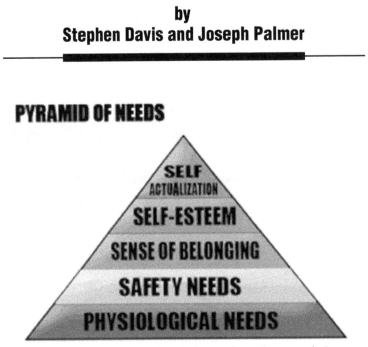

Image © ducu59us, 2012. Used under license from Shutterstock, Inc.

Abraham Maslow's (1970) **hierarchy of needs** combines biological and psychological aspects of motivation. According to Maslow, five categories of motivated behavior can be ordered in a hierarchical fashion along two dimensions: (a) the *type* of motivation (from innate physiological motives to more psychological learned motives) and (b) the *strength* of the motivation (from strongest to weakest). The strongest and most physiologically based motives involve satisfying basic or survival needs such as hunger and thirst.

According to Maslow, we attempt to satisfy stronger motives before trying to satisfy motives that are higher in the hierarchy. Thus *physiological* needs (such as hunger) must be met before safety needs (security) can be satisfied. Safety needs are satisfied by a stable job, insurance, and financial reserves for emergencies. For the few people who successfully satisfy their physiological, safety, belongingness, and esteem needs, yet another need, *self-actualization*, emerges. **Self-actualization** comes from developing one's unique potential to its fullest extent. Each of us strives to become the very best (carpenter, truck driver, and so on) that our potential allows us to become. Because our struggle to satisfy needs that are lower in the hierarchy is a continuing one, only a small number of people achieve self-actualization.

Maslow's theory is often characterized as a *growth theory of motivation* because people strive to satisfy successively higher needs. As we satisfy needs at progressively higher levels of the hierarchy, we grow as individuals; this growth influences how we behave when we are later forced to confront

Section Four—Content-Area

lower-level needs again. Although we might expect prisoners of war to be concerned only with their survival, many prisoners in Nazi concentration camps gave their food, clothing, and even their lives for others.

Critics note that not everyone proceeds through the hierarchy as Maslow outlined. What's more, in some societies people have difficulty meeting basic needs, yet they may be able to satisfy higher needs, as when a couple struggles to establish a family and to make ends meet while growing closer to each other as a result of their struggle.

Based on Maslow's hierarchy of needs, we might predict that prisoners in Nazi concentration camps would be motivated by their basic survival needs. In contrast to this prediction, some prisoners in Nazi concentration camps, such as one at Mittlebau Dora in Nordhausen, Germany (1945), put the survival of others before their own and offered food, clothing, and, at times, even their own lives.

I. Reading Comprehension Activities

My Title: _____

Main Idea Statement: This story is about _____

_____

_____

Supporting Details / Specific Info / Facts & Details (5W's + H) :

1. _____

2. _____

3. _____

4. _____

5. _____

6. _____

7. _____

8. _____

9. _____

10. _____

Inferences (Educated Guesses/Possibilities/R-B-T-L):

1. _____

2. _____

3. _____

4. _____

5. _____

6. _____

7. _____

8. _____

II. Using Vocabulary In Context

1. Write a complete sentence using 'unknown' word in context: _____

_____

    A. New Word/Unknown Word: _____

    B. Dictionary Definition: _____

    _____

    C. Synonyms: i. _____

               ii. _____

2. Write a complete sentence using 'unknown' word in context: _____

_____

    A. New Word/Unknown Word: _____

    B. Dictionary Definition: _____

    _____

    C. Synonyms: i. _____

               ii. _____

3. Write a complete sentence using 'unknown' word in context: _____

_____

    A. New Word/Unknown Word: _____

    B. Dictionary Definition: _____

    _____

    C. Synonyms: i. _____

               ii. _____

4. Write a complete sentence using 'unknown' word in context: _____

_____

    A. New Word/Unknown Word: _____

    B. Dictionary Definition: _____

    _____

    C. Synonyms: i. _____

               ii. _____

III. Critical Reading & Thinking, Part One

A. The author's purpose in writing this was to _____

_____

_____

B. I know this because of the following traits included in this reading: _____

_____

C. Of the following tone words, discuss with a partner or in your group which words more appropriately describe the tone of the selection. Support your choices—reasons why you made the choice that you did.

accurate	factual	impartial	truthful	matter-of-fact
calm	angry	direct	dramatic	serious
informal	formal	optimistic	pessimistic	biased
neutral	objective	subjective	emotional	unbiased

D. A graphic organizer is the most effective way to show the visual connection between ideas. The best graphic organizer to use for this selection would be:

_____

_____

Why? _____

_____

E. Complete a graphic organizer, a map, or an outline of main points of selection.

IV. Critical Reading
& Thinking, Part Two

Directions: Your instructor will guide you based on which of the sections below students will be working on (individually or in groups). Students are to use the back of this page (Notes Page) to list their information and ideas based on evaluation, analysis, or discussion of the chosen Issues, Readings, or Topics below. This is a teacher-guided activity.

Argument is the ability to exchange ideas, opinions, and conclusions between two or more students based on readings or writings that cover contemporary issues or author's ideas.

Issue #1: _____

Issue #2: _____

Issue #3: _____

Issue #4: _____

Inferences are educated guesses or educated possibilities based on what is already known (past information or background information). These are not assumptions, opinions, or personal points of view.

Reading #1: _____

Reading #2: _____

Reading #3: _____

Reading #4: _____

Points of View are ideas that students come to conclude (draw conclusions) based on their own personal experience or information gained from past knowledge or experiences. These ideas can be personal opinions if they have an educational foundation and are not just personal feelings or beliefs.

Topic #1: _____

Topic #2: _____

Topic #3: _____

Topic #4: _____

V. Summary Page –or– Precis Page

Summary / Precis (Circle One): This story is about _____

_____

_____

_____

_____

_____

_____

_____

_____

_____

_____

_____

_____

_____

_____

_____

_____

_____

_____

_____

_____

_____

_____

_____

Source Information (Citation):

Title of Selection: _____

Author: _____

Publisher: _____

Copyright Date: _____

Notes: _____

_____

_____

_____

_____

_____

_____

_____

_____

_____

_____

_____

_____

_____

_____

_____

_____

_____

_____

_____

_____

_____

_____

_____

_____

_____

_____

_____

_____

_____

_____

_____

Therapy and Therapists

by
Stephen Davis and Joseph Palmer

Image © Yulia Glam, 2012. Used under
license from Shutterstock, Inc.

Not everyone who seeks therapy suffers from a psychological disorder. Some people need help to cope with such lifestyle events as the loss of a job, school-related difficulties, or family disagreements. During a 1-year period, nearly 30% of U.S. adults (about 60 million) would qualify for a diagnosis of some psychological disorder, and 15% received some mental health service. Of those people who had a disorder, however, only about 30% sought treatment. Of the people who sought treatment, 55% were suffering from a disorder. The remainder did not meet the diagnostic criteria for any psychological disorder during the year, although many had a previous disorder during their lifetimes. Clearly, actual mental health services provided fall short of the potential need (Regier, Kaelber et al., 1998; Regier, Rae et al., 1988).

What factors influence the decision to seek (or not to seek) mental health treatment? One key factor is the nature of the disorder. For example, the use of mental health services is high among people diagnosed with schizophrenia (64%), bipolar disorder (61%), and panic disorder (59%). By contrast, only 24% of individuals with a substance-use disorder seek help. In addition, people with multiple disorders are more likely to seek treatment (Regier, Kaelber et al., 1998; Regier, Rae et al., 1988).

Research has underscored the importance of seeking treatment. It is estimated that living with a serious mental illness may shorten a person's life by as much as 25 years (Novotney, 2008). Clearly, it is important for people to seek treatment when they need it.

Where do people go to receive treatment? Most receive outpatient rather than in-patient treatment: 5% of patients receive inpatient care only, 10% receive a combination of inpatient (usually hospital) and outpatient treatment, and 85% are exclusively outpatients (Melton, Petrila, Poythress, & Slobogin, 1997).

There are more than 400 different treatments for psychological disorders. These treatments can be divided into two broad categories: **biomedical therapies** and **psychological therapies**. The biomedical therapies use psychotropic drugs (drugs that affect the brain), electroconvulsive therapy, and psychosurgery to alter brain functioning and thus reduce symptoms. Psychological therapies range from "talk therapies" to treatments based on the principles of learning.

Psychotherapy is a general term that describes psychological treatments designed to help people resolve behavioral, emotional, and interpersonal problems and improve the quality of their lives (Leftwich, 2008a). The primary means of achieving these goals is for a therapist to engage a client in discussions and interactions. Some of these forms of therapy, often called *behavior therapy*, are based on the principles of classical conditioning, operant conditioning, and modeling.

TYPES OF THERAPISTS. Members of several professions as well as paraprofessionals provide psychotherapeutic services. The term *therapist* encompasses a diverse group of people with different backgrounds. Included here are people with a master's or doctoral degree in psychology and people with a medical degree and special training in psychiatry, as well as self-designated psychotherapists (Nevid & Greene, 2001). Among the most common types of licensed psychotherapists are clinical and counseling psychologists, psychiatric nurses, psychiatrists, and social workers.[1]

TYPES OF THERAPISTS AND THEIR TRAINING

Clinical psychologists	Have earned a doctoral degree (Ph.D., Psy.D., or Ed.D.), which usually takes 4 or more years after an undergraduate degree. Their training includes completion of a dissertation based on research and a 1-year internship in a mental hospital or community mental health center. During their schooling, they take courses on the diagnosis and treatment of psychological disorders. They must meet state certification or licensing requirements that typically require doctoral training, an internship, a number of hours of supervised clinical work in addition to the internship, and a national licensing examination.
Counselors	Have a range of educational backgrounds, from a bachelor's degree to a doctorate. They may be members of the clergy (pastoral counselors) or professional educators; some counselors are trained to work with specific populations such as drug and alcohol abusers. Some people who identify themselves as counselors, however, have little formal training in providing psychotherapeutic services.
Marriage and family therapists	Usually, but not always, complete a 2-year master's program. Their training focuses on therapy with couples and families and is typically followed by 2 or more years of supervised work. These therapists are specially trained to deal with marital problems and child-parent conflicts. Some states license marriage and family therapists.
Psychiatric nurses	Are registered nurses who usually have earned a master's degree from a psychiatric nursing program, which usually takes about 2 years. Psychiatric

---

[1] describes the qualifications and roles of these and other mental health professionals.

nurses are especially proficient in evaluating the effects of a person's environment and physical functioning on his or her mental health status.

Psychiatrists

Are medical doctors (holders of an M.D.) who have completed a 3-year residency in psychiatry, usually in a psychiatric hospital or community mental health center. As physicians, they can prescribe drugs and hospitalize patients. They treat problems ranging from mild emotional problems to severe psychotic disorders. In addition to drug and other medical treatments, they can use a full range of individual and group psychotherapies; some psychiatrists also use behavior therapy.

Psychoanalysts

Often (but not always) hold an M.D. and have additional training in the psychoanalytic tradition of therapy developed by Sigmund Freud. A person without an M.D. can qualify as a psychoanalyst by completing the required training and undergoing psychoanalysis, a costly and time-consuming process.

Social workers

Constitute the largest group of professionals in the mental health field. Most have earned a master's degree in social work (M.S.W.), which usually takes 2 years of full-time study; a few social workers have earned a doctorate. Their course work includes practical experience (called *field placement*) in social work agencies or mental health facilities. As part of their training, they learn to use the services of agencies and groups to meet their clients' needs, They may direct clinics or have private practices. Licensing requirements vary from state to state. Psychiatric social workers specialize in treating mentally ill patients.

I. Reading Comprehension Activities

My Title: _____

Main Idea Statement: This story is about _____

_____

_____

Supporting Details / Specific Info / Facts & Details (5W's + H) :

1. _____

2. _____

3. _____

4. _____

5. _____

6. _____

7. _____

8. _____

9. _____

10. _____

Inferences (Educated Guesses/Possibilities/R-B-T-L):

1. _____

2. _____

3. _____

4. _____

5. _____

6. _____

7. _____

8. _____

II. Using Vocabulary In Context

1. Write a complete sentence using 'unknown' word in context: _____

_____

_____

   A. New Word/Unknown Word: _____

   B. Dictionary Definition: _____

   _____

   C. Synonyms: i. _____

               ii. _____

2. Write a complete sentence using 'unknown' word in context: _____

_____

   A. New Word/Unknown Word: _____

   B. Dictionary Definition: _____

   _____

   C. Synonyms: i. _____

               ii. _____

3. Write a complete sentence using 'unknown' word in context: _____

_____

   A. New Word/Unknown Word: _____

   B. Dictionary Definition: _____

   _____

   C. Synonyms: i. _____

               ii. _____

4. Write a complete sentence using 'unknown' word in context: _____

_____

   A. New Word/Unknown Word: _____

   B. Dictionary Definition: _____

   _____

   C. Synonyms: i. _____

               ii. _____

III. Critical Reading & Thinking, Part One

A. The author's purpose in writing this was to _____

_____

_____

B. I know this because of the following traits included in this reading: _____

_____

C. Of the following tone words, discuss with a partner or in your group which words more appropriately describe the tone of the selection. Support your choices—reasons why you made the choice that you did.

accurate	factual	impartial	truthful	matter-of-fact
calm	angry	direct	dramatic	serious
informal	formal	optimistic	pessimistic	biased
neutral	objective	subjective	emotional	unbiased

D. A graphic organizer is the most effective way to show the visual connection between ideas. The best graphic organizer to use for this selection would be:

_____

_____

Why? _____

_____

E. Complete a graphic organizer, a map, or an outline of main points of selection.

IV. Critical Reading & Thinking, Part Two

Directions: Your instructor will guide you based on which of the sections below students will be working on (individually or in groups). Students are to use the back of this page (Notes Page) to list their information and ideas based on evaluation, analysis, or discussion of the chosen Issues, Readings, or Topics below. This is a teacher-guided activity.

Argument is the ability to exchange ideas, opinions, and conclusions between two or more students based on readings or writings that cover contemporary issues or author's ideas.

Issue #1: _____

Issue #2: _____

Issue #3: _____

Issue #4: _____

Inferences are educated guesses or educated possibilities based on what is already known (past information or background information). These are not assumptions, opinions, or personal points of view.

Reading #1: _____

Reading #2: _____

Reading #3: _____

Reading #4: _____

Points of View are ideas that students come to conclude (draw conclusions) based on their own personal experience or information gained from past knowledge or experiences. These ideas can be personal opinions if they have an educational foundation and are not just personal feelings or beliefs.

Topic #1: _____

Topic #2: _____

Topic #3: _____

Topic #4: _____

V. Summary Page –or– Precis Page

Summary / Precis (Circle One): This story is about _____

_____

_____

_____

_____

_____

_____

_____

_____

_____

_____

_____

_____

_____

_____

_____

_____

_____

_____

_____

_____

_____

_____

_____

_____

_____

Source Information (Citation):

Title of Selection: _____

Author: _____

Publisher: _____

Copyright Date: _____

Notes: _____

Section Four—Content-Area

Paranormal Phenomena

by
Stephen Davis and Joseph Palmer

Image © Stocksnapper, 2012. Used under license from Shutterstock, Inc.

Thousands of handbills were distributed, posters were displayed, and newspaper advertisements were placed to announce the first public appearance of a famous psychic who had spent years being tested in laboratories around the world. Extra chairs were brought in to accommodate the huge crowd that wanted to see and hear the lecture and demonstration. The psychic began by showing plants perceiving animosity or affection from people. Next, he drew some geometric figures that matched those drawn by a member of the audience. Finally, from about 20 feet away and using only the power of his mind, he caused a large heavy rocking chair to move back and forth (Gordon, 1987). *What do people believe is the cause of such phenomena?*

Surveys have indicated that over 90% of adult Americans believe in at least one *paranormal* (literally, "beyond normal") or psychic phenomenon, and almost half believe in five or more. Belief in such phenomena is widespread among college students. One-third of them express belief in reincarnation; a similar number believe that communication with the dead is possible. Over half believe that their dreams predict events such as the death of a family member or a natural disaster (Messer & Griggs, 1989).

Undoubtedly you have heard about **extrasensory perception (ESP)**, which refers to experiences or behaviors that occur without sensory contact—in other words, without the use of our sensory receptors. The term *ESP* is reserved for paranormal phenomena that do not involve the senses. The most frequently mentioned examples of ESP are clairvoyance, telepathy, and precognition. *Clairvoyance* (from the French for "clear seeing") is the claimed ability to "see" information from objects or events without direct contact with the senses. If you could tell us what was in a closed box that you had never seen, you might be demonstrating clairvoyance. *Telepathy* is the claimed ability to perceive the thoughts or emotions of others without the use of recognized senses. *Precognition* is knowledge of a future event or circumstance obtained by paranormal means. *Psychokinesis* (once known as *telekinesis*) is the claimed power of the mind to influence matter directly. Because psychokinesis does not involve perception, some researchers do not consider it an example of ESP. The term *parapsychology* is often used to refer to "the study of paranormal phenomena, which are considered to be well outside the bounds of established science."

I. Reading Comprehension Activities

My Title: _____

Main Idea Statement: This story is about _____

_____

_____

Supporting Details / Specific Info / Facts & Details (5W's + H) :

1. _____

2. _____

3. _____

4. _____

5. _____

6. _____

7. _____

8. _____

9. _____

10. _____

Inferences (Educated Guesses/Possibilities/R-B-T-L):

1. _____

2. _____

3. _____

4. _____

5. _____

6. _____

7. _____

8. _____

II. Using Vocabulary In Context

1. Write a complete sentence using 'unknown' word in context: _____

_____

_____

    A. New Word/Unknown Word: _____

    B. Dictionary Definition: _____

    _____

    C. Synonyms: i. _____

              ii. _____

2. Write a complete sentence using 'unknown' word in context: _____

_____

    A. New Word/Unknown Word: _____

    B. Dictionary Definition: _____

    _____

    C. Synonyms: i. _____

              ii. _____

3. Write a complete sentence using 'unknown' word in context: _____

_____

    A. New Word/Unknown Word: _____

    B. Dictionary Definition: _____

    _____

    C. Synonyms: i. _____

              ii. _____

4. Write a complete sentence using 'unknown' word in context: _____

_____

    A. New Word/Unknown Word: _____

    B. Dictionary Definition: _____

    _____

    C. Synonyms: i. _____

              ii. _____

III. Critical Reading & Thinking, Part One

A. The author's purpose in writing this was to _____

_____

_____

B. I know this because of the following traits included in this reading: _____

_____

C. Of the following tone words, discuss with a partner or in your group which words more appropriately describe the tone of the selection. Support your choices—reasons why you made the choice that you did.

accurate	factual	impartial	truthful	matter-of-fact
calm	angry	direct	dramatic	serious
informal	formal	optimistic	pessimistic	biased
neutral	objective	subjective	emotional	unbiased

D. A graphic organizer is the most effective way to show the visual connection between ideas. The best graphic organizer to use for this selection would be:

_____

_____

Why? _____

_____

E. Complete a graphic organizer, a map, or an outline of main points of selection.

IV. Critical Reading & Thinking, Part Two

Directions: Your instructor will guide you based on which of the sections below students will be working on (individually or in groups). Students are to use the back of this page (Notes Page) to list their information and ideas based on evaluation, analysis, or discussion of the chosen Issues, Readings, or Topics below. This is a teacher-guided activity.

Argument is the ability to exchange ideas, opinions, and conclusions between two or more students based on readings or writings that cover contemporary issues or author's ideas.

Issue #1: _____

Issue #2: _____

Issue #3: _____

Issue #4: _____

Inferences are educated guesses or educated possibilities based on what is already known (past information or background information). These are not assumptions, opinions, or personal points of view.

Reading #1: _____

Reading #2: _____

Reading #3: _____

Reading #4: _____

Points of View are ideas that students come to conclude (draw conclusions) based on their own personal experience or information gained from past knowledge or experiences. These ideas can be personal opinions if they have an educational foundation and are not just personal feelings or beliefs.

Topic #1: _____

Topic #2: _____

Topic #3: _____

Topic #4: _____

V. Summary Page –or– Precis Page

Summary / Precis (Circle One): This story is about _____

_____

_____

_____

_____

_____

_____

_____

_____

_____

_____

_____

_____

_____

_____

_____

_____

_____

_____

_____

_____

_____

_____

_____

_____

_____

Source Information (Citation):

Title of Selection: _____

Author: _____

Publisher: _____

Copyright Date: _____

Notes:

Section Four—Content-Area

Selection 29

Indian Removal

by
Goldfield, Abbott, Anderson, et al.

Image © tukkki, 2012. Used under license from Shutterstock, Inc.

Any support Jackson might have lost among market-minded entrepreneurs and farmers in the West by his Maysville veto was more than made up by the popularity of his Indian removal policy. Some 125,000 Indians lived east of the Mississippi when Jackson became president. The largest concentration was in the South, where five Indian nations, the Cherokees, Creeks, Choctaws, Chickasaws, and Seminoles, controlled millions of acres of land in what soon would become the great cotton frontiers of southwestern Georgia and central Alabama and Mississippi. That, of course, was the problem: Native Americans held land that white farmers coveted for their own economic gain.

Pressure from the states to remove the Indians had been building since the end of the War of 1812. It was most intense in Georgia. In early 1825, Georgia authorities finalized a fraudulent treaty that ceded most of the Creek Indians' land to the state. In 1828, Georgia moved against the Cherokees, the best-organized and most advanced (by white standards) of the Indian nations. By now a prosperous

GOLDFIELD/ABBOTT/ ANDERSON/ARGERSINGER/BARNEY/WEIR, THE AMERICAN JOURNEY: TEACHING AND LEARNING CLASSROOM EDITION, VOLUME 1, 5th Edition, © 2009. Reprinted by permission of Pearson Education, Inc., Upper Saddle River, NJ.

society of small farmers with their own newspaper and schools for their children, the Cherokees wanted to avoid the fate of their Creek neighbors. In 1827, they adopted a constitution declaring themselves an independent nation with complete sovereignty over their land. The Georgia legislature reacted by placing the Cherokees directly under state law, annulling Cherokee laws and even the right of the Cherokees to make laws, and legally defining the Cherokees as tenants on land belonging to the state of Georgia. By also prohibiting Indian testimony in cases against white people, the legislature stripped the Cherokees of any legal rights. Alabama and Mississippi followed Georgia's lead in denying Indians legal rights.

Thus the stage was set for what Jackson always considered the most important measure of the early days of his administration, the **Indian Removal Act**. Jackson had long considered the federal policy of negotiating with the Indians as sovereign entities a farce. But it was awkward politically for the president to declare that he had no intention of enforcing treaty obligations of the U.S. government. The way out of this dilemma was to remove Native Americans from the center of the dispute. In his first annual message, Jackson sided with state officials in the South and advised the Indians "to emigrate beyond the Mississippi or submit to the laws of those States."

Congress acted on Jackson's recommendation in the Indian Removal Act of 1830. The act appropriated $500,000 for the negotiation of new treaties under which the southern Indians would surrender their territory and be removed to land in the trans-Mississippi area (primarily present-day Oklahoma). Although force was not authorized and Jackson stressed that removal should be voluntary, no federal protection was provided for Indians harassed into leaving by land-hungry settlers.

And so most of the Indians left the eastern United States, the Choctaws in 1830, the Creeks and Chickasaws in 1832, and the Cherokees in 1838, that won the federal contracts for transporting and Thousands of Indians, perhaps as many as one-fourth of those who started the trek, died on the way to Oklahoma, the victims of cold, hunger, disease, and the general callousness of the white people they met along the way. "It is impossible to conceive the frightful sufferings that attend these forced migrations," noted a Frenchman who observed the Choctaw removal. It was indeed, as recalled in the collective memory of the Cherokees, a **Trail of Tears**.

Tribes that resisted removal were attacked by white armies. Federal troops joined local militias in 1832 in suppressing the Sauk and Fox Indians of Illinois and Wisconsin in what was called **Black Hawk's War**. More a frantic attempt by the Indians to reach safety on the west bank of the Mississippi than an actual war, this affair ended in the slaughter of 500 Indian men, women, and children by white troops and their Sioux allies. The Seminoles, many of whose leaders were runaway slaves adopted into the tribe, fought the army to a standstill in the swamps of Florida in what became the longest Indian war in U.S. history.

Jackson forged ahead with his removal policy despite the opposition of eastern reformers and Protestant missionaries. Aligned with conservatives concerned by Jackson's cavalier disregard of federal treaty obligations, they came within three votes of defeating the removal bill in the House of Representatives. Jackson ignored their protests (see American Views: Native Americans Speak Out) as well as the legal rulings of the Supreme Court. In *Cherokee Nation v. Georgia* (1831) and *Worcester v. Georgia* (1832), the Court ruled that Georgia had violated the U.S. Constitution in extending its jurisdiction over the Cherokees. Aware that southerners and westerners were on his side, Jackson ignored the Supreme Court rulings and pushed Indian removal to its tragic conclusion.

I. Reading Comprehension Activities

My Title: _____

Main Idea Statement: This story is about _____

_____

_____

Supporting Details / Specific Info / Facts & Details (5W's + H) :

1. _____

2. _____

3. _____

4. _____

5. _____

6. _____

7. _____

8. _____

9. _____

10. _____

Inferences (Educated Guesses/Possibilities/R-B-T-L):

1. _____

2. _____

3. _____

4. _____

5. _____

6. _____

7. _____

8. _____

II. Using Vocabulary In Context

1. Write a complete sentence using 'unknown' word in context: _____

_____

_____

    A. New Word/Unknown Word: _____

    B. Dictionary Definition: _____

    _____

    C. Synonyms: i. _____

              ii. _____

2. Write a complete sentence using 'unknown' word in context: _____

_____

    A. New Word/Unknown Word: _____

    B. Dictionary Definition: _____

    _____

    C. Synonyms: i. _____

              ii. _____

3. Write a complete sentence using 'unknown' word in context: _____

_____

    A. New Word/Unknown Word: _____

    B. Dictionary Definition: _____

    _____

    C. Synonyms: i. _____

              ii. _____

4. Write a complete sentence using 'unknown' word in context: _____

_____

    A. New Word/Unknown Word: _____

    B. Dictionary Definition: _____

    _____

    C. Synonyms: i. _____

              ii. _____

III. Critical Reading & Thinking, Part One

A. The author's purpose in writing this was to _____

_____

_____

B. I know this because of the following traits included in this reading: _____

_____

C. Of the following tone words, discuss with a partner or in your group which words more appropriately describe the tone of the selection. Support your choices—reasons why you made the choice that you did.

accurate	factual	impartial	truthful	matter-of-fact
calm	angry	direct	dramatic	serious
informal	formal	optimistic	pessimistic	biased
neutral	objective	subjective	emotional	unbiased

D. A graphic organizer is the most effective way to show the visual connection between ideas. The best graphic organizer to use for this selection would be:

_____

_____

Why? _____

_____

E. Complete a graphic organizer, a map, or an outline of main points of selection.

IV. Critical Reading & Thinking, Part Two

Directions: Your instructor will guide you based on which of the sections below students will be working on (individually or in groups). Students are to use the back of this page (Notes Page) to list their information and ideas based on evaluation, analysis, or discussion of the chosen Issues, Readings, or Topics below. This is a teacher-guided activity.

Argument is the ability to exchange ideas, opinions, and conclusions between two or more students based on readings or writings that cover contemporary issues or author's ideas.

Issue #1: _____

Issue #2: _____

Issue #3: _____

Issue #4: _____

Inferences are educated guesses or educated possibilities based on what is already known (past information or background information). These are not assumptions, opinions, or personal points of view.

Reading #1: _____

Reading #2: _____

Reading #3: _____

Reading #4: _____

Points of View are ideas that students come to conclude (draw conclusions) based on their own personal experience or information gained from past knowledge or experiences. These ideas can be personal opinions if they have an educational foundation and are not just personal feelings or beliefs.

Topic #1: _____

Topic #2: _____

Topic #3: _____

Topic #4: _____

V. Summary Page –or– Precis Page

Summary / Precis (Circle One): This story is about _____

_____

_____

_____

_____

_____

_____

_____

_____

_____

_____

_____

_____

_____

_____

_____

_____

_____

_____

_____

_____

_____

_____

_____

_____

_____

Source Information (Citation):

Title of Selection: _____

Author: _____

Publisher: _____

Copyright Date: _____

Notes:

Native Americans Speak Out

by
Goldfield, Abbott, Anderson, et al.

Image © -AnnA-, 2012. Used under license from
Shutterstock, Inc.

MEMORIAL AND PROTESTS OF THE CHEROKEE NATION, 1836

Of the major tribes in the Southeast, the Cherokees fought longest and hardest against the Jacksonian policy of Indian removal, Led by their principal chief, John Ross, the son of a Scot and a mixed-blood Cherokee woman, they submitted the following protest to Congress against the fraudulent 1835 Treaty of New Echota forced on them by the state of Georgia. Although clearly opposed by an overwhelming majority of the Cherokees, this treaty provided the legal basis for the forced removal of the Cherokee people from Georgia to the Indian Territory.

- **On what** legal grounds did the Cherokees base their protest? What pledges had been made to them by the U.S. government?

- **What** did the Cherokees mean when they said they had been "taught to think and feel as the American citizen"? If the Cherokees had become "civilized" by white standards, why did most whites still insist on their removal?

- **Why** would President Jackson have allowed white intruders to remain on land reserved by treaties for the Cherokees?

- **Do** you feel that the Cherokees were justified in believing that they had been betrayed by the U.S. government?

The undersigned representatives of the Cherokee nation, east of the river Mississippi, impelled by duty, would respectfully submit . . . the following statement of facts: It will be seen, from the numerous treaties between the Cherokee nation and the United States, that from the earliest existence of this government, the United States, in Congress assembled, received the Cherokees and their nation into favor and protection; and that the chiefs and warriors, for themselves and all parts of the Cherokee nation, acknowledged themselves and the said Cherokee nation to be under the protection of the United States of America, and of no other sovereign whatsoever: they also stipulated, that the said Cherokee nation will not hold any treaty with any foreign power, individual State, or with individuals of any State: that for, and in consideration of, valuable concessions made by the Cherokee nation, the United States solemnly guaranteed to said nation all their lands not ceded, and pledged the faith of the government, that "all white people who have intruded, or may hereafter intrude, on the lands reserved for the Cherokees, shall be removed by the United States, and proceeded against, according to the provisions of the act, passed 30th March, 1802," entitled "An act to regulate trade and intercourse with the Indian tribes, and to preserve peace on the frontiers." It would be useless to recapitulate the numerous provisions for the security and protection of the rights of the Cherokees, to be found in the various treaties between their nation and the United States. The Cherokees were happy and prosperous under a scrupulous observance of treaty stipulations by the government of the United States, and from the fostering hand extended over them, they made rapid advances in civilization, morals, and in the arts and sciences. Little did they anticipate, that when taught to think and feel as the American citizen, and to have with him a common interest, they were to be despoiled by their guardian, to become strangers and wanderers in the land of their fathers, forced to return to the savage life, and to seek a new home in the wilds of the far west, and that without their consent. An instrument purporting to be a treaty with the Cherokee people, has recently been made public by the President of the United States, that will have such an operation, if carried into effect. This instrument, the delegation aver before the civilized world, and in the presence of Almighty God, is fraudulent, false upon its face, made by unauthorized individuals, without the sanction, and against the wishes, of the great body of the Cherokee people. Upwards of fifteen thousand of those people have protested against it, solemnly declaring they will never acquiesce.

Source: U.S. Congress, *Executive Documents* (1836)

I. Reading Comprehension Activities

My Title: _____

Main Idea Statement: This story is about _____

_____

_____

Supporting Details / Specific Info / Facts & Details (5W's + H) :

1. _____

2. _____

3. _____

4. _____

5. _____

6. _____

7. _____

8. _____

9. _____

10. _____

Inferences (Educated Guesses/Possibilities/R-B-T-L):

1. _____

2. _____

3. _____

4. _____

5. _____

6. _____

7. _____

8. _____

II. Using Vocabulary In Context

1. Write a complete sentence using 'unknown' word in context: _____

_____

_____

    A. New Word/Unknown Word: _____

    B. Dictionary Definition: _____

    _____

    C. Synonyms: i. _____

                ii. _____

2. Write a complete sentence using 'unknown' word in context: _____

_____

    A. New Word/Unknown Word: _____

    B. Dictionary Definition: _____

    _____

    C. Synonyms: i. _____

                ii. _____

3. Write a complete sentence using 'unknown' word in context: _____

_____

    A. New Word/Unknown Word: _____

    B. Dictionary Definition: _____

    _____

    C. Synonyms: i. _____

                ii. _____

4. Write a complete sentence using 'unknown' word in context: _____

_____

    A. New Word/Unknown Word: _____

    B. Dictionary Definition: _____

    _____

    C. Synonyms: i. _____

                ii. _____

III. Critical Reading & Thinking, Part One

A. The author's purpose in writing this was to _____

_____

_____

B. I know this because of the following traits included in this reading: _____

_____

C. Of the following tone words, discuss with a partner or in your group which words more appropriately describe the tone of the selection. Support your choices—reasons why you made the choice that you did.

accurate	factual	impartial	truthful	matter-of-fact
calm	angry	direct	dramatic	serious
informal	formal	optimistic	pessimistic	biased
neutral	objective	subjective	emotional	unbiased

D. A graphic organizer is the most effective way to show the visual connection between ideas. The best graphic organizer to use for this selection would be:

_____

_____

Why? _____

_____

E. Complete a graphic organizer, a map, or an outline of main points of selection.

IV. Critical Reading & Thinking, Part Two

Directions: Your instructor will guide you based on which of the sections below students will be working on (individually or in groups). Students are to use the back of this page (Notes Page) to list their information and ideas based on evaluation, analysis, or discussion of the chosen Issues, Readings, or Topics below. This is a teacher-guided activity.

Argument is the ability to exchange ideas, opinions, and conclusions between two or more students based on readings or writings that cover contemporary issues or author's ideas.

Issue #1: _____

Issue #2: _____

Issue #3: _____

Issue #4: _____

Inferences are educated guesses or educated possibilities based on what is already known (past information or background information). These are not assumptions, opinions, or personal points of view.

Reading #1: _____

Reading #2: _____

Reading #3: _____

Reading #4: _____

Points of View are ideas that students come to conclude (draw conclusions) based on their own personal experience or information gained from past knowledge or experiences. These ideas can be personal opinions if they have an educational foundation and are not just personal feelings or beliefs.

Topic #1: _____

Topic #2: _____

Topic #3: _____

Topic #4: _____

V. Summary Page –or– Precis Page

Summary / Precis (Circle One): This story is about _____

_____

_____

_____

_____

_____

_____

_____

_____

_____

_____

_____

_____

_____

_____

_____

_____

_____

_____

_____

_____

_____

_____

_____

Source Information (Citation):

Title of Selection: _____

Author: _____

Publisher: _____

Copyright Date: _____

Notes:

Section Four—Content-Area

Politics and Public Opinion

by
T. R. Dye and B. H. Sparrow

Image © Igor Petrov, 2012. Used under license from Shutterstock, Inc.

For most Americans, politics is not as interesting as football or basketball, or the sex lives of celebrities, or prime-time television entertainment. Although politicians, pollsters, and commentators frequently assume that Americans have formed opinions on major public issues, in fact, most have not given them very much thought. Nevertheless, **public opinion** commands the attention of politicians, the news media, and political scientists.

Public opinion is given a lot of attention in democracies because democratic government rests on the consent of the governed. The question of whether public opinion *should* direct government policy has confounded political philosophers for centuries. Edmund Burke, writing in 1790, argued that democratic representatives should serve the *interests* of the people, but not necessarily conform to their *will*, in deciding questions of public policy. In contrast, other political philosophers have evaluated the success of democratic institutions by whether or not they produce policies that conform to popular opinion.

Major shifts in public opinion in the United States generally translate into policy change. Both the president and Congress appear to respond over time to *general* public preferences for "more" or "less"

DYE, THOMAS R.; SPARROW, BARTHOLOMEW H., POLITICS IN AMERICA, 8th Edition, © 2009. Reprinted by permission of Pearson Education, Inc., Upper Saddle River, New Jersey.

government regulation, "more" or "less" government spending, "getting tough on crime," "reforming welfare," and so on. But public opinion is often weak, unstable, ill informed, or nonexistent on *specific* policy issues. Consequently, elected officials have greater flexibility in dealing with these issues—and, at the same time, there is an increase in the influence of lobbyists, interest groups, reporters, commentators, and others who have direct access to policy makers. Moreover, the absence of well-formed public opinion on an issue provides interest groups and the media with the opportunity to influence policy indirectly by shaping popular opinion.

I. Reading Comprehension Activities

My Title: _____

Main Idea Statement: This story is about _____

_____

_____

Supporting Details / Specific Info / Facts & Details (5W's + H) :

1. _____

2. _____

3. _____

4. _____

5. _____

6. _____

7. _____

8. _____

9. _____

10. _____

Inferences (Educated Guesses/Possibilities/R-B-T-L):

1. _____

2. _____

3. _____

4. _____

5. _____

6. _____

7. _____

8. _____

II. Using Vocabulary In Context

1. Write a complete sentence using 'unknown' word in context: _____

_____

   A. New Word/Unknown Word: _____

   B. Dictionary Definition: _____

   _____

   C. Synonyms: i. _____

             ii. _____

2. Write a complete sentence using 'unknown' word in context: _____

_____

   A. New Word/Unknown Word: _____

   B. Dictionary Definition: _____

   _____

   C. Synonyms: i. _____

             ii. _____

3. Write a complete sentence using 'unknown' word in context: _____

_____

   A. New Word/Unknown Word: _____

   B. Dictionary Definition: _____

   _____

   C. Synonyms: i. _____

             ii. _____

4. Write a complete sentence using 'unknown' word in context: _____

_____

   A. New Word/Unknown Word: _____

   B. Dictionary Definition: _____

   _____

   C. Synonyms: i. _____

             ii. _____

III. Critical Reading & Thinking, Part One

A. The author's purpose in writing this was to _____
_____
_____

B. I know this because of the following traits included in this reading: _____
_____

C. Of the following tone words, discuss with a partner or in your group which words more appropriately describe the tone of the selection. Support your choices—reasons why you made the choice that you did.

accurate	factual	impartial	truthful	matter-of-fact
calm	angry	direct	dramatic	serious
informal	formal	optimistic	pessimistic	biased
neutral	objective	subjective	emotional	unbiased

D. A graphic organizer is the most effective way to show the visual connection between ideas. The best graphic organizer to use for this selection would be:
_____
_____

Why? _____
_____

E. Complete a graphic organizer, a map, or an outline of main points of selection.

IV. Critical Reading & Thinking, Part Two

Directions: Your instructor will guide you based on which of the sections below students will be working on (individually or in groups). Students are to use the back of this page (Notes Page) to list their information and ideas based on evaluation, analysis, or discussion of the chosen Issues, Readings, or Topics below. This is a teacher-guided activity.

Argument is the ability to exchange ideas, opinions, and conclusions between two or more students based on readings or writings that cover contemporary issues or author's ideas.

Issue #1: _____

Issue #2: _____

Issue #3: _____

Issue #4: _____

Inferences are educated guesses or educated possibilities based on what is already known (past information or background information). These are not assumptions, opinions, or personal points of view.

Reading #1: _____

Reading #2: _____

Reading #3: _____

Reading #4: _____

Points of View are ideas that students come to conclude (draw conclusions) based on their own personal experience or information gained from past knowledge or experiences. These ideas can be personal opinions if they have an educational foundation and are not just personal feelings or beliefs.

Topic #1: _____

Topic #2: _____

Topic #3: _____

Topic #4: _____

V. Summary Page –or– Precis Page

Summary / Precis (Circle One): This story is about _____

_____

_____

_____

_____

_____

_____

_____

_____

_____

_____

_____

_____

_____

_____

_____

_____

_____

_____

_____

_____

_____

_____

_____

_____

_____

Source Information (Citation):

Title of Selection: _____

Author: _____

Publisher: _____

Copyright Date: _____

Notes:

Section Four—Content-Area

Can We Believe the Polls?

by
T. R. Dye and B. H. Sparrow

Image © SFerdon, 2012. Used under license from Shutterstock, Inc.

Survey research is a flourishing political enterprise. The national news media—notably CBS, NBC, ABC, FOX, and CNN television networks, the *New York Times* and the *Washington Post*, and *Time* and *Newsweek* magazines—regularly sponsor independent national surveys, especially during election campaigns. Major survey organizations—the American Institute of Public Opinion (Gallup), Louis Harris and Associates, National Opinion Research Center (NORC), the Roper Organization, National Election Studies (University of Michigan)—have been in business for a long time and have files of survey results going back many years. Political candidates also contract with private marketing and opinion research firms to conduct surveys in conjunction with their campaigns.

Public opinion surveys depend on the selection of a *random sample* of persons chosen in a way which ensures that every person in the *universe* of people about whom information is desired has an equal chance of being selected for interviewing. National samples, representative of all adults or all voters, usually include only about 1,000 persons. First, geographical areas (for example, counties or telephone area codes) that are representative of all such areas in the nation are chosen. Then residential telephone numbers are randomly selected within these areas. Once the numbers have been selected at random, the poll taker does not make substitutions but calls back several times if necessary to make contact so as not to bias the sample toward people who stay at home. An increasingly troublesome problem in survey research: nearly 15 percent of U.S. households cannot now be reached by the typical telephone survey because they have only a cell phone and no landline telephone. While there is no

DYE, THOMAS R.; SPARROW, BARTHOLOMEW H., POLITICS IN AMERICA, 8th Edition, © 2009. Reprinted by permission of Pearson Education, Inc., Upper Saddle River, New Jersey.

conclusive evidence yet that cell-only users respond differently to poll questions than landline users, survey researchers must soon address this problem.

Even when random-selection procedures are closely followed, the sample may not be truly representative of the universe. But survey researchers can estimate the *sampling error* through the mathematics of probability. The sampling error is usually expressed as a percentage range—for example, plus or minus 3 percent—above and below the sample response within which there is a 95 percent likelihood that the same response would be found if the entire universe were questioned. For example, if 65 percent of the survey respondents favor the death penalty and the sampling error is calculated at plus or minus 3 percent, then we can say there is a 95 percent probability that a survey of the whole population (the universe) would produce a response of between 62 and 68 percent in favor of the death penalty.

"Loaded" or "leading" questions are often used by unprofessional pollsters simply to produce results favorable to their side of an argument. An even worse abuse in telephone polling is the "push poll"—questions asked by political campaign workers posing as independent pollsters, deliberately worded to create an opinion—for example, "If you knew that Congressman Smith would soon be indicted for child molestation, would you vote for him?"

Professional pollsters strive for questions that are clear and precise, easily understood by the respondents, and as neutral and unbiased as possible. Nevertheless, because all questions have a potential bias, it is often better to examine *changes over time* in response to identically worded questions. Perhaps the best-known continuing question in public opinion polling is the presidential approval rating: "Do you approve or disapprove of the way _____ is handling his job as president?" Changes over time in public response to this question alert scholars, commentators, and presidents themselves to their public standing (see Chapter 11).

A survey can only measure opinions *at the time* it is taken. A few days later public opinion may change, especially if major events that receive heavy television coverage intervene. Some political pollsters conduct continuous "tracking" surveys until election night in order to catch last-minute opinion changes.

An altogether different type of poll is the *exit poll*, during which election day voters are personally interviewed as they leave the voting booth. Exit polls are used by the media to "call" winners early on election night even before all votes are counted. Television networks now jointly contract with an independent company, VNS, to select voting precincts at random, interview voters, and fast-forward the results to the networks. The networks analyze the results and make their own "calls" in response to criticism that early calls reduce voter turnout, the networks have agreed not to call a state result until the polls close in that state.

I. Reading Comprehension Activities

My Title: _____

Main Idea Statement: This story is about _____

_____

_____

Supporting Details / Specific Info / Facts & Details (5W's + H) :

1. _____

2. _____

3. _____

4. _____

5. _____

6. _____

7. _____

8. _____

9. _____

10. _____

Inferences (Educated Guesses/Possibilities/R-B-T-L):

1. _____

2. _____

3. _____

4. _____

5. _____

6. _____

7. _____

8. _____

II. Using Vocabulary In Context

1. Write a complete sentence using 'unknown' word in context: _____

_____

_____

    A. New Word/Unknown Word: _____

    B. Dictionary Definition: _____

                               _____

    C. Synonyms: i. _____

                 ii. _____

2. Write a complete sentence using 'unknown' word in context: _____

_____

    A. New Word/Unknown Word: _____

    B. Dictionary Definition: _____

                               _____

    C. Synonyms: i. _____

                 ii. _____

3. Write a complete sentence using 'unknown' word in context: _____

_____

    A. New Word/Unknown Word: _____

    B. Dictionary Definition: _____

                               _____

    C. Synonyms: i. _____

                 ii. _____

4. Write a complete sentence using 'unknown' word in context: _____

_____

    A. New Word/Unknown Word: _____

    B. Dictionary Definition: _____

                               _____

    C. Synonyms: i. _____

                 ii. _____

III. Critical Reading & Thinking, Part One

A. The author's purpose in writing this was to _____

_____

_____

B. I know this because of the following traits included in this reading: _____

_____

C. Of the following tone words, discuss with a partner or in your group which words more appropriately describe the tone of the selection. Support your choices—reasons why you made the choice that you did.

accurate	factual	impartial	truthful	matter-of-fact
calm	angry	direct	dramatic	serious
informal	formal	optimistic	pessimistic	biased
neutral	objective	subjective	emotional	unbiased

D. A graphic organizer is the most effective way to show the visual connection between ideas. The best graphic organizer to use for this selection would be:

_____

_____

Why? _____

_____

E. Complete a graphic organizer, a map, or an outline of main points of selection.

IV. Critical Reading & Thinking, Part Two

Directions: Your instructor will guide you based on which of the sections below students will be working on (individually or in groups). Students are to use the back of this page (Notes Page) to list their information and ideas based on evaluation, analysis, or discussion of the chosen Issues, Readings, or Topics below. This is a teacher-guided activity.

Argument is the ability to exchange ideas, opinions, and conclusions between two or more students based on readings or writings that cover contemporary issues or author's ideas.

Issue #1: _____

Issue #2: _____

Issue #3: _____

Issue #4: _____

Inferences are educated guesses or educated possibilities based on what is already known (past information or background information). These are not assumptions, opinions, or personal points of view.

Reading #1: _____

Reading #2: _____

Reading #3: _____

Reading #4: _____

Points of View are ideas that students come to conclude (draw conclusions) based on their own personal experience or information gained from past knowledge or experiences. These ideas can be personal opinions if they have an educational foundation and are not just personal feelings or beliefs.

Topic #1: _____

Topic #2: _____

Topic #3: _____

Topic #4: _____

V. Summary Page –or– Precis Page

Summary / Precis (Circle One): This story is about _____

_____

_____

_____

_____

_____

_____

_____

_____

_____

_____

_____

_____

_____

_____

_____

_____

_____

_____

_____

_____

_____

_____

_____

_____

_____

_____

Source Information (Citation):

Title of Selection: _____

Author: _____

Publisher: _____

Copyright Date: _____

Notes:

Are We One Nation "Under God"?

by
T. R. Dye and B. H. Sparrow

Image © Edwin Verin, 2012. Used under license from Shutterstock, Inc.

For over 100 years the Pledge of Allegiance has been recited in public school rooms at the beginning of each day. In 1954, at the height of the Cold War, Congress added the words "under God" after "one nation," to emphasize that the United States acknowledged spiritual values in contrast to "godless communism." President Dwight D. Eisenhower, upon signing the bill, said it would strengthen "those spiritual weapons which forever will be our country's most powerful resource in peace and war."

As early as 1943, the Supreme Court declared that public school pupils could not be *required* to recite the pledge. The opinion was widely praised as an expression of our constitutional freedoms: "If there is any fixed star in our constitutional constellation, it is that no official, high or petty, can prescribe what shall be orthodox in politics, nationalism, religion, or other matters of opinion, or force citizens to confess by word or act their faith therein."[1] Pupils who did not wish to take the pledge were free to stand silent in the classroom while the pledge was being recited.

The Supreme Court was called upon to review the phrase "under God" in 2002 when the father of a public school pupil argued that these words constituted an establishment of religion by an instrument of the government, namely the schools, whether or not his daughter was required to participate in the ceremony. He argued that the pledge with "under God" constituted "a ritual proclaiming that there is a

---

[1] *West Virginia Board of Education v. Barnette*, 319 U.S. 624 (1943).

God" and therefore violated the Establishment Clause of the 1st Amendment. The Words "under God" asserted monotheism and possibly offended atheists, the nonreligious, and others who did not wish to swear an oath of allegiance to a monotheistic deity.

The U.S. Court of Appeals for the Ninth Circuit (with jurisdiction for California and other West Coast states and arguably the most liberal Circuit Court in the nation) agreed that the words "under God" were not neutral and represented a swearing of allegiance to monotheism. The effect of this appeals court's opinion was to remove the words "under God" from the Pledge. However, subsequently it was revealed that the father (who was divorced) did not have custody over his daughter, and that the custodial mother did not wish her daughter to bring suit over this issue. The Surpreme Court, therefore, dismissed the case on this technicality and avoided the substantive issue of whether or not the words "under God" in the Pledge of Allegiance violated the Establishment Clause.[2] The effect of the Supreme Court's decision was to retain the words.

It can be argued that these words do not refer to any specific religion or deity but simply acknowledge the nation's religious heritage. References to God have long been part of our national identity. Our coins invoke the blessing "In God We Trust," chaplains are provided for the Armed Forces, prayers open the sessions of both chambers of Congress as well as the Supreme Court itself. A strong majority (84 percent) of Americans support the inclusion of the words "under God" in the Pledge of Allegiance.

---

[2] *Elk Grove United School District v. Newdow*, 542 U.S. 277 (2004).

I. Reading Comprehension Activities

My Title: _____

Main Idea Statement: This story is about _____

_____

_____

Supporting Details / Specific Info / Facts & Details (5W's + H) :

1. _____

2. _____

3. _____

4. _____

5. _____

6. _____

7. _____

8. _____

9. _____

10. _____

Inferences (Educated Guesses/Possibilities/R-B-T-L):

1. _____

2. _____

3. _____

4. _____

5. _____

6. _____

7. _____

8. _____

II. Using Vocabulary In Context

1. Write a complete sentence using 'unknown' word in context: _____

_____

_____

    A. New Word/Unknown Word: _____

    B. Dictionary Definition: _____

_____

    C. Synonyms: i. _____

              ii. _____

2. Write a complete sentence using 'unknown' word in context: _____

_____

    A. New Word/Unknown Word: _____

    B. Dictionary Definition: _____

_____

    C. Synonyms: i. _____

              ii. _____

3. Write a complete sentence using 'unknown' word in context: _____

_____

    A. New Word/Unknown Word: _____

    B. Dictionary Definition: _____

_____

    C. Synonyms: i. _____

              ii. _____

4. Write a complete sentence using 'unknown' word in context: _____

_____

    A. New Word/Unknown Word: _____

    B. Dictionary Definition: _____

_____

    C. Synonyms: i. _____

              ii. _____

III. Critical Reading & Thinking, Part One

A. The author's purpose in writing this was to _____

_____

_____

B. I know this because of the following traits included in this reading: _____

_____

C. Of the following tone words, discuss with a partner or in your group which words more appropriately describe the tone of the selection. Support your choices—reasons why you made the choice that you did.

accurate	factual	impartial	truthful	matter-of-fact
calm	angry	direct	dramatic	serious
informal	formal	optimistic	pessimistic	biased
neutral	objective	subjective	emotional	unbiased

D. A graphic organizer is the most effective way to show the visual connection between ideas. The best graphic organizer to use for this selection would be:

_____

_____

Why? _____

_____

E. Complete a graphic organizer, a map, or an outline of main points of selection.

IV. Critical Reading & Thinking, Part Two

Directions: Your instructor will guide you based on which of the sections below students will be working on (individually or in groups). Students are to use the back of this page (Notes Page) to list their information and ideas based on evaluation, analysis, or discussion of the chosen Issues, Readings, or Topics below. This is a teacher-guided activity.

Argument is the ability to exchange ideas, opinions, and conclusions between two or more students based on readings or writings that cover contemporary issues or author's ideas.

Issue #1: _____

Issue #2: _____

Issue #3: _____

Issue #4: _____

Inferences are educated guesses or educated possibilities based on what is already known (past information or background information). These are not assumptions, opinions, or personal points of view.

Reading #1: _____

Reading #2: _____

Reading #3: _____

Reading #4: _____

Points of View are ideas that students come to conclude (draw conclusions) based on their own personal experience or information gained from past knowledge or experiences. These ideas can be personal opinions if they have an educational foundation and are not just personal feelings or beliefs.

Topic #1: _____

Topic #2: _____

Topic #3: _____

Topic #4: _____

V. Summary Page –or– Precis Page

Summary / Precis (Circle One): This story is about _____

_____

_____

_____

_____

_____

_____

_____

_____

_____

_____

_____

_____

_____

_____

_____

_____

_____

_____

_____

_____

_____

_____

<u>Source Information (Citation):</u>

Title of Selection: _____

Author: _____

Publisher: _____

Copyright Date: _____

Notes:

Is Welfare Reform Working?

by
T. R. Dye and B. H. Sparrow

Image © SunnyS, 2012. Used under license from Shutterstock, Inc.

Welfare reform, officially Temporary Assistance to Needy Families, was passed by Congress in 1996; its provisions took effect in 1997. By early 1998 the Clinton administration, as well as Republican congressional sponsors of welfare reform, was declaring it a success.

The number of cash welfare recipients in the nation has dropped below 5 million—the lowest number in more than 25 years. Only about 2 percent of Americans are now on cash welfare—the smallest proportion since 1970. No doubt some of this decline is attributable to growth of the economy: declines in welfare rolls began *before* Congress passed its welfare reform law, and some decline may have occurred without reform. Many states had initiated their own reforms under "waivers" from the federal government even before Congress acted.

All states have now developed work programs for welfare recipients. Applicants for welfare benefits are now generally required to enter job-search programs, to undertake job training, and to accept jobs or community service positions.

Yet, although nearly everyone agrees that getting people off welfare rolls and onto payrolls is the main goal of reform, there are major obstacles to the achievement of this goal. First of all, a substantial portion (perhaps 25 to 40 percent) of long-term welfare recipients have handicaps—physical disabilities, chronic illnesses, learning disabilities, alcohol or drug abuse problems—that prevent them from holding a full-time job. Many long-term recipients have no work experience (perhaps 40 percent), and two-thirds of them did not graduate from high school. Almost half have three or more children, making day-care arrangements a major obstacle. It is unlikely that any counseling, education, job training, or job placement programs could ever succeed in getting these people into productive employment.

Early studies of people who left the welfare rolls following welfare reform suggest that over half and perhaps as many as three-quarters have found work, although most at minimum or near-minimum wages.

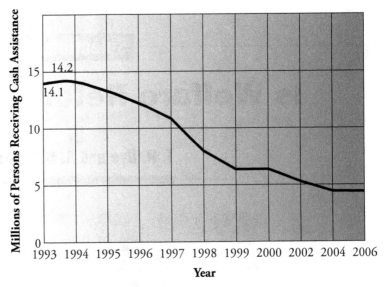

Source: Department of Health and Human Services, 2006.

I. Reading Comprehension Activities

My Title: _____

Main Idea Statement: This story is about _____

_____

_____

Supporting Details / Specific Info / Facts & Details (5W's + H) :

1. _____

2. _____

3. _____

4. _____

5. _____

6. _____

7. _____

8. _____

9. _____

10. _____

Inferences (Educated Guesses/Possibilities/R-B-T-L):

1. _____

2. _____

3. _____

4. _____

5. _____

6. _____

7. _____

8. _____

Selection 34:   Is Welfare Reform Working?

II. Using Vocabulary In Context

1. Write a complete sentence using 'unknown' word in context: _____

_____

_____

    A. New Word/Unknown Word: _____

    B. Dictionary Definition: _____

    _____

    C. Synonyms: i. _____

                 ii. _____

2. Write a complete sentence using 'unknown' word in context: _____

_____

    A. New Word/Unknown Word: _____

    B. Dictionary Definition: _____

    _____

    C. Synonyms: i. _____

                 ii. _____

3. Write a complete sentence using 'unknown' word in context: _____

_____

    A. New Word/Unknown Word: _____

    B. Dictionary Definition: _____

    _____

    C. Synonyms: i. _____

                 ii. _____

4. Write a complete sentence using 'unknown' word in context: _____

_____

    A. New Word/Unknown Word: _____

    B. Dictionary Definition: _____

    _____

    C. Synonyms: i. _____

                 ii. _____

III. Critical Reading & Thinking, Part One

A. The author's purpose in writing this was to _____

_____

_____

B. I know this because of the following traits included in this reading: _____

_____

C. Of the following tone words, discuss with a partner or in your group which words more appropriately describe the tone of the selection. Support your choices—reasons why you made the choice that you did.

accurate	factual	impartial	truthful	matter-of-fact
calm	angry	direct	dramatic	serious
informal	formal	optimistic	pessimistic	biased
neutral	objective	subjective	emotional	unbiased

D. A graphic organizer is the most effective way to show the visual connection between ideas. The best graphic organizer to use for this selection would be:

_____

_____

Why? _____

_____

E. Complete a graphic organizer, a map, or an outline of main points of selection.

IV. Critical Reading & Thinking, Part Two

Directions: Your instructor will guide you based on which of the sections below students will be working on (individually or in groups). Students are to use the back of this page (Notes Page) to list their information and ideas based on evaluation, analysis, or discussion of the chosen Issues, Readings, or Topics below. This is a teacher-guided activity.

Argument is the ability to exchange ideas, opinions, and conclusions between two or more students based on readings or writings that cover contemporary issues or author's ideas.

Issue #1: _____

Issue #2: _____

Issue #3: _____

Issue #4: _____

Inferences are educated guesses or educated possibilities based on what is already known (past information or background information). These are not assumptions, opinions, or personal points of view.

Reading #1: _____

Reading #2: _____

Reading #3: _____

Reading #4: _____

Points of View are ideas that students come to conclude (draw conclusions) based on their own personal experience or information gained from past knowledge or experiences. These ideas can be personal opinions if they have an educational foundation and are not just personal feelings or beliefs.

Topic #1: _____

Topic #2: _____

Topic #3: _____

Topic #4: _____

V. Summary Page –or– Precis Page

Summary / Precis (Circle One): This story is about _____

_____

_____

_____

_____

_____

_____

_____

_____

_____

_____

_____

_____

_____

_____

_____

_____

_____

_____

_____

_____

_____

_____

_____

_____

Source Information (Citation):

Title of Selection: _____

Author: _____

Publisher: _____

Copyright Date: _____

Notes:

The Supremacy Clause at Work: Marijuana for Medical Use

by
T. R. Dye and B. H. Sparrow

Image © Gary Blakeley, 2012. Used under license from Shutterstock, Inc.

THE SUPREMACY CLAUSE AT WORK: MARIJUANA FOR MEDICAL USE?

Currently, marijuana prohibition applies to everyone across the nation, including the sick and dying. But many doctors, patients, and organizations contend that marijuana, medically known as cannabis, is valuable in the treatment of glaucoma, HIV-AIDS, nausea, and pain relief, especially in cancer patients. As of 2008, twelve states—Alaska, California, Colorado, Hawaii, Maine, Maryland, Montana, Nevada, New Mexico, Oregon, Rhode Island, Vermont, and Washington—have enacted medical marijuana laws reversing state-level penalties for possession and cultivation when patients possess written documentation from physicians stating that they benefit from its medical use. Wherever the issue has appeared on state referenda, it has passed by large margins. National polls regularly report

DYE, THOMAS R.; SPARROW, BARTHOLOMEW H., POLITICS IN AMERICA, 8th Edition, © *2009.* Reprinted by permission of Pearson Education, Inc., Upper Saddle River, New Jersey.

that 75 percent of the American public support making marijuana legally available to seriously ill patients.

Congress, however, has never exempted the medical use of marijuana from its Controlled Substance Act, which makes it a federal crime "to manufacture, distribute, or dispense, or possess . . . a controlled substance." Various petitions to the federal Drug Enforcement Agency to declassify marijuana as a controlled substance and allow physicians to legally prescribe its use have been rejected.

Clearly, federal law is in direct conflict with the laws of many states on this issue. But the Supremacy Clause of the Constitution clearly requires that federal law prevail over state law in cases of conflict.

The issue reached the U.S. Supreme Court in 2001. The Court recognized that whether or not the activities of individuals or organizations regarding marijuana were legal under California law, they nonetheless violated federal law, notably the Controlled Substance Act. The Court further held that "medical necessity" does not allow anyone to violate the Controlled Substance Act; Congress made no exemption in this act for medical necessity. The Supreme Court recognized that the states have concurrent powers with the federal government in regulating drugs and medications. However, "Under the Supremacy Clause, any state law, however clearly within a state's acknowledged power, which interferes with or is contrary to federal laws must yield."[1]

Politically, the federal Drug Enforcement Agency realizes that prosecuting seriously ill patients or their doctors for using marijuana medically is very unpopular. Many individuals, especially in those states that have tried to legalize the medical use of marijuana, have continued to use the drug, knowing that they are violating federal law.

---

[1] *United States v. Oakland Cannabis Buyers Cooperatives* 523 U.S. 483 (2001).

I. Reading Comprehension Activities

My Title: _____

Main Idea Statement: This story is about _____

_____

_____

Supporting Details / Specific Info / Facts & Details (5W's + H) :

1. _____

2. _____

3. _____

4. _____

5. _____

6. _____

7. _____

8. _____

9. _____

10. _____

Inferences (Educated Guesses/Possibilities/R-B-T-L):

1. _____

2. _____

3. _____

4. _____

5. _____

6. _____

7. _____

8. _____

II. Using Vocabulary In Context

1. Write a complete sentence using 'unknown' word in context: _____

_____

_____

   A. New Word/Unknown Word: _____

   B. Dictionary Definition: _____

                   _____

   C. Synonyms: i. _____

                 ii. _____

2. Write a complete sentence using 'unknown' word in context: _____

_____

   A. New Word/Unknown Word: _____

   B. Dictionary Definition: _____

                   _____

   C. Synonyms: i. _____

                 ii. _____

3. Write a complete sentence using 'unknown' word in context: _____

_____

   A. New Word/Unknown Word: _____

   B. Dictionary Definition: _____

                   _____

   C. Synonyms: i. _____

                 ii. _____

4. Write a complete sentence using 'unknown' word in context: _____

_____

   A. New Word/Unknown Word: _____

   B. Dictionary Definition: _____

                   _____

   C. Synonyms: i. _____

                 ii. _____

               Section Four—Content-Area

III. Critical Reading & Thinking, Part One

A. The author's purpose in writing this was to _____

_____

_____

B. I know this because of the following traits included in this reading: _____

_____

C. Of the following tone words, discuss with a partner or in your group which words more appropriately describe the tone of the selection. Support your choices—reasons why you made the choice that you did.

accurate	factual	impartial	truthful	matter-of-fact
calm	angry	direct	dramatic	serious
informal	formal	optimistic	pessimistic	biased
neutral	objective	subjective	emotional	unbiased

D. A graphic organizer is the most effective way to show the visual connection between ideas. The best graphic organizer to use for this selection would be:

_____

_____

Why? _____

_____

E. Complete a graphic organizer, a map, or an outline of main points of selection.

IV. Critical Reading & Thinking, Part Two

Directions: Your instructor will guide you based on which of the sections below students will be working on (individually or in groups). Students are to use the back of this page (Notes Page) to list their information and ideas based on evaluation, analysis, or discussion of the chosen Issues, Readings, or Topics below. This is a teacher-guided activity.

Argument is the ability to exchange ideas, opinions, and conclusions between two or more students based on readings or writings that cover contemporary issues or author's ideas.

Issue #1: _____

Issue #2: _____

Issue #3: _____

Issue #4: _____

Inferences are educated guesses or educated possibilities based on what is already known (past information or background information). These are not assumptions, opinions, or personal points of view.

Reading #1: _____

Reading #2: _____

Reading #3: _____

Reading #4: _____

Points of View are ideas that students come to conclude (draw conclusions) based on their own personal experience or information gained from past knowledge or experiences. These ideas can be personal opinions if they have an educational foundation and are not just personal feelings or beliefs.

Topic #1: _____

Topic #2: _____

Topic #3: _____

Topic #4: _____

V. Summary Page –or– Precis Page

Summary / Precis (Circle One): This story is about _____

_____

_____

_____

_____

_____

_____

_____

_____

_____

_____

_____

_____

_____

_____

_____

_____

_____

_____

_____

_____

_____

_____

_____

_____

_____

<u>Source Information (Citation):</u>

Title of Selection: _____

Author: _____

Publisher: _____

Copyright Date: _____

Notes:

Section Four—Content-Area

Washington Bails Out Wall Street

by
T. R. Dye and B. H. Sparrow

Image © sgame, 2012. Used under license from Shutterstock, Inc.

For years Americans lived on easy credit. Families ran up credit card debt and borrowed heavily for cars, tuition, and especially home buying. Mortgage lenders approved loans for borrowers without fully examining their ability to pay. Federally chartered corporations, Fannie Mae and Freddie Mac, encouraged mortgage loans to low-income home buyers. Some mortgages were "predatory" with initial low payments followed by steep upwardly adjustable rates. To make matters worse, banks and financial institutions bundled mortgages together and sold these mortgage-backed securities as "derivatives." Banks, insurers, and lenders all assumed that housing prices would inevitably rise. Housing construction boomed.

Eventually the bubble burst. Housing prices fell dramatically. The number of houses for sale greatly exceeded the number of people willing to buy them. Homeowners found themselves holding "upside down" mortgages—mortgages that exceeded the value of their homes. Many were unable or unwilling to meet their mortgage payments. Foreclosures and delinquencies spiraled upward. Investors who held mortgage-backed securities began to incur heavy losses. Investment banks, such as Bear Stearns, and mortgage insurers, including Fannie Mae and Freddie Mac, found themselves in serious financial trouble. Bankruptcies and federal bailouts multiplied. The stock market plummeted.

President Bush sent Secretary of the Treasury Henry Paulson, Federal Reserve Chairman Ben Bernanke, and the Securities and Exchange Commission Chairman Chris Cox, to Congress to

DYE, THOMAS R.; SPARROW, BARTHOLOMEW H., POLITICS IN AMERICA, 8th Edition, © *2009.* Reprinted by permission of Pearson Education, Inc., Upper Saddle River, New Jersey.

plead for a massive $700 billion bailout of banks, insurance companies, and investment firms that held mortgage-backed "illiquid assets." They argued that their proposal was absolutely essential to safeguard the financial security of the nation. Steep recession, if not a full-blown depression, would result if the federal government failed to purchase these troubled assets.

Congress responded with their own ideas: no Wall Street CEOs should benefit from government rescue (no "golden parachutes"); congressional oversight of the bailout; taxpayers must share in any recovery that might eventually occur; and the money must be made available in staggered amounts.

The nation's top leadership—President Bush, the Treasury Secretary, the Fed Chairman, House and Senate Democratic and Republican leaders, and even the presidential candidates—all supported the bill as amended. But polls show that most Americans oppose a "Wall Street bailout." Congress members were being asked by their leaders to ignore the folks back home. The initial House vote stunned Washington and Wall Street: "nay" votes prevailed. The stock market plunged alarmingly.

Predictions of economic catastrophe inspired a renewed effort to pass the bill. The Senate responded by passing it with a comfortable margin, while adding various sweeteners, mostly tax benefits to gain House support. Tensions ware high when the House voted on the Senate version of the bill. In a sharp reversal of its earlier action, the House approved the Emergency Economic Stabilization Act of 2008. President Bush promptly signed it: "By coming together on this legislation, we have acted boldly to help prevent the crisis on Wall Street from becoming a crisis in communities across the country."

I. Reading Comprehension Activities

My Title: _____

Main Idea Statement: This story is about _____

_____

_____

Supporting Details / Specific Info / Facts & Details (5W's + H) :

1. _____

2. _____

3. _____

4. _____

5. _____

6. _____

7. _____

8. _____

9. _____

10. _____

Inferences (Educated Guesses/Possibilities/R-B-T-L):

1. _____

2. _____

3. _____

4. _____

5. _____

6. _____

7. _____

8. _____

II. Using Vocabulary In Context

1. Write a complete sentence using 'unknown' word in context: _____

_____

_____

    A. New Word/Unknown Word: _____

    B. Dictionary Definition: _____

    _____

    C. Synonyms: i. _____

              ii. _____

2. Write a complete sentence using 'unknown' word in context: _____

_____

    A. New Word/Unknown Word: _____

    B. Dictionary Definition: _____

    _____

    C. Synonyms: i. _____

              ii. _____

3. Write a complete sentence using 'unknown' word in context: _____

_____

    A. New Word/Unknown Word: _____

    B. Dictionary Definition: _____

    _____

    C. Synonyms: i. _____

              ii. _____

4. Write a complete sentence using 'unknown' word in context: _____

_____

    A. New Word/Unknown Word: _____

    B. Dictionary Definition: _____

    _____

    C. Synonyms: i. _____

              ii. _____

                                         Section Four—Content-Area

III. Critical Reading & Thinking, Part One

A. The author's purpose in writing this was to _____

_____

_____

B. I know this because of the following traits included in this reading: _____

_____

C. Of the following tone words, discuss with a partner or in your group which words more appropriately describe the tone of the selection. Support your choices—reasons why you made the choice that you did.

accurate	factual	impartial	truthful	matter-of-fact
calm	angry	direct	dramatic	serious
informal	formal	optimistic	pessimistic	biased
neutral	objective	subjective	emotional	unbiased

D. A graphic organizer is the most effective way to show the visual connection between ideas. The best graphic organizer to use for this selection would be:

_____

_____

Why? _____

_____

E. Complete a graphic organizer, a map, or an outline of main points of selection.

IV. Critical Reading & Thinking, Part Two

Directions: Your instructor will guide you based on which of the sections below students will be working on (individually or in groups). Students are to use the back of this page (Notes Page) to list their information and ideas based on evaluation, analysis, or discussion of the chosen Issues, Readings, or Topics below. This is a teacher-guided activity.

Argument is the ability to exchange ideas, opinions, and conclusions between two or more students based on readings or writings that cover contemporary issues or author's ideas.

Issue #1: _____

Issue #2: _____

Issue #3: _____

Issue #4: _____

Inferences are educated guesses or educated possibilities based on what is already known (past information or background information). These are not assumptions, opinions, or personal points of view.

Reading #1: _____

Reading #2: _____

Reading #3: _____

Reading #4: _____

Points of View are ideas that students come to conclude (draw conclusions) based on their own personal experience or information gained from past knowledge or experiences. These ideas can be personal opinions if they have an educational foundation and are not just personal feelings or beliefs.

Topic #1: _____

Topic #2: _____

Topic #3: _____

Topic #4: _____

V. Summary Page –or– Precis Page

Summary / Precis (Circle One): This story is about _____

_____

_____

_____

_____

_____

_____

_____

_____

_____

_____

_____

_____

_____

_____

_____

_____

_____

_____

_____

_____

_____

_____

_____

_____

Source Information (Citation):

Title of Selection: _____

Author: _____

Publisher: _____

Copyright Date: _____

Notes:

Section Five

Teaching Guides

I. Motivation for Reading & Student Responsibility

Prof. John A. Garcia, Ed.R.S., ABD [Harvard Reading Specialist]

I—Do you have a personal philosophy or rule that you follow?

Garcia's Academic Philosophies:

A—Success consists of getting up one more time than you fall!

B—Obstacles are what we see when we take our eyes off our goals!

C—Dreams are nothing more than goals waiting to be fulfilled!

D—You never miss your water until the well runs dry!

E—Success is much better without stress!

F—Success doesn't matter if you don't enjoy yourself!

G—Diamonds: Jagged pieces of coal put under extreme pressure!

II—Create your own personal philosophy to follow or borrow one from the above list.

III—Students' Responsibilities:

A—No cell phone, food, or distractions in class!

B—Pay attention; be focused; listen to your 'little' voice!

C—RESPECT, RESPECT, RESPECT—No back talk and no attitude!

D—Make a connection with professors—'Letters of Recommendation' later on.

E—Study Schedule—you can have more FUN even with study time!

IV—THE MYTH: You're going to community college? Why?

Friends tease or tell you that a 'university' is better. Not!

Don't believe everything your friends tell you—Jealousy!!

SOURCE: *SuperStudy III: A Reading & Learning Strategies Workbook for College Success*; Prof. John A. Garcia, Ed.R.S., ABD [Harvard Reading Specialist], 2010.

II. TIME MANAGEMENT / STUDY SCHEDULE

STUDENT: _____

SEMESTER: _____

[FORMULA: _____ CREDITS x 2 hrs. Study/hr. + 4 additional STUDY = _____ TOTAL STUDY Hours/Week]

	MONDAY	TUESDAY	WEDNESDAY	THURSDAY	FRIDAY	SATURDAY	SUNDAY
5–6 a.m.							
6–7 a.m.							
7–8 a.m.							
8–9 a.m.							
9–10 a.m.							
10–11 a.m.							
11–12 p.m.							
12–1 p.m.							
1–2 p.m.							
2–3 p.m.							
3–4 p.m.							
4–5 p.m.							
5–6 p.m.							
6–7 p.m.							
7–8 p.m.							
8–9 p.m.							
9–10 p.m.							
10–11 p.m.							
11–12 a.m.							
12–1 a.m.							
1–2 a.m.							
2–3 a.m.							
3–4 a.m.							
4–5 a.m.							

SOURCE: *SuperStudy III: A Reading & Learning Strategies Workbook for College Success*; Prof. John A. Garcia, Ed.R.S., ABD [Harvard Reading Specialist], 2010.

III. VOCABULARY ENRICHMENT

Prof. John A. Garcia, Ed.R.S., ABD [Harvard Reading Specialist]

[NOTE: WRITTEN PERMISSION TO COPY MUST BE GRANTED BY AUTHOR FOR FACULTY OR STUDENT USE]

P N E U M O N O U L T R A M I C R O S C O P I C S I L I C O V O L C A N O C O N I O S I S

or

Pneumono / ultra-microscopic / silico / volcano / coniosis

'Longest Word' Separated Into "Working" Syllables (Working Chunks):

Pneumo or pneumono	=	having to do with the lungs
Ultra	=	beyond the range or limits, more than
Microscopic	=	very small, minute, fine
Ultra-microscopic	=	miniscule, particle-like, dust-like
Silico	=	compounds in oils, plastics (silicone)
Volcano	=	burnt material resulting in smoke or ash
Coniosis	=	disease or extreme illness

'8' PRACTICAL STEPS TOWARDS WORD MASTERY

In your 'new' repertoire of improving, enhancing, enriching, and adding these 'new' words, let me give you 8 techniques that can easily and readily be applied to all college-level reading material to figure out the meanings of "unknown or unfamiliar" words. By mastering these techniques, you can rapidly increase your chances of success in college without the added stress! The reading vocabulary-strengthening techniques are as follows:

1—Using 'Known' Prefixes, Roots, and Suffixes [Beginning/Middle/Ending]

2—Using Proper Pronunciation and a "Working" Syllabication,

3—Figuring out the Parts of Speech,

4—Applying Contextual Analysis [Four Types of Context],

5—Using Correct Spelling in Your Writing,

6—Asking Your Instructor To Use 'Unknown' Word In A Sentence,

7—Using the Dictionary or Thesaurus (Only As A Last Resort)

8—Incorporating 'New' Vocabulary Into Your Written & Spoken Language.

SOURCE: *SuperStudy III: A Reading & Learning Strategies Workbook for College Success*; Prof. John A. Garcia, Ed.R.S., ABD [Harvard Reading Specialist], 2010.

IV. READING COMPREHENSION SYSTEMS

Prof. John A. Garcia, Ed.R.S., ABD [Harvard Reading Specialist]

[NOTE: WRITTEN PERMISSION TO COPY ANY SYSTEMS MUST BE GRANTED BY AUTHOR(s)
FOR FACULTY OR STUDENT USE.]

There are a variety of reading and/or note-taking systems that a student can use to build reading comprehension and taking effective lecture notes in a college or university classroom. Below are four systems students can choose from, depending on the type of course information that he/she is presented in a lecture. Each one has its advantages. Each student must figure out which system will be the most beneficial in analyzing and retaining information, when reading and studying for college/ university exams. These Reading Comprehension Systems and effective Note-taking Systems are as follows:

I—'MIFIV' Reading Comprehension System #1 (J. A. Garcia, Ed.R.S., ABD): This system involves listing all information that is considered important or valuable during the lecture. The areas are divided into columns listed as follows—MAIN IDEA (Title) plus a MAIN IDEA STATEMENT (sentence that gives the overall general view of notes). *Column #1*: "FACTS & DETAILS" (Facts = Important points; Details = Explanation of the points; Points are easy to find—use the "5w's + H" of Supporting Points involve figuring out what information to list in notes. The "5W's + H" are the WHO, WHAT, WHEN, WHERE, WHY, and HOW of notes. Pick one (WHO) and use the others to explain that person. *Column #2*: "INFERENCES" which are 'educated guesses' or possibilities of the situations listed in notes (what do you think happened or why—this is similar to 'point of view'). *Column #3:* "Unknown Vocabulary" and a synonym or synonym phrase to help with the meaning of words—increases college vocabulary. For further information: HarvardAlum83@aol.com

II—'ATP' Reading Comprehension System #2 (J. A. Garcia, Ed.R.S., ABD): This is a system that will assist students in raising their reading comprehension levels. It also serves as an effective Note-taking System for college lectures. This is SUPER STUDY SYSTEM #2 taken from J. Garcia's 'SUPER STUDY III' textbook. For further information: HarvardAlum83@aol.com

III—'SUMMARY SHEET' Reading Comprehension System #3 (J. A. Garcia, Ed.R.S., ABD): This is a system that will assist students in raising their reading comprehension levels. It also serves as an effective Note-taking System for college lectures. This is SUPER STUDY SYSTEM #3 taken from J. Garcia's 'SUPER STUDY' series. For further information: HarvardAlum83@aol.com

SOURCE: *SuperStudy III: A Reading & Learning Strategies Workbook for College Success*; Prof. John A. Garcia, Ed.R.S., ABD [Harvard Reading Specialist], 2010.

'MIFIV' READING COMPREHENSION SYSTEM #1

Prof. John A. Garcia, Ed.R.S. ABD [Harvard Reading Specialist]

Main Idea
(Title of Story): _____

My Own Title: _____

Main Idea Statement: This story is about _____

_____

_____ .

FACTS & DETAILS	+	INFERENCES
1. _____	A.	_____
_____		_____
2. _____	B.	_____
_____		_____
3. _____	C.	_____
_____		_____
4. _____	D.	_____
_____		_____
5. _____	E.	_____
_____		_____

PLUS

VOCABULARY

Unknown Word		Synonym or Synonym Phrase
1. _____	/	_____
2. _____	/	_____
3. _____	/	_____
4. _____	/	_____
5. _____	/	_____

SOURCE: *SuperStudy III: A Reading & Learning Strategies Workbook for College Success*; Prof. John A. Garcia, Ed.R.S., ABD [Harvard Reading Specialist], 2010.

'ATP' READING COMPREHENSION SYSTEM #2

[Analytical Thought Process]

Prof. John A. Garcia, Ed.R.S., ABD [Harvard Reading Specialist]

I—Important Point (FACT—use '5W's + H' process):
- A. Supporting Detail (Explanation of Point)
- B. Supporting Detail
- C. Supporting Detail
- D. Supporting Detail

Inferences/Point of View:
- 1. Educated Guess (Possibility according to 'Fact')
- 2. Educated Guess

II—Important Point (FACT)
- A. Supporting Detail
- B. Supporting Detail
- C. Supporting Detail
- D. Supporting Detail

Inferences/Point of View:
- 1. Educated Guess
- 2. Educated Guess

III—Important Point (FACT)
- A. Supporting Detail
- B. Supporting Detail
- C. Supporting Detail
- D. Supporting Detail

Inferences/Point of View:
- 1. Educated Guess
- 2. Educated Guess

IV—Important Point (FACT)
- A. Supporting Detail
- B. Supporting Detail
- C. Supporting Detail
- D. Supporting Detail

Inferences/Point of View:
- 1. Educated Guess
- 2. Educated Guess

OVERVIEW of NOTES:_____

_____

_____

_____.

SOURCE: *SuperStudy III: A Reading & Learning Strategies Workbook for College Success*; Prof. John A. Garcia, Ed.R.S., ABD [Harvard Reading Specialist], 2010.

'SUMMARY SHEET' READING COMPREHENSION SYSTEM #3

Prof. John A. Garcia, Ed.R.S., ABD [Harvard Reading Specialist]

Main Idea Statement (MIS): This story is about _____

_____

_____ .

SUMMARY of READING [Precis—use some details in your writing]: _____

_____

_____

_____

_____

_____

_____

_____

_____

_____

_____

POINT of VIEW [Drawing Conclusions]: _____

_____

_____

_____

_____

_____

_____

_____

_____

SOURCE: *SuperStudy III: A Reading & Learning Strategies Workbook for College Success*; Prof. John A. Garcia, Ed.R.S., ABD [Harvard Reading Specialist], 2010.

V. CRITICAL READING: THE FUN BEGINS WITH 'INFERENCES'

Prof. John A. Garcia, Ed.R.S., ABD [Harvard Reading Specialist]

MAKING INFERENCES: An *inference* is a statement you create, based on background information that has been provided in a reading or handout. It is also information you may have already been aware of (based on past knowledge or information). It is a type of 'educated guess' which is based on 'what is going on' or what could happen (not something you assume—do not assume). The best thing about inferences is you can never be completely wrong with your statement (answer)—as long as it is a strong possibility, you are going to be alright with the statement you make. Therefore, *inferences are possibilities!*

Inferences also help us arrive at conclusions (drawing conclusions) and using logic with critical reading and writing. Sometimes it takes no more than a bit of common sense, so don't be discouraged when an inference you make is not completely correct. Making the attempt at making an inference is what it's all about! When students do this, it assists them in developing critical reading and thinking skills that can be used in either classroom discussions or on college writing papers.

I always remember an old television series called "Family Matters" which included a nerdy character named Erkle (IRCL). Because many of your peers or friends believe you are a 'nerd' if you show any semblance of intelligence or 'smarts' when speaking or writing, I used a form of his name (IRCL) to remember 'key elements' for reading or writing college papers.

> **I** = **Inferences (Making Inferences)**
> **R** = **Reasoning**
> **C** = **Conclusions (Drawing Conclusions)**
> **L** = **Logic**

Below are some 'fun' situations that can get you 'warmed up' for critical reading and thinking. Let's see how many you can come up with—use your mental processes only—do not use the Internet. If you let the computer or Internet 'think' for you, you are not doing any critical thinking. The computer then deserves the grade for coming up with correct responses to the situations below:

1—On a snowy mountain peak in New Mexico (9,500 feet), a group is stranded and will have to spend a few nights in a small cabin they came across while hiking. The large storm has left no way out. In the cabin, they have a pile of newspapers, a fireplace with kindling and wood, a large kerosene lamp, and a wood stove. What do they have to light first in order to stay warm throughout the night and survive their ordeal?

2—What three coins will always total 80 cents ($0.80) if one coin *cannot* be a quarter (25 cents)? We are talking about American (U.S.) currency and not any other form of currency in the world.

3—Circle only the numbers below that are equally divisible by the number 2. Look at them carefully before circling your answer. This may not be as easy as it appears!

1, 2, 3, 4, 5, 6, 7, 8, 9, 10, 11, 12, 13, 14, 15, 16, 17, 18, 19, 20.

4—How many cubic feet of dirt are in a hole that is 2 ft. long, 2 ft. wide, and 1 ft. deep? Use your math skills!

5—Before Mount Everest was ever discovered, what was the highest mountain peak on earth?

6—What one word does every Harvard, Yale, Stanford, Notre Dame, University of Texas, and Eastfield College student pronounce wrong every time?

7—**"Railroad crossing here comes a car! Never drive onto the tracks after leaving a bar!** There are ten R's in these two phrases. Try to spell these two sentences without using an 'R'—you must maintain the same comprehension. You can only use English, not any other language. Think carefully—it is not difficult, but it is rather challenging!!

SOURCE: *SuperStudy III: A Reading & Learning Strategies Workbook for College Success*; Prof. John A. Garcia, Ed.R.S., ABD [Harvard Reading Specialist], 2010.

VI. MEMORY TRAINING—Mnemonics for College Study

Prof. John A. Garcia, Ed.R.S., ABD [Harvard Reading Specialist]

[NOTE: WRITTEN PERMISSION TO COPY MUST BE GRANTED BY AUTHOR(s)
FOR FACULTY OR STUDENT USE.]

I have developed a system using 'mnemonics' (clues to assist with recalling info and retaining it) so that students can have access to something that will make their study-time less stressful. This system is guaranteed to help when studying for tests in English or when writing papers for any class that requires research writing. In fact, this system will assist students anytime they write, whether it be a paper for class or a memo for their job. The following is a guide for avoiding run-on sentences, comma splices, and some fragment phrases:

'8' Punctuation Patterns for College Writing (Garcia, 1982)

1. IC. IC.   Every complete sentence (independent clause) is followed by a period.

2. DC, IC. [FRAG]   A dependent clause is followed by a comma and a complete sentence.

3. IC DC. [FRAG]   A complete sentence that is followed by a dependent clause only requires a period—no comma before dependent clause.

4. IC, (cw) IC. [RO]   Two complete sentences can be divided by a comma and a 'connecting word' (coordinating conjunction).

5. IC; IC. [RO]   Two complete (related) sentences can be divided by a semi-colon.

6. IC; (scw), IC. [RO]   Two complete sentences can be divided by a semi-colon, a stronger connecting word (joining word) and a comma (period at the end).

7. IC. (Scw), IC. [RO]   Same as #6—you can use a period after the first sentence and then capitalize the stronger connecting word.

8. IC, IC. [CS]   Two sentences are NEVER separated by a comma (comma splice)—use one of the other methods above to correctly punctuate the sentences.

#2 & #3   **'A BUDUWISAW'** (no this is not a beverage)

A = Although
B = Before, Because
U = Until
D = During (used as prepositional phrase)
U = Unless
W = While
I = If
S = Since
A = After
W = When, Whenever

#4   **'FABNOSY' or 'FANBOYS'**

F = For
A = And
B = But
N = Nor
O = Or
S = So
Y = Yet

#5 & #6   **'THe Funny CON MAN' (caps only)**

T = Therefore
H = However
e

F = Furthermore
u
n
n
y

C = Consequently
O = Otherwise
N = Nevertheless

M = Moreover
A = Accordingly
'I' N = In Addition

Sample Sentences Using the Punctuation Patterns Listed on Previous Page

[NOTE: WRITTEN PERMISSION TO COPY MUST BE GRANTED BY AUTHOR FOR FACULTY OR STUDENT USE]

1. **IC . IC .**

   The children played at the park. They got exhausted running back and forth.

2. **DC , IC .**

   After the Psychology exam, I went to the mall with my friends.

3. **IC DC .**

   I went to the mall with my friends *after* the Psychology exam.

4. **IC , (cw) IC .**

   Tia is going to Guadalajara on Spring Break, *but* she doesn't want to go alone.

5. **IC ; IC .**

   My parents took us to the aquarium; we saw a stingray and two sharks.

6. **IC ; (scw) , IC .**

   The surgeon wants to schedule surgery for December; *however,* I would rather wait until May.

7. **IC . (Scw) , IC .**

   The surgeon wants to schedule surgery for December. *However,* I would rather wait until May.

8. **IC , IC . [Comma Splice—incorrect sentence]**

   The football team has won five games, they haven't lost a single game yet. (This sentence is INCORRECT—it is known as a Comma Splice.)

SOURCE: *SuperStudy III: A Reading & Learning Strategies Workbook for College Success*; Prof. John A. Garcia, Ed.R.S., ABD [Harvard Reading Specialist], 2010.

VII. Active Reading + Textbook Marking Systems

["HQA5R" and "HQAR"]

Prof. John A. Garcia, Ed.R.S., ABD [Harvard Reading Specialist]

"HQA5R" for Enhanced Study & Comprehension

"An Active Reading & Textbook Marking System for College Success"

By
Prof. John A. Garcia, Ed.R.S., ABD [Harvard Reading Specialist]

NOTE TO STUDENTS:

The following reading systems have been very effective and efficient for students who are seeking to raise their levels of comprehension in college or who need to prepare for exams by becoming active readers (DOING not just READING) in their textbooks. Furthermore, if students follow the 'HQA5R' system as it is explained (step-by-step without any shortcuts), then this system is guaranteed to bring the student the success that he/she seeks.

I have seen average or below average students go from 'C' and 'D' grades (and failing grades) to grades of 'B' and 'A' on quizzes & tests, midterm exams, and final exams. If the 'HQA5R' system does not work for you, please contact me at HarvardAlum83@aol.com. It may be that you took a shortcut, or you didn't do precisely what was asked while applying it to your textbooks, handouts, or lecture notes. I would be more than willing to assist you, if needed, so that you get the 'success' you have sought. Your ultimate success is my reward!

H HIGHLIGHT in YELLOW (Skim & Scan Only—Chapter) :

Use 'Skimming & Scanning' technique to find Titles & Subtitles plus words in **bold print** and *italics* that require definitions. This can be used for chapters in the course textbook, instructors' handouts, research printouts, or lecture notes. Remember: This system of HIGHLIGHTING is done in small chunks—do not highlight entire sentences or paragraphs, as most students probably were accustomed to doing in the past! Also, DO NOT READ the entire set of material or chapter at this time!

Q QUESTIONS (Mark Your 'Q' Next to Highlighting—Notebook Study Guide) :

Develop a set of 'possible' test questions from the HIGHLIGHTED information above, develop questions using the '5W's + H' guide. Write these out in a separate notebook (study guide) as questions, skipping 5–6 lines between each question. Mark these as 'Q1' and 'Q2' so that each question in the study guide corresponds to the same 'Q1' and 'Q2' in the written material.

A ANSWERS in BLACK (Underline and Mark Your 'A'—Notebook Study Guide) :

Read only as much as you need to *find the answer* to each of the questions that were developed. After finding the answer in the material, UNDERLINE that answer using a BLACK felt-tip pen (mark as 'A1' and 'A2' and so on). Then, write the answer (student's own words is preferred—paraphrase) in the spaces provided under each question. Make sure that you have corresponding 'A1' and 'A2' and so on in the text material.

NOTE: STUDENTS NOW HAVE A BASIC STUDY GUIDE for the CHAPTER or other ASSIGNED READING MATERIAL, with a 'PRELIMINARY' SET of QUESTIONS based on that material!

R RECITE (Aloud—Study From Notebook Study Guide) :

Students should spend time 'going over' these Q's and A's they have developed and written out in their study guides. This process requires that students read Q's and A's aloud. By doing this, students will keep their "little voice" silent—this is a way to focus on the material with little to no distractions. Mark off the Q's and A's that are known or easily remembered—spend a bit more time with those that are causing some difficulty.

R READ (1st Time You Read Entire Chapter—Do All Again + Notebook Study Guide) :

It isn't until NOW that the student will actually READ the entire chapter or set of material. The MAIN reason for READING the chapter at this time is to 'DISCOVER' what was possibly missed during the 'Skimming & Scanning' process done at the beginning of the chapter. During this step, students will do all of the above steps, i.e., HIGHLIGHT Question, WRITE OUT Question in STUDY GUIDE, UNDERLINE Answer in chapter, WRITE answer in STUDY GUIDE, and mark each corresponding 'Q' and 'A' in text and Study Guide.

NOTE: Students need a "purpose" for reading. Reading a chapter because "it was assigned" or it "was due" is not a valid purpose. They want to "read to discover and learn" as they go through information in the chapter or material assigned for reading!

R REASONING (Essay Q + A—Notebook Study Guide—More Than One Page) :

During this step, students should develop one/two open-ended ESSAY QUESTIONS based on the reading material. These ESSAY Questions should be general enough to cover the most important point(s) in the chapter or reading. This process follows the development of all the other Q's and A's from the above steps. Each ESSAY Question should be an "open-ended" question and should have an answer that is at least one (1) page in length. Use the ENGLISH technique for 'Basic Essay Writing' to develop the response for Essay Questions (Introduction, Body, Conclusion).

R REVIEW (Several Times Over—Now Study From Notebook Study Guide) :

The textbook is no longer necessary as a study tool. The student should now feel confident that he/she has developed Q's and A's of the most important information in the reading material. The student can now 'go over' the material (review Q's and A's) as many times as he/she feels is necessary. Students will discover that they are retaining much more information now than before, and more importantly, they are retaining the most important areas of the chapter that their instructor actually wanted them to learn and remember.

NOTE: Going back and studying material from text, especially when the student believes that he/she will ONLY read what was HIGH-LIGHTED is not a wise decision. This is where TEST ANXIETY results from—a person cannot read ONLY what is HIGH-LIGHTED. The human eye will take in all of the information on the printed page, not just the information that the student be-lieves he/she is focusing on. Then, when it is time for the test, a 'flood' of information comes out and gets the student confused and frustrated. Thus, TEST PANIC and ANXIETY set in—this results in a poor grade on the test!

R (W)RITE (Write All You Know or Remember; Test Yourself) :

This is the step where a student can self-check himself or herself to see what they actually remember from their studying (reviewing Q's and A's). The student writes as much as he/she remembers from their study guide. Any format is allowed, i.e., paragraph, Q's & A's, important point + explanation, etc. . . The idea here is for students to write as much as possible—this serves as a 'self-test' before the actual test is taken in class!

SOURCE: *SuperStudy III: A Reading & Learning Strategies Workbook for College Success*; Prof. John A. Garcia, Ed.R.S., ABD [Harvard Reading Specialist]; Revised, 2010 (Original, 1982).

"HQAR" for Enhanced Study & Comprehension

"An Active Reading & Textbook Marking System without Study Guide"

By
Prof. John A. Garcia, Ed.R.S., ABD [Harvard Reading Specialist]

NOTE TO STUDENTS:

This system, which is a variation of the 'HQA5R' active reading system, is one that works for students who do not want to follow the other system by creating study guides from their chapters in their textbook or from handouts or lecture notes. Using this system is a 'shortcut' to study, one that I simply will not be able to guarantee in terms of significantly raising reading comprehension levels or raising grades on those tests. It will require students to study directly from their textbook, which is something that I do not advocate.

While I cannot or will not guarantee this system to make rapid advancements in reading comprehension levels or to raise grades substantially on tests, I will let you know that it is much better than the methods now employed by students for studying from textbooks. In the past (or the current method students use for reading textbook assignments), students have always done the same 'old' thing—they read the chapter and then go about their regular daily business. When asked 'why' they read the chapter(s), the replies are almost always the same—"I read the chapter because it was assigned!" I believe that students do exactly as they are told (most times)—when asked to read a chapter or when they are given an assignment to read, they do exactly that—READ!! There is hardly any work done to retain the information read, and once done, they rarely can recall what the chapter or information was about. So, if a student does not want to use the guaranteed 'HQA5R' for reading and study purposes because it takes a bit longer than just reading the chapter, then I suggest this less-effective active reading method, the 'HQAR' system.

With this system, a student will not need to develop a study guide nor will the student have to study from a notebook study guide which contains possible test questions and answers. They can study right from the textbook—this is something that I am totally against and believe that retaining the information will only be slightly better using this system. I am convinced (and my studies have proven this) that students cannot study effectively from a text or set of reading materials. Their peripheral vision does not permit a student to focus ONLY on the material that is relevant and will be on a test. While students tell themselves that they are going to read ONLY the material highlighted, their eyes take in the entire page (remember Science class and how parts of the eye function like a camera and take in the entire page). This is why students suffer from test anxiety and test panic when they encounter questions that have them perplexed—many times, even though they have covered the material, they simply cannot come up with the answers (on the tip of my tongue).

Finally, if you decide not to heed my advice and use the 'HQA5R' system which will guarantee your success, then feel free to use the 'HQAR' method. While it will never provide the results that the 'HQA5R' system will bring a student, it is still better than not using a system at all by resorting to the *old* but unreliable method of 'just reading a chapter.'

The 'HQAR' active reading system (for elevating comprehension levels or studying out of the textbook) is as follows:

"HQAR" Active Reading Method—Studying From Text

H HIGHLIGHT in YELLOW (Read Entire Chapter and Highlight All Necessary Information) :

As you read the chapter, mark (highlight) the Titles & Subtitles that you think might be included on test as test questions. Also, highlight any words in **bold** print and *italics* that have definitions along side them. This can be used for chapters in the course textbook, instructors' handouts, research printouts, or lecture notes. Remember: This system of HIGHLIGHTING is done in small chunks—do not highlight entire sentences or paragraphs, as most students probably were accustomed to doing in the past! That's called coloring!

Q QUESTIONS (Mark Your 'Q' Next to Highlighting as You READ the CHAPTER) :

Develop a set of 'possible' test questions as you HIGHLIGHT information (see above)—use '5W's + H' guide. Mark these as 'Q1' and 'Q2' and go on to find answers as you read. See the next part—'R' for retrieving answers!

A RETRIEVE the ANSWERS—Underline in BLACK; Mark Your 'A' :

As you read the chapter and highlight possible test questions, look for the answer to the highlighted questions, and UNDERLINE those answers in BLACK. Remember, after finding the answer in the material, UNDERLINE that answer using a BLACK felt-tip pen (mark as 'A1' and 'A2' and so on). Make sure that the 'A1' and 'A2' underlined answers correspond to the 'Q1' and 'Q2' (possible test questions) and so on

R REVIEW 'Q' and 'A' INFORMATION FROM TEXT (Over and Over Again) :

Students can now review their questions and answers directly from the text. While I know that they will be trying to read ONLY what was highlighted and underlined, that is not always what happens. But, this is better than just reading the chapter. It will help remember some of the material but not all of it. Using this method for studying will not reduce anxiety or test panic, but it will help to know much of the material in general. This system is good for remembering information for classes where discussions are the norm or study groups are used for dissecting information from a text. Then, a student is more prepared than before when they *JUST* read the chapter and *HOPED* to know what the instructor or other students were talking about during discussions or question-answer sessions. Good Luck!!

SOURCE: *SuperStudy III: A Reading & Learning Strategies Workbook for College Success*; Prof. John A. Garcia, Ed.R.S., ABD [Harvard Reading Specialist], 2010 (Original 1982).

VIII. OVERCOMING TEST ANXIETY AND STRESS

[MORE SUCCESS with LESS STRESS]

Prof. John A. Garcia, Ed.R.S., ABD [Harvard Reading Specialist]

[NOTE: WRITTEN PERMISSION TO COPY MUST BE GRANTED BY AUTHOR FOR FACULTY OR STUDENT USE]

PHILOSOPHIES OF STRESS

1—Stress is the result of too many 'items in life' piling up from day to day!

2—Learn how to deal with and manage the 'piles' of items in your life!

3—Reduce your 'piles' of stressors, and move on to enjoy your life!

4—Don't let the small stuff get to you; spend your time on larger life problems!

5—If you think about it, there really is no large stuff; it's all small stuff in our life!!

DEALING WITH ANXIETY & STRESS

These little things or items that pile up and sometimes manage to overtake your life and control your every waking minute are known as 'stressors.' These 'stressors' can range from the upcoming test in your Psychology class to not having enough cash to pay your current electric bill. Every time something bothers us, it is usually the result of stress. According to Webster's Collegiate Dictionary, **stress** *is the physical, mental, or emotional pressures or tensions resulting from an outside force, i.e., a stressor, and can be one of the major factors in disease causation.* These **stressors**, if not handled and dealt with quickly and changed into something manageable, can cause us undo pain, suffering, and distress. Very often these stressors manifest themselves in something that is all too often a physical or emotional burden. The solution is to 'get rid' of these at the very least or to completely eliminate them by finding a speedy resolution to them.

There, that should be simple enough! Well, now let's dig a little deeper into what these stressors are and how we can reduce them to make life more physically, mentally, and emotionally healthy. The last thing you want to do is to get backed into a corner where your daily repertoire makes you start up a diet of Mylanta and Prozac.

What is known about 'stressors' in a person's life is that they can often become a danger to that person's overall health and well-being. Studies have shown that the stress, brought on us by everyday problems, can be extremely critical when dealing with all types of cancer and other 'terminal' illnesses. As a matter of fact, 'stressors' can make up to 75% or more of the malignancies that affect people much worse, and in some cases, it can be the actual cause of a malignancy or illness. These studies have gone further in showing that cases of fatigue or the sudden onset of an ailment can lead to Acute Stress Disorder or Chronic Stress Syndrome, both of which are the direct result of the stress that takes over our body and normal everyday functions. This can cause havoc with our physical, mental, and emotional capabilities. It then overloads our already full mental 'baggage' of items and can get to the point where we become so overwhelmed that, at the very least, it creates that all-to-frequent 'visceral' feeling called 'butterflies' that can make many people constantly sick to their stomach with severe nausea and vomiting. Sometimes we even get short of breath, leaving us utterly speechless! All this from a simple case of stress, something no one ever believed was harmful!

I always wondered why, when a person is told that he or she is afflicted with a deadly disease or cancer, the disease is made worse or the cancer metastasizes almost twice as fast. It isn't too long after that that the person begins showing signs of deterioration and soon after that is close to death. This doesn't happen in all cases, but it does occur in a great many of these instances. It didn't take too much longer for me to figure out, after reading up on the causes and speaking to medical experts that, the greater number of instances is all due to stress. People find out there is something terribly wrong with them, and then, because of worry and emotional distress, they quickly make a downward spiral into a slow, suffering existence.

There are two types of stress: positive and negative. We usually associate stress with the negative only, such as income taxes, overwork, illness, divorce, financial problems, homework, or failing grades; however, no one ever talks about 'positive stressors.' These may include a wedding, a first date, an award ceremony, a vacation trip, waiting for your IRS refund, or lottery tickets. How we deal with stress depends on whether it has the positive or negative effects on us. Many psychologists and researchers agree that, in order to manage stress effectively and reduce its ill effects, we must do several things. The ways we will be reviewing shortly are ones that I practice daily and ones that I advocate to everyone. By implementing these ways into your daily life, you will be able to see a marked difference in how you approach stress from here on out and how well you take care of yourself.

Do you ever wonder about the one or two students in every class that almost thrive at the thought of an upcoming exam? They actually look forward to the challenge—no grimacing, no ill feelings, and no 'freaking out' at the mere mention of 'quiz' or 'test.' I am sure they do experience the 'butterflies' before the exam (I know that, when I have to give a presentation to a large audience even after countless presentations, I still experience that 'visceral' feeling); however, they know the same thing that I know! We make the 'stress' work for us! We don't let it control us! By knowing how to reduce and control our 'stressors,' we can then spend the rest of our energy and time working on something more productive. Our energies are spent better when we focus on other things we need to get done: keeping mentally and physically happy and healthy, finding how to make ourselves more successful, focusing on our strengths instead of our weaknesses, and further building up our self-image, discipline, and self-esteem.

FIVE WAYS TO REDUCE STRESS

1—Work to develop positive and mental conditioning to assist with attitudes about ourselves and our environment. We also have to figure out and prioritize, in order of importance, the things that affect us the most.

2—Follow a well-balanced, healthy exercise routine at least several times per week. Try to do this on a daily basis if your 'hectic' lifestyle permits it. Remember, we can always come up with excuses why we don't have time to exercise.

3—Begin today to eat healthier by reducing your caloric and high fat intake and replacing 'snack' calories with more nutritious foods. It is important to limit your cholesterol intake and to balance your large carbohydrate meals. Nowadays, there are so many 'wise' foods that are both delicious and nutritious.

4—Manage and control the amount of stressful items you deal with all at once. Also, it is a very important priority to limit the types of 'stressors' we tend to categorize as 'all huge problems' and break them down into smaller annoyances that can be solved with a few 'brainstorming' sessions meant to help us find alternatives that will ease or eliminate the problem. The 'little' things will always take care of themselves!!

5—Develop and follow a workable schedule, one that is comfortable and leaves us without thoughts of not having enough time to get things done. There is plenty of time to do what we need to get done; we just have to figure out how to fit these 'tasks' into a plan without running ourselves 'wild' and feeling scattered in all directions trying to get them done and not even coming close! This will reduce needless stress!!

PERSONAL PHILOSOPHY: Always strive for more personal success with least amount of stress!!

CHECKLIST OF 'STRESSORS'

STRESSOR	Affecting Me At Current Time	I Can Take Care of or Manage	I Need Help In Finding Ways to Handle
1—Financial Problems or Concerns	_____	_____	_____
2—Family Problems or Crises	_____	_____	_____
3—School-related Problems	_____	_____	_____
4—Job or Career Problems	_____	_____	_____
5—Transportation Problems	_____	_____	_____
6—Budgeting and Money Management	_____	_____	_____
7—Health-related Issues	_____	_____	_____
8—Legal Problems or Issues	_____	_____	_____
9—Relationship or Marital Problems	_____	_____	_____
10—Emotional or Spiritual Crises	_____	_____	_____
11—Daycare or Childcare Issues	_____	_____	_____
12—Other Problems at Home	_____	_____	_____

OVERCOMING TEST ANXIETY

This could also be called the section where 'Test-Taking is Made Easy'! You may be feeling a bit more confident as you progress through some of these new skills and chapters. You also might've leaned toward believing my tenet for success in school, "College is not stressful and can really be a blast!" We feel good about ourselves when we succeed. We tend to be friendlier, take on added challenges and responsibilities, and realize that we are doing something worthwhile in life (maybe for the first time). We even find that some of the goals we have set are much closer to achieving and are not unrealistic. For all this to happen, we must first face the truth about college—it is going to take a lot of hard work and discipline because of the amount of homework, exams, and papers that await us—however, it is all within reach and manageable!! It becomes easier when you realize that there is help out there!! Below is a list of things you can do to help when faced with what you believe is almost 'constant testing' and homework. These will also help allay the fears you will definitely encounter as you prepare for those 'dreaded' exams. You might even get to the point where you think of exams as more of an activity and a challenge than a 'loss of appetite' and 'lack of sleep' type of problem or formal occurrence. These tips have become valuable assets to thousands of students; they have come to know how to deal with stress and anxiety. They know that tests are a sure thing, as sure as the sun coming up every morning; however, they have come to figure out the key to college and exams. That 'key' is taking them as you would a normal, everyday classroom activity and not panicking just because they are called, in formal academic language, an exam, a quiz, or a test. The follow-up to this 'key' is to have more fun 'doing' college than stressing out about it!!

PERSONAL PHILOSOPHY: <u>Stress</u> is all created in your mind and can quickly and easily be forgotten and put behind you if you work at it and use the 'Be Here Now' method!!

TIPS FOR OVERCOMING TEST PANIC

1—Prepare well in advance of the exam. Remember, 'study time' is not only for the times you receive homework assignments, but unbeknownst to many students, it is also a time to review, self-test, and keep material 'fresh' and current in our memory banks.

2—Know the time and the place of each of your exams. Make sure you arrive on time, or better yet, ahead of time with plenty of opportunity to relax and get your 'mind' set for the exam. A sure-fire way to do poorly or fail an exam is to arrive late and in a 'panic.' By not arriving on time, you are setting yourself up for failure; you are finding ways to create test anxiety, not a way to overcome it!!

3—Do not talk about the test or do that 'quick review' right before you enter class to take the test. When you do this with classmates or friends, it can make you wonder if you missed some of the information, which could lead you directly into test panic as you take the exam. What if someone mentions a step that you didn't cover in your study; they believed this was a step mentioned in the material when all along it was confused with another portion of the material? This can quickly send you into the 'anxiety' mode! Do not do the things that will raise your levels of anxiety and panic!!

4—Plan your 'approach to the test' by reading it over first. Do this before actually beginning to answer any of the questions. Get 'comfortable' with the format of the test and the type of questions being asked. Keep in mind that you already know all of the material and have no reason to panic. Figure out the time you will need for each section of the test, how many points the questions are worth (if possible), and which items are the easiest to answer first!!

5—If you recognize that a problem exists on the test or you're not sure what is being asked on the test, ask your instructor for further explanation or clarification. Do not wait until you are sure the test was set up to 'fool' you or 'intimidate' you and you have gone into a panic to ask for the instructor's assistance. There really isn't any type of 'stupid' question when you are asking for clarification or explanation!! Ask your questions quickly; do not waste valuable time you could use on the exam!!

6—If you do not know the answer to a question, don't worry about it! Go on and answer the ones that you do know. You can always come back to try those you don't know. Sometimes, by going on, you 'click' on other material that will generate ideas, connections, or answers for the ones you skipped. This is a common success tip in taking exams!!

7—Relax yourself physically and mentally during the test. Don't tighten up! Loosen up by taking deep breaths and doing some 'stretches' right where you sit—these are sometimes called 'Isometric Exercises,' which can be done right from where you sit!. These exercises are based on the theory of 'muscle tension and force' and that 'two opposite forces in equal proportion to the tension applied will create a reverse tension and pressure directly where the forces meets.' To do this, take the palms of your hands, and while applying equal pressure to each palm with the other in the center of the body, you will create tension. This further creates a muscle strengthening force that, when released after five seconds, will produce not only additional power but a relaxed sensation. Try it! Another example is to apply pressure to the floor, where you sit at your desk, with the balls of your feet. It must be an equal pressure. Press against the floor for five seconds and release! Repeat this two or three time with each foot. You can do this with many parts of your body, i.e., your neck and the palm of your hand, your arm and your desk, or knee against the leg of your desk!

8—Pay attention to the test. Do not focus on other distractions. Focus on what you are doing and are required to do. You must give each test your best shot. You will not get this opportunity again with the tests you are taking. Once they are over, they are over! You have one chance to do your best. Do not worry about how others are doing on the test or how rapidly they are progressing through the test. Just worry about you and how well you plan on doing on the test. Do not blame yourself or give up on yourself for not knowing items on the test. Worrying about it and blaming yourself will only open the door for test panic!!

9—Your regular environment is important and directly related to how well you will do on the test. Sit in the desk or seat where you sit during regular class sessions. Any changes in your regular seating habits or attitude can 'block out' information that you had previously been sure of. It can be devastating when you realize that you are 'forgetting' information faster than completing the exam. You must breathe deeply and realize that the test isn't over yet! You can still recover from the 'forgetting' and focus on recalling the material you know you have mastered. Positive thinking, not worrying, will assist you in your drive for that grade!!

10—After each of your tests have been graded, find out who the students are that are getting the A's on the tests. These are the ones you want to 'hook up' with in study groups. They are the ones that are the most likely to help you towards achieving your goals of succeeding. They are the ones that I would 'partner up' with for assistance. Find out their methodologies on preparing and taking exams. It's my philosophy that we always learn best from the best!!

11—Once again, test preparation and how well you accomplish this is what is going to get you past that exam and get you the grade you want. If you believe you deserve the best ('A'), you better do your best! Use the methods of "Recite, Review, and Self-Test" to get yourself ready and assist you with the mastery of the material which is what learning and knowledge is all about!! These methods are practiced by many and really do work well when applied!!

12—Finally, know how to answer certain items on the exam. What is the instructor actually asking and what does he or she expect in an answer?? It is the wise student who will review the methods of testing and the types of test he/she will be confronted with in college. By knowing precise 'things' that are asked of you, you can be sure you will be more than ready when it comes time for the test. Remember, by doing the 'small' things that will get you by on the exam, you are piling up additional points that will get you the 'A' you seek!!

TEST-TAKING: TYPES OF EXAMS AND HOW TO TAKE THEM

ESSAY EXAMS: =Anticipate, develop, and answer 'possible' test questions.

=Create 'quick' outlines for each essay question before beginning.

=Use the "H2W" method for essay exams (How? What? Why?)

=Know 'precisely' what is being asked for each question, such as:

COMPARE	Show the similarities, use valid examples!
CONTRAST	Show the differences, use valid examples!
DEFINE	Give complete definition or meaning with examples!
DESCRIBE	Explain fully (description) using supporting details!!
DIAGRAM	Create a 'drawing' or 'picture;' label it, explain it!
ENUMERATE	List points (1, 2, 3) and explain each fully, examples!
EVALUATE	Assess a topic or subject, use pros & cons, examples!
DISCUSS	Explain in detail the various aspects with examples!
INTERPRET	Explain using analysis, inference, and experiences!
JUSTIFY	Give valid reasons why something is as it is!
LIST	Give a series of items or points and add examples!
RELATE	Show valid connections and comparisons!
SUMMARIZE	Provide a brief, condensed version of main points!
TRACE	List in order of progression—history, background!
OUTLINE	Organize general (I, II, III) and specifics (A, B, C) of a topic using main points and supporting details!

MULTIPLE-CHOICE TESTS:

1—Always remember to choose the 'best' or 'closest' answer from all of the available choices or 'alternatives.' Sometimes an instructor will not list 'exact wording' answers that you had read in the text or from lecture material. You will, on occasion, see that there are several answers that are very close to correct but only one that is actually 'complete' and correct.

2—As you proceed through the exam and the alternative choices for each question, cross out (mentally if you cannot write on the test) and eliminate the answers that are incorrect or are not sure possibilities.

3—Do not mark the first answer you read that you think is 'probably' the one you are looking for. Make sure you read through all the alternatives first, and then when you are sure, go ahead and mark the correct one.

4—Use 'guessing' only as a last resort and when you have no idea of the correct answer. If you're not sure, don't leave the answer blank; guess at it!!

5—If time permits, read the question over again, after you read each of the alternatives. Many times, this technique will provide a mental connection between the question and the answer.

6—The longest answers are very likely, and many times, the correct ones, or the correct answer will provide the most information and detail.

7—Watch for two answers that have opposite meanings. There is a very high probability that one of them is the correct answer.

8—Watch for these words or phrases: most of the time, probably, possibly, sometimes, usually, is often the case, many times, in most cases, in many instances. These tend to be 'correct' more often than they are incorrect. Answers that tend to be 'incorrect' are the ones that begin with 'never' or 'always.'

TRUE / FALSE TESTS:

- Much to your dismay, there is no 'sure-fire' way to answer these unless you are well versed with the material you have studied. You must know the material; if you guess, you only have a 50-50 chance of getting it right!!

- Be aware of the following words: always, everybody, everyone, all, none, never, no one, nobody. These might be providing a FALSE answer.— might be providing a 'FALSE' answer.

- Take note that words such as—sometimes, generally, possibly, probably, usually, generally, often— might be providing a 'TRUE' answer.

MATCHING TESTS:

- Read the terms or phrases in the left column with the corresponding answers in the right column before beginning to match any of them.

- Find out from your instructor if some answers can be used more than once, even if there are just as many answers as there are questions in each column.

- Count both sides to see if they are equal. Many times, instructors will provide more answers (in one column) than there are questions, terms or phrases to match (in the other column). Knowing what you are dealing with and asked to do, right from the beginning, can help eliminate or reduce your chances of 'bringing on' stress or anxiety.

FILL-IN-THE-BLANK TESTS:

- Make up your own type of 'fill-in' tests when studying. These are easy and use the principles of 'cloze' testing. Find examples of 'cloze tests' that you can review and learn how to develop. If you can't find any, begin by creating a paragraph and leave every *'n'th* word out or every term that you need to know (leave it out, and put it in a list). As you read the paragraph when studying, use the list to provide you with 'possible' answers. Make the paragraphs lengthy enough so that they become challenging. This is an excellent method for 'self-testing' yourself before you actually take your exam in class!!

- Answers must 'fit in' grammatically and logically when you are reading each alternative on the test. Repeat the phrase, and as you pick a word from your answer list (alternatives), try to recall what it sounded like or what it should sound like as you 'verbalize' it silently.

- Find out, from your instructor, if one blank indicates only one word per blank or if you are allowed to enter a phrase. Sometimes, when you know this ahead of time, you make new connections and reduce confusion as you enter answers. You don't want to reduce your options—if you studied material in phrases for answers and then you can only use a single word or term, you want to make sure you use all possible methods of recall and connection and don't end up in a test panic!!

STUDY TIPS TO IMPROVE EXAM GRADES

1— Organize your time and figure out <u>exactly</u> when you will study. This is the technique that you should've already mastered (time management). It also allows for you to pick the best and the most opportune times for yourself, according to the other priorities in your life.

2—Find a study place that suits you and is conducive to learning. Don't pick a place that is too relaxing and puts you to sleep or a place that has too much 'traffic' through it and keeps you distracted and from focusing on your studies.

3—Choose your setting both mentally and physically—what type of 'mood' or environment best suits me for what I have to study? Do I need absolute quiet for studying Literature or can I have music on while I study Biology?

4—Practice makes perfect! Use the methods of 'tuning in' to studying and 'tuning out' distractions!

5—Use the 'FOCUS' method when you are studying. If you lose focus or concentration and simply cannot regain it, take a minute to 'visualize' the successes you will achieve from finishing your task at hand and from learning the material in front of you.

6—Choose and apply the study system that best suits your needs and that is BEST for you: The **'SuperStudy'** Notetaking & Comprehension Systems, the **'HQA5R'** Active Reading System, and the **'HQAR'** Textbook Marking System. Determine which one system or which ones are applicable to your particular circumstances or your course, its material, and your study needs!!

7—Set up goals for studying. What is the amount of material that you plan on covering in a given time? How many days and hours are going to be required to master certain test material? Exactly what is going to be required for a particular course? How much 'play' time will I be required to 'give up' to make education and college a priority? What is best for me and for my future?

8—Do not procrastinate! Putting off for tomorrow what you know you need to get done today is a very bad habit and can become a practice that is difficult to break. If you put it off until later, all that you have accomplished is keeping it on your mind no matter what else you do! You could be with friends, strolling through the mall, shopping, and having fun; however, every once in a while your 'little voice' reminds you that you still have a 'chore' to get done. You end up stressing out instead of really enjoying your 'play' time!!

9—Take frequent breaks whenever you feel it is necessary and valid. Do not study for more than 1 ½ to 2 hours without some type of break to get your mind completely off the material you're studying. You are wasting your time if you study more than 2 hours without a break! The material doesn't get 'soaked in' to your memory banks because of the 'overload' factor. Ideal breaks should not be less than 5 minutes or more than 10 minutes! Too long of a study block without a break will decrease your retention levels and powers of concentration!!

10—Always be prepared well in advance (especially for those surprise quizzes)! You never know when an instructor will decide to give you a test—be and stay ready!! Whatever you do, never cram!!

PHILOSOPHY FOR SUCCESSFUL TEST-TAKING: If you can do it under any type of pressure, you will be able to do it at anytime and in any situation, regardless of the circumstances you face or the cards you are dealt!

[GOOD LUCK ON ALL OF YOUR EXAMS!!]

SOURCE: *SuperStudy III: A Reading & Learning Strategies Workbook for College Success*; Prof. John A. Garcia, Ed.R.S., ABD [Harvard Reading Specialist], 2010.

CPSIA information can be obtained
at www.ICGtesting.com
Printed in the USA
BVHW091719100722
641601BV00003B/4

9 781465 231482